W9-BHL-087

Center for Basque Studies
Basque Classics Series, No. 9

Selected Basque Writings:
The Basques and
Announcement of a Publication

Wilhelm von Humboldt

With an Introduction by
Iñaki Zabaleta Gorrotxategi

Translated by
Andreas Corcoran

Center for Basque Studies
University of Nevada, Reno
Reno, Nevada

This book was published with generous financial support obtained by the Association of Friends of the Center for Basque Studies from the Provincial Government of Bizkaia.

Basque Classics Series, No. 9
Series Editors: William A. Douglass, Gregorio Monreal, and Pello Salaburu

Center for Basque Studies
University of Nevada, Reno
Reno, Nevada 89557
http://basque.unr.edu

Copyright © 2013 by the Center for Basque Studies
All rights reserved. Printed in the United States of America

Cover and series design © 2013 by Jose Luis Agote
Cover painting: "Aurresku ante la Iglesia" [*Aurresku* in front of Church] by José Arrúe. © Bilboko Arte Ederren Museoa–Museo de Bellas Artes de Bilbao.

Library of Congress Cataloging-in-Publication Data

Humboldt, Wilhelm, Freiherr von, 1767-1835.
 Selected basque writings : the Basques and announcement of a publication / Willhelm von Humboldt with an Introduction by Inaki Zabaleta Gorrotxategi ; translated by Andreas Corcoran.
    pages cm. -- (Basque classics series, no. 9)
 Includes bibliographical references and index.
 Summary: "Classic texts on the Basque people and language by the German man of letters Wilhelm von Humboldt with a new scholarly introduction to his Basque works"-- Provided by publisher.
 ISBN 978-1-935709-44-2 (pbk.) -- ISBN 978-1-935709-45-9 (cloth) 1. Basques--History. 2. Basques--Social life and customs. 3. Basque language I. Title.

GN549.B3H85 2013
305.899'92--dc23

2013036442

Contents

Selected Basque Writings of Wilhelm von Humboldt

The Basques

Note on Basque Orthography

The standard form to refer to the Basque language today is Euskara. Most English-language texts on the Basque Country have traditionally employed only the French and Spanish orthographic renderings of Basque place names. Here, in light of the standard Basque orthographic renderings of these same place names by the Basque Language Academy (Euskaltzaindia), we will endeavor to use these Basque versions, with an addition in parentheses of the French or Spanish equivalents on first mention in each chapter.

Some exceptions to this rule include the use of Navarre (Nafarroa in Basque, Navarra in Spanish) and Lower Navarre (Nafarroa Beherea in Basque, Basse Navarre in French); the hyphenated bilingual cases of Donostia-San Sebastián, Vitoria-Gasteiz, and Iruñea-Pamplona; and occasions where French or Spanish place name variants are used to make a linguistic point. In the latter case, the Basque equivalents appear in parentheses after the French or Spanish place name.

Additionally, on occasion we anglicize certain Basque terms, rather than use the original Basque, French, or Spanish terms themselves. Thus, for example, inhabitants of Zuberoa (Soule), instead of being rendered as *zuberotarrak* or *xiberotarrak* (from the Basque alternative Xiberoa), or *Souletines* (in French), are described here as Zuberoans.

Occasionally, Humboldt cites words and phrases in Basque to make a point. We have preserved his original renderings, but where applicable added the standard modern Basque variants of these words and phrases in parentheses. For longer phrases—proverbs and sayings for example—we have maintained the original orthography.

It should be noted that, for much of the period under study here, there was little consistency in the rendering of either place names or personal names in any of these languages; a fact of life that is apparent in a region of Europe where multiple cultures and identities overlap. We see such lack of consistency as a more flexible way of appreciating this diversity.

Wilhelm von Humboldt and the Basques

IÑAKI ZABALETA GORROTXATEGI

Wilhelm von Humboldt, the older brother of the renowned geographer and naturalist Alexander von Humboldt, was born in Potsdam, Prussia, on June 22, 1767 and died in Tegel, near Berlin, on April 8, 1835. During Humboldt's lifetime the philosophy of Immanuel Kant emerged and became widespread. A contemporary of other great German idealists and romantics, Humboldt, however, developed his own relatively independent line of thinking on the basis of a moderate critique of Kantian formalism, idealistic speculation, and romantic exaggeration. Wilhelm von Humboldt is in fact the most prominent representative of Germany's Neohumanist movement, given that he offered the most vigorous defense of a theory of human education based on the individual (*Bildung*), a theory that had important practical implications in a wide variety of fields. It is within this humanistic context that he conducted his research on the Basques and their language, and produced the two studies that are presented in this book.

It is impossible to overemphasize the importance of the fact that Humboldt was not an academic in the traditional sense. Instead, he was a practical man, something that can be seen even in his theorizing. This trait gives both his life and work an unmistakably constructive character. His anthropological thinking, for example, does not address unsolvable questions such as the definition of human "essential being," but instead focuses primarily on "real becoming." Through an interest in a wide range of human and social sciences, Humboldt continually sought to increase his anthropological knowledge; yet such knowledge was always put at the service of providing mileposts for individual development. His conceptualization of linguistics was similar. Specifically, his theory of language is based on the practical research of languages, and is oriented toward the educational practices of individual human beings. Humboldt thus combined theoretical-philosophical studies on language and practical-theoretical research on languages, ever mindful of the fact that the educational development of human beings cannot ignore—and indeed to a large extent depends on—their linguistic development. Humboldt's political thought was not limited to the reflections of an ivory-tower academic.

Humboldt is in fact remembered for his political activity on behalf of the Prussian state. As the Prussian minister of education he founded the University of Berlin, advocated educational reform, and proposed a new constitution. The political commitments of Humboldt were in fact firmly grounded in his humanism—a humanism that led him to reflect upon both the limits of state action and the importance of the nation on human development. What we therefore see in Humboldt is a man who thought so that he could act, and whose thinking was in turn driven by action. Thus, all of his theoretical reflections arose within the frame of reference of an anthropology that aimed to be humanizing in the truest sense of the word.

Humboldt's interest in the Basques can only be fully understood within the context of his humanistic approach. Thus, his travels within the Basque Country and his research on the Basque nation and its language can be seen as constituting a part of an anthropological project of far greater scope. This is something that is reflected in the two texts presented in this book: *Die Vasken, oder Bemerkungen auf einer Reise durch Biscaya und das französische Basquenland im Frühling des Jahrs 1801* (The Basques, or Observations on a Journey through Bizkaia and the French Basque Country in the Spring of 1801, 1805; hereafter, *The Basques*) and *Ankündigung einer Schrift über die Vaskische Sprache und Nation, nebst Angabe des Gesichtspunctes und Inhalts derselben* (Announcement of a Publication on the Basque Language and Nation, Amid an Outline of the Perspective and Content of the Same, 1812; hereafter *Announcement of a Publication*).[1]

For these reasons, the present introduction attempts to offer answers to a number of important questions. Why was Humboldt interested in the Basques? What did Humboldt's research on the Basques consist of? What place do Humboldt's Basque studies have in his thinking in general?

---

1. In Humboldt, *Gesammelte Schriften*, vol. 13, 1–197 and vol. 3, 288–300.

From Comparative Anthropology to Euskal Herria

The broad outlines of Humboldt's "anthropology," which he himself termed "comparative," can be found in a number of writings that he completed prior to moving to Paris in 1797. The most important of these are *Plan einer vergleichenden Anthropologie* (Outline of a Comparative Anthropology, 1797) and *Das achtzehnte Jahrhundert* (The Eighteenth Century, 1796–1797).[2] The overarching aim of these works was nothing less than that of proposing a new kind of anthropology—one based on a comparison of different individuals and nations.

A New Paradigm for Anthropology

Humboldt's initial reflections on anthropology, which date back to the end of the eighteenth century, took place at a time when an important debate was being waged within anthropological philosophy regarding the principles of that discipline. Johann Gottfried Herder contended that "historicity" was an inherent element of human nature, and therefore he questioned the then-dominant Kantian view, which, like his philosophy in general, saw anthropology as a pure science aimed at discovering the universal elements of human beings with a view to arriving at general and normative principles. Such a view tended to disregard historical circumstances as irrelevant. This was the exact opposite of Herder's view. For Herder, the "here" and the "now" of human beings—of each individual human being—are not matters of secondary or circumstantial importance, but rather defining characteristics of their "real being" and "real becoming." It is for this reason that, according to Herder's view, anthropological theory could not only not afford to dispense with concrete research—in real time and in real space—of human phenomena, but needed to make such studies the very lodestar of their enterprise. For Herder, what was important was to emphasize a view of human beings as individuals, and for such a view to constitute a fundamental point of reference in the search for general patterns and universal types. In thus introducing this factor of historicism, Herder changed both the way of viewing human beings and of approaching anthropological research: Henceforth, human "facts" would be studied from the standpoint of their "becoming." Reflecting a similar line of thinking, Humboldt wrote:

---

2. In Humboldt, *Gesammelte Schriften*, vol. 1, 377–410, and vol. 2, 1–112.

XII *Selected Basque Writings*

"What we need most right now is an individualizing knowledge of human beings."[3]

Humboldt's point of departure is this same historicist perspective and, following the same line as other thinkers, he fashioned his own particular kind of anthropology, which was characterized by its uniting "knowledge" with "humanization," and using the former in the service of the latter. The recognition of the unfinished character of human beings (in other words, given that history forms an integral part of their nature) means that Humboldt's anthropology shifts from a theoretical-cognitive plane to a practical-educational plane, thus situating itself in a place between what human beings already are and what they are capable of becoming. In reality, Humboldt saw his task as that of mediating between "individual reality" and "ideal possibility." In other words, Humboldt tried to show different ways of both "idealizing human reality" (or, to express the same idea in a different way, to construct that reality in accordance with one's ideas) and of "realizing the human ideal" (or revising one's ideas in accordance with one's lived reality). According to Humboldt, such tasks are feasible, given his view that there are as many ideas as there are individuals. Many years later, he developed this line of thinking in a letter he wrote on December 2, 1822 to his friend Charlotte Diede: "Each human being, however wonderful he truly is, carries within himself another human being who is even better, and who most surely constitutes his 'even-more-real-Self.'" It is for this reason that, in Humboldt's view, anthropology should not be a merely descriptive science that depicts only that which has taken concrete form in human beings, but should also be a "teleological" science that dares to represent that which can or should be components of that form. Yet such a standpoint is unattainable if different anthropological studies remain entrenched in their respective specialties. In other words, anthropology cannot become truly humanizing if the social sciences and the human sciences are not capable of mutual interaction. Humboldt expresses this idea as follows: "In order to at one and the same time arrive at an understanding of man as he is and also to freely speculate on what he might become, practical observation and the philosophical spirit must work hand in hand."[4]

---

3. Humboldt, "Plan einer vergleichenden Anthropologie" (1795), *Gesammelte Schriften*, vol. 1, 383.

4. Ibid., 378.

Specifically, Humboldt's anthropology proposes as its goal the "understanding" of human beings in their particularity, and is characterized by its utilization of a methodology that "compares" various human manifestations with one another. The reality is that the dynamism characteristic of human individuals makes it impossible to know them at a conceptual level. It is for this very reason that anthropological research should focus on understanding human beings at a symbolic level. Given the impossibility of arriving at immutable truths regarding mutable human beings, Humboldt proposes the more realistic goal of drawing progressively closer to the reality of human beings by means of "images." In fact, the task of anthropology consists of "a comprehensive collection of all the evidence that clearly differentiates one subject from other subjects. In other words, it is more a matter of sketching a portrait of a subject's character than of conceptualizing the subject."5 It is within the context of this historicist approach, which rejects definitive universal points of reference, that Humboldt perceives the necessity of redefining the method of anthropological investigation, by anchoring it firmly in a comparative methodology. For him, comparison is necessary in order to recognize the distinctive traits of individuals, to detect similarities and differences, to properly categorize different kinds of character, and, most importantly, to visualize universal reference points of humanization. In his own words, "The individual can only represent the ideal of human perfection from a single angle (i.e., from his own uniqueness). However, comparative observation of many of these partial and different representations draws us closer to a clear idea of a comprehensive view of Man."6 Thus, Humboldt offers a comparative anthropology that, from the moment that he theoretically reflects on human comprehension, is closely tied to the new philosophical hermeneutics introduced by Friedrich Schleiermacher.

Nations and Journeys in Comparative Anthropology

Humboldt's "comparative anthropology," which seeks to humanize by means of knowledge, specifically seeks to base the understanding of human beings on a comparison "of" and "between" all human manifestations. Thus, the very construction of an anthropological theory requires a

---

5. Humboldt, "Das achtzehnte Jahrhundert" (1796–1797), *Gesammelte Schriften*, vol. 2, 95.

6. Ibid., 38.

direct and ongoing reference to the practical research of human diversity. It is precisely within this context that the idea of nations and field observation take on a fundamental importance for Humboldt. The questions raised here are fundamentally important, not only for a full appreciation of Humboldt's particular anthropology, but also for understanding what led him to take an interest in the Basques and other peoples. I will now attempt to clarify these issues.

As his writings unequivocally show, a large part of Humboldt's anthropology is devoted to comparative research on various nations that, within the context of his humanistic views, clearly play a fundamental role in educating individuals. At its root, this is a natural consequence of a rigorous acceptance of the historical nature of human beings, and therefore of their inherent sociocultural dimensions, factors that must be taken into account by any kind of anthropology with the future within its purview. Humboldt wrote, "We need to be presented as a vital link in a concatenation of causes that act collectively," in other words, "at one and the same time as both the product of forces that exercised their effects before us, and as a source of other sources that will manifest themselves after we are no longer here."[7] This is what leads him to make reference to the "individuality" and "unique character" of different nations. In this regard, it is important to emphasize that, for Humboldt, "nation" is not so much a political concept (for a start, it has nothing to do with the state) as it is a sociocultural concept that serves to identify a specific community *in* and *through* its linguistic dimension. This is because, for him, "language" and "nation" are indeed so "intertwined"[8] that they really need to be thought of as a single interactive dynamic. According to Humboldt, a nation is nothing less than "a spiritual form of humanity that is characterized by a single language."[9] In this regard, "all languages offer clues as to the character of their nations."[10] Thus, the study of different nations is not merely one option among others but rather the fundamental task of a comparative anthropology that continually links the

---

7. Ibid., 1.

8. Humboldt, "Über den Nationalcharakter der Sprachen" (1812), *Gesammelte Schriften*, vol. 4, 424.

9. Humboldt, "Über die Verschiedenheiten des menschlichen Sprachbaues" (1827–1829), *Gesammelte Schriften*, vol. 6, 126.

10. Humboldt, "Ueber die Verschiedenheit des menschlichen Sprachbaues und ihren Einfluss auf die geistige Entwicklung des Menschengeschlechts" (1830–1835), *Gesammelte Schriften*, vol. 7, 172.

concepts of "human education," "linguistic education," and "national education."

Given Humboldt's contention that different nations constitute a fundamental subject of research for comparative anthropology, travel to and observation within particular nations were for him an indispensable means of conducting research about them. Human existence only takes on a reality, and assumes a comprehensible form in the context of a variety of different kinds of individuals and nations. This is a fundamental tenet of the historicist perspective, and it is also the reason that such a perspective requires the anthropologist to travel in order to capture human existence as it really is. This is why Humboldt poses the following question: "Would it not be worth an effort greater than we have thus far seen to endeavor to understand and depict forms of nature and humanity—to see what the first human beings produced, and what humanity's final specimens might be capable of achieving?"[11] Humboldt's travels that brought him into direct contact with human diversity—travels that, as he wrote in a letter to Friedrich Schiller dated October 10, 1797, had an "ultimate scientific purpose." Humboldt was well aware that human individuality, at both the personal and national level, does not reveal itself through "dead words" but instead becomes manifest, in partial and imperfect ways, via "living images." Travel and direct observation were therefore of vital importance for him. "In order to understand a foreign nation, in order to decipher the code that reveals its unique manifestation within each of its individual specimens, and even merely to fully understand many of that nation's writers, it is absolutely necessary to have visited and seen it with one's own eyes."[12] This kind of direct observation allows us to connect with the nation directly, and to become familiar with its customs and way of life. Travel accounts therefore play a fundamentally important role in Humboldt's anthropological research, allowing one to "gather and store every impression" in order to succeed in obtaining a true "image" of each nation.[13]

To summarize the main points made thus far, Humboldt's vision of "comparative anthropology" proposes, in a manner consistent with its fundamental principles, that human beings be studied in all of their

11. Humboldt, "Der Montserrat bei Barcelona" (1800), *Gesammelte Schriften*, vol. 3, 32.

12. Ibid., 30.

13. Ibid., 32.

national diversity, with journeys for the purposes of direct observation forming a critical part of research. As soon as Humboldt became aware that human beings contained more "history" than "essence," it was inevitable that consideration of human sociocultural diversity through the study of different nations would constitute a pillar of his program. For this same reason, Humboldt's anthropology involved research that focused more on "description" than on "definition." In other words, his program consisted of investigations that, by means of travel and direct observation, enable us to visualize (but not to define in any exact terms) the essential character of each nation. This is the indisputable anthropological context of Humboldt's decision to visit the Basque Country, where he journeyed on two separate occasions for the clear purpose of characterizing the Basque people in terms of their national identity.

Humboldt's Visits to the Basque Country in 1799 and 1801

For Humboldt, each and every nation is unique in its own right. And in terms of his particular conception of anthropology, which sought to engender a humanizing knowledge on the basis of comparisons, each nation constitutes an invaluable and irreplaceable entity. His visits to the Basque Country, as well as the texts that emerged from these direct contacts, are thus part of a broad-based anthropological project that strove to transcend the bounds of mere theorizing, and that therefore necessarily involved research in the real world. Thus Humboldt's interest in the Basques, while not extraordinary in and of itself, had an important comparative value because of the uniqueness and distinctiveness of the Basque people. He embarked upon his two visits to the Basque Country, one rather brief and casual and the other more unequivocally research-oriented, at a time when he was living in Paris with his family, and before he turned his considerable energies and talent to Prussian politics.

Humboldt's first visit to the Basque Country lasted no more than one week: specifically, from October 10–18, 1799. This short stay was part of a longer "Spanish tour" that he took with his entire family, and that lasted more than seven months. It should be borne in mind that, by that time, the fundamental principles of his comparative anthropology had already been formulated, and that this is what led him to give tangible expression to his project by means of an extended trip through southern Europe. Humboldt's initial plan was to visit Italy, but a variety of circumstances led him to design a new tour that mainly involved travel within Spain. It is important to note that Humboldt's encounter with the Basques during this first trip was by no means accidental or undertaken as a result of some perceived external obligation. Instead, the visit had been carefully planned and eagerly anticipated by Humboldt. In fact, as part of his meticulous preparations for this trip in Paris, Humboldt developed a specific interest in the Basques, and especially in their language. This interest is reflected in a letter that he wrote to Schiller on April 26, 1799: "At the very least, one can safely say that it is the only country in Europe that has a genuinely original tongue. . . . And the grammar of this language is of supreme interest." Some six months later, Humboldt set foot in the Basque Country for the first time and, despite the brevity of his visit, the land, and its people and their language, made a deep impression upon him. But the most important impact of his trip was that it led to Humboldt's appreciation of the link between "human beings" and "human language" (that is, between nations and their respective languages) and to the beginnings of a reorientation of his anthropological research toward linguistic matters. On December 20, 1799, Humboldt wrote to the philologist Friedrich August Wolf from Madrid: "I think that, in the future, I am going to devote my energies even more exclusively to the study of language."

Humboldt's second sojourn among the Basques lasted five weeks, from April 27 through June 3, 1801. This was part of a planned "Basque journey" that he undertook alone. As noted, the first visit had sparked his intense interest in the Basques, leading him to avidly track down all possible information and material about this people after his return to Paris. "Altogether," Humboldt wrote, "this greatly heightened my desire to journey through this country."[14] The opportunity to do just that arose a short time later, when his friend Georg Wilhelm Bockelmann (who had to travel to Cádiz on business) invited Humboldt to accompany him as far as Bilbao. Humboldt accepted the invitation immediately, and, after looking for contacts who could help him, set off for the Basque Country with the clear intention of visiting all of the Basque provinces in both Spain and France, and of fashioning an "image" of the national character of the Basques. It is important to note here that his curiosity about Euskara, the Basque language (which had developed even before his first trip) had matured into a genuine interest, which was especially catalyzed when he became aware that little had been written up to that time either in or about that language. Humboldt wrote: "it became clear to me that a language that is only spoken cannot be learned anywhere else but in

---

14. See page 12.

situ."[15] Yet one should recall that his interest in learning the Basque language was above all else an anthropological interest. What this means is that, for him, the Basque *language* served as a means of characterizing the Basque *people*. The Basque language was thus "a desirable object of study"[16] during this second trip. It is for this reason that he established contact with people such as the Durango parish priest Pablo de Astarloa who could teach him something about the language.[17]

Humboldt's initial observations during his two journeys to the Basque Country can be found in his corresponding travel journals, specifically his "Tagebuch der Reise nach Spanien" (Journal of a Trip to Spain, 1799–1800) and his "Tagebuch der baskischen Reise" (Journal of the Basque Journey, 1801).[18] He expanded upon these reflections in his vast correspondence during his travels and the letters that he wrote to his wife Caroline during his second trip are especially noteworthy in this respect. It could thus be said that Humboldt's letters constituted a kind of supplementary travel diary. As a source of Humboldt's first contact with the Basques there is also a partially preserved account bearing the title "Cantabrica" (Cantabrica, 1800).[19] Yet his most important text about the Basque Country is *The Basques*, a work that, while mainly based on his second trip, also includes experiences from his previous trip.

Humboldt's Research in the Basque Country

Humboldt's travels to the Basque Country in 1799 and 1801 reflect the comparative anthropology that had been his brainchild. These journeys, and the texts that resulted from them, constitute the raw materials that he would use to characterize the Basques as a nation. The first text presented in this book, *The Basques*, is the first and most detailed component of his research on the Basque people and their language.

---

15. See page 12.

16. See page 11.

17. See "Pablo Pedro de Astarloa y Aguirre," in *Anthology of Apologists and Detractors of the Basque Language*, ed. Madariaga Orbea, 431–43. Humboldt's relationship with Astarloa is also discussed in the chapter, "Wilhelm Freiherr von Humboldt," 492–508, in the same work.

18. In Humboldt, *Gesammelte Schriften*, vol. 15, 47–355 and vol. 15, 356–451.

19. In Humboldt, *Gesammelte Schriften*, vol. 3, 114–36.

The Basque Nation as an Object of Study

The first thing that caught Humboldt's attention in the Basque Country, and that led him to write *about* and become interested *in* the Basque nation, was nothing other than the "unique tribal characteristics"[20] that he observed in them. Humboldt wrote that it was hardly necessary to delve deeply into their history to appreciate the fact that the Basques, despite the many obstacles in their path, had "ceaselessly retained the idiosyncrasies of their national character" as well as a "spirit of freedom and Independence."[21] Yet, at the same time that he discovered the distinct originality of the Basques—and therefore, ipso facto, their distinctiveness as a nation—Humboldt steadfastly maintained that they were "not simply poor mountain shepherds or even oppressed serfs."[22] Evidence of this was that, in contrast to the other ancient peoples of Europe, the Basques were able to create an "independent political constitution" for themselves, and to attain a "flourishing wealth," which they had conserved until Humboldt's day.[23] Humboldt even went so far as to say that the Basques had succeeded in "transplanting many of the most beneficial fruitions of the Enlightenment right into their wildest of lands; all that without forfeiting their uniqueness and original simplicity."[24] But most significant for Humboldt was the fact that, in the Basques, he discovered a people that, ensconced "between the mountains and the ocean," lived "alone like an island" in their own small territory—a people "quite independent of external and accidental influences. . . . What qualifies the Basques as a pure and separate national tribe is their language, constitution, custom, physiognomy, in short, everything that surrounds them, the scenery of the country not excluded."[25] It was undoubtedly this realization that led Humboldt to appreciate the possibility of studying the Basque people's national character.

What is particularly interesting in this connection is the fact that Humboldt wrote the German *Vasken* with a "V" rather than the expected "B." By doing this, Humboldt showed that he was first and foremost interested in the Basques to the extent that they formed a "nation." He

---

20. See page 11.
21. See page 99.
22. See page 10.
23. See page 6.
24. See page 6.
25. See page 10.

himself explains in a footnote on the first page of *Die Vasken* the reason that he uses an unusual spelling (as unusual in his time as it is in our own) to designate the name of this people. For him, the choice primarily grew out of his realization that there was no single word that encompassed all persons of Basque origin. He wrote: "One is at a loss should one want to apply one name to the whole tribe of the '*biscayische*' nation." One searches in vain for a name that has been accepted uniformly by Spanish, French, and Germans."[26] The Basques currently refer to themselves generically as *euskaldunak* (literally meaning those who possess, or speak, Euskara, the Basque language), but they also designated themselves "according to the provinces where they reside."[27] For their part, the French use the terms "*Biscayen*" and "*Basques*," as a means of designating the Spanish Basques and French Basques respectively. And the Spanish refer to "*las provincias vascongadas*" (the Basque provinces in Spain), a term which only includes those Basques residing within Spain's national borders. Such a state of affairs troubled Humboldt: "this unfortunate tribe has even lost the unity of its name."[28] Because Humboldt's goal was that of comparing different nations with one another, over and apart from other political reflections, it was important for him to have at his disposal a common name for the Basques that was also embraced by the Basque people themselves. This led Humboldt to make the following decision regarding the terminology used: "When speaking of the whole tribe scattered across the Basque Country, Biscay, and Navarre: Basques; when I speak of the Spanish part of the country: Biscay; when I speak of the Basques that are subjugated by the French Republic: French Basques."[29]

It is also important to note that Humboldt's observations do not lead him to be especially optimistic about the future of the Basque nation and language and that, although he stated his opinion with a heavy heart, he in fact believed that their disappearance was only a matter of time. He certainly did not see extinction as an immediate prospect. He wrote that "no likely violent commotion lies ahead of them today though"

---

26. See page 5n1.

27. Humboldt, "Berichtigungen und Zusätze zum ersten Abschnitte des zweiten Bandes des *Mithridates* über die kantabrische oder baskische Sprache" (1811), *Gesammelte Schriften*, vol. 3, 224.

28. See page 5n1.

29. See page 5n1. See editorial comment in note 1 of the main text on the rendering of these terms in English in the present work —ed.

and he even foresaw, at least in the short term, "a rise in population and affluence."[30] However, in the medium term and long term, Humboldt is rather less sanguine, citing the "slow influences that . . . will surely augur [their] demise." He offers the following explanation: "These influences more and more drive out their language and so, inevitably, their national character is lost at the same time . . . [and this] will occur at an even faster pace from now on."[31] It is true that Humboldt was more confident in his prediction of degeneration in France than in Spain, and that he even went so far as to claim that "the unique tribal characteristics of the Basques," (or, at least, of "a part of these idiosyncrasies") would survive and "remain for a long time to come."[32] For this reason, he thought it important to immediately address a pressing political issue: prescribing a treatment of the Basques by the states in which they resided that would best promote national diversity. But, again, Humboldt is generally pessimistic and resigned regarding the future: "Basque will possibly have vanished from the list of living languages in less than a century."[33] Humboldt's conviction that the Basque language's extinction was a very real possibility, as well as the fact that the loss of that language would lead to the loss of the nation, served as yet further motivation for him to seek a comprehensive characterization of the Basque nation.

Ethnographic Observations: Physiognomy, Culture, and Politics

The observations in Humboldt's *The Basques*, as well as in other related texts, do not follow any discernible plan or order of presentation. In fact, and consistent with his own conception of anthropology, Humboldt prefers to let the natural events of his journey determine his presentation, and thus avoid giving undue weight to preconceived notions. This lack of organization obliges one to impose some semblance of order on his observations for the purposes of this introductory essay. Thus, I will first address Humboldt's ethnographic material and follow this with his observations regarding the Basque language.

First let us consider Humboldt's observations of the physiognomy of Basque people and of the features of Basque territory. During his first visit, he had already noticed "the wonderful alternation between pleas-

---

30. See page 8.

31. See page 8.

32. See page 11.

33. See page 8.

antly covered hills and sweetly cultivated valleys," and, above all, "the vivacious and appealing physiognomy of the inhabitants."[34] While, unlike the influential Swiss physiogonmist Johann Kaspar Lavater, Humboldt did not consider physiognomist in and of itself to be a genuine source of knowledge, he did think it useful as a factor of secondary importance that could help orient the observer. The natural environment of the land of the Basques first caught his attention. Thus, we find abundant mention in his writings of mountains, ocean, farmlands, and so on, which he saw as reflecting the "character of this area."[35] Here we see Humboldt engaging in an exercise of drawing closer to what really interests him: a characterization of the Basque *people* in their own uniqueness. Indeed, it is in this context that he writes without qualification of their "striking national physiognomy."[36] Humboldt wrote to Goethe on November 28, 1799: "I've never seen a people that has preserved such an authentic national character, or a physiognomy that appeared so distinctive at first glance." And yet it is important to stress here that these physiognomical observations, however striking, merely serve the purpose of raising other questions that actually do result in progress toward a national characterization of the Basques.

Let us now move to Humboldt's observations regarding the way of life of the Basques, a people that, according to him, "have preserved a state of original simplicity regarding their customs" and that also serve to explain his anthropological interest in them.[37] The first thing that stands out in this respect is the variety of occupations he came across. There are, consequently, interesting observations regarding mining and, to a lesser extent, fishing, and—most of all—concerning agriculture. These constitute the basis for his conclusion—stated in a letter to Caroline on May 9, 1801—that the nucleus and origin of the nation are "the rural inhabitants who are dispersed among the hills." Secondly, there are observations regarding different kinds of leisure pastimes and entertainments enjoyed by the Basques. In this regard, Humboldt wrote of the "*zortzicos*" (which he defines as "eight-lined Basque national songs"), of traditional dancing (which he sees as reflecting "the character of a

34. See page 12.

35. See page 49.

36. Humboldt, "Tagebuch der Reise nach Spanien" (1799–1800), *Gesammelte Schriften*, vol. 15, 128.

37. See page 6.

completely popular merriment") and especially Basque *pelota* (which Humboldt identifies without hesitation as the "the Biscayans' greatest enjoyment" par excellence).[38] Finally, he offers other reflections regarding the "character" of the Basques, namely the ways that they educate themselves and come to see themselves as part of the same people. In fact, Humboldt emphasizes the "natural" and "egalitarian" aspects of their education, while also noting their "local pride" as well as their "national pride."[39] These are all clearly general observations regarding the "popular culture" of the Basques, understood in the broadest possible sense. This popular culture clearly both forms a part of their national identity, while at the same time constituting an important expression of that very identity.

In addition, Humboldt expressed particular surprise at the Basques having preserved and developed "an independent political constitution."[40] In this regard, there are a great many observations in his writings of a historical and political character, most of which offer detailed descriptions of the Basque *fueros* and the *juntas generales* (General Assemblies) of Gipuzkoa, Bizkaia, and Araba.[41] The *fueros* refer to centuries-old written laws that regulate Basque political and social life. Humboldt wrote that these *fueros* are based on the "personal liberty" cherished by the Basque people, and that they constitute "the nation's code of law."[42] For their part, the *juntas generales* are provincial parliaments that engage in a practical political activity that also captures Humboldt's imagination. He thus writes of the "pure and perfect democracy" of Gipuzkoa (in contrast to "a representative system") and of the "free constitution of the rural inhabitants" of Bizkaia (in contrast to a "feudal constitution of landowners"). On the other hand, Humboldt sees both positive and

---

38. On the significance of Basque dance in general and the *zortzikoa* in particular, see Bikandi, *Alejandro Aldekoa*, chap. 4 and chap. 5, esp. 171–73; for an explanation of pelota and its historical and cultural importance, see González Abrisketa, *Basque Pelota*, esp. part I.

39. Humboldt, "Tagebuch der baskischen Reise" (1801), *Gesammelte Schriften*, vol. 15, 395.

40. See page 6.

41. On the meaning and significance of the *fueros* and *juntas generales* in the Basque Country, see Monreal Zia, *The Old Law of Bizkaia*; Agirreazkuenaga, *The Making of the Basque Question*; Ibarra Güell and Irujo Ametzaga, *Basque Political Systems*.

42. See page 138.

negative aspects of the "brotherhoods" (guilds) of Araba.[43] Humboldt's observations regarding Basque politics also offer other characterizations and assessments of the native inhabitants. Specifically, he writes of "the harshness and envy of Spain's treatment of the 'Biscayan Provinces,'" and of how "the French Revolution has cast aside particular constitutions" of the "Basque Provinces."[44] Humboldt also reflects on the differences between the French and Spanish Basques, noting how a political border and, more specifically, the coincidental belonging of individuals to different states, had "wrenched them from their common setting and come to dominate their feelings."[45] We should remember in this regard that, as previously noted, Humboldt was not especially optimistic regarding the future of the Basques.

The Basque Language in Humboldt's Diaries and Travel Accounts

Humboldt's travel notes regarding Euskara, the Basque language, need to be considered as a separate question, given the fact that it was "a desirable object of study" during his second visit to the Basque Country. His quest to inform himself about Euskara was by no means easy, mainly because knowledge of the language was not widespread among the Basques themselves, and its use was mainly confined to the countryside (or, as Humboldt put it rather picturesquely, "to the mountain cabins."[46]) Humboldt also writes that the French Revolution in the French Basque territories and some Spanish laws in the Spanish Basque territories had sullied the purity of the Basque language. He even goes so far as to write of the "mutilation" and "disfigurement" of Basque words that have been incorporated into French or Spanish.[47] Yet these phenomena simply served to further pique his interest in the language. His travel journal is in fact chockfull with notes, observations, and comments on Euskara's vocabulary,

---

43. See page 90.

44. Humboldt, "Tagebuch der baskischen Reise" (1801), *Gesammelte Schriften*, vol. 15, 395.

45. See page 29. On the context of Humboldt's comments about the Basque Country in France see the classic study by Veyrin, *The Basques*; and more contemporary accounts in Jacob, *Hills of Conflict*, esp. chap. 1, and Ahedo Gurrutxaga, *The Transformation of National Identity in the Basque Country of France*, esp. chap. 1.

46. Humboldt, "Tagebuch der baskischen Reise" (1801), *Gesammelte Schriften*, vol. 15, 412.

47. See page 20n5.

especially regarding the etymology of toponyms in the Basque Country. Recalling his experiences in the Basque Country many years later, Humboldt wrote: "Within the territory, one could come to appreciate that the land itself offered the richest and most trustworthy dictionary [that] had conserved many words that had fallen into disuse."[48] For this reason, and with the assistance of people like Astarloa, he keenly studied the etymology of various Basque toponyms and names. Leaving aside the matter of the accuracy of his linguistic analysis, he clearly appears to have bought into the spurious notion that Euskara was an "original language." "Dating back to the dawn of civilization," Humboldt wrote in his first travel journal that the Basque language had conserved a striking "uniformity" that "constituted proof of its antiquity."[49]

From the very start, Humboldt was also struck by a "uniqueness" of Euskara that he saw as a reflection of the uniqueness of the Basque people themselves. He wrote in "Cantabrica": "The language is unique in terms of its words, morphology, and pronunciation. The tongue is incomprehensible to foreigners, and this is true of its most insignificant words and even its place names, which for the most part are derived from the Basque language. This uniqueness also applies, at least in part, to its oldest root words, which strike foreigners as strange and unusual."[50] Humboldt in fact saw Euskara as the "natural property"[51] of an ethnic group, and this led him to the conclusion that, in general terms, the study of a language should focus more on how it is spoken by the common people than on the written production of scholars. Humboldt was of the opinion that, while "literacy and science" clearly invested a language with "vibrancy, power, and depth," such a phenomenon only occurred after said language had served to express "their most immediate needs, their most natural sensations, most childish fantasies, even the rawest of their passions."[52] The study of Euskara thus led Humboldt to the realization that a language is not any less of a language because it has not yet matured academically (namely, the status of a language is not diminished because it cannot claim an impressive literature). In his conceptu-

---

48. Humboldt, "Über die Verschiedenheiten des menschlichen Sprachbaues" (1827–1829), *Gesammelte Schriften*, vol. 6, 139.

49. Humboldt, "Cantabrica" (1800), *Gesammelte Schriften*, vol. 3, 123.

50. Ibid., 122–23.

51. See page 9.

52. See page 9.

alization, every language constitutes an organic whole that seems to have arisen "suddenly out of nothing."[53] It is for this reason that he felt that the most fundamental questions regarding a language had to do with their evolution, not with their origin. It is precisely this view that sparked Humboldt's abiding interest in the linguistic and national particularity of the Basques. He wrote: "It is precisely because the Basque language is a vernacular, and because one must look among the Basques for sound judgment rather than any scientific education, for natural, warm and lively feeling rather than refined sensibility, that this language and this nation becomes for us highly interesting."[54]

It was this line of thinking that led Humboldt to reflect—first in relation to the Basque Country and later in more general terms—on the close bond between a nation and its language. "The identity of a tribe can never be proven with certitude beyond the identity of its language and the only thing that one can undoubtedly and without contest conclude from its appearance and examination is the fact that all Basques constitute a nation."[55] For Humboldt, Euskara constituted "the defining trait" of "a unique people," and this led him to write in a general way of "the intimate connection between the character of a people, its language, and its land."[56] He believed that language determines nationhood. In this regard it is telling that, in reference to Spanish and French components of the Basque people, he discerns a national unity that transcends political borders. Thus, in referring to the westernmost province of one side of the border and the easternmost province of the other side, he writes the following: "The . . . raw Bizkaian and the delicate Zuberoan . . . speak one tongue . . . [and] recognize each other as brothers belonging to one and the same nation."[57] As previously noted, Humboldt asserts that the provincial constitutions have played an important role in preserving Basque identity. Yet he also claims, and even more forcefully, that such a phenomenon can largely be explained by the Basque language. Thus, in reference to the Franco-Spanish border running through Basque territory, and the meaning of that border for the Basque people throughout

---

53. See page 103.

54. Ibid., 11.

55. Ibid., 181.

56. Humboldt, "Über die Verschiedenheiten des menschlichen Sprachbaues" (1827–1829), *Gesammelte Schriften*, vol. 6, 138.

57. Humboldt, "Die Vasken" (1805), *Gesammelte Schriften*, vol. 13, 195. Readers interested in Basque dialectical variation should see Zuazo, *The Dialects of Basque*.

the course of their history, Humboldt stresses the fact that it has been above all "on account of its very ancient, pure, and original language that this people has maintained a sense of independence within its national boundaries."[58] For this reason, it is hardly surprising that, in both the diaries and travel journals chronicling his time in the Basque Country, Humboldt continually insisted that "the diversity of languages and cultures" in fact constituted a more fundamental "kind of natural boundary among various nations."[59]

From the Basque Country to "Linguistic Anthropology"

Humboldt's research on the Basque people goes far beyond the descriptions that he recorded in his diaries and travel journals. In fact, the latter serve as nothing more than a point of departure for a more extensive project that includes other linguistic and historical studies of the Basque people. What is important in this connection is that the experience he obtained in his research on the Basques ultimately led Humboldt to pursue his professional endeavors within the framework of linguistic anthropology.

The Unfinished Monograph

Humboldt begins *Announcement of a Publication*, the second work presented in this book, with a description of a project aimed at providing a "complete description, a real *Monograph on the Basque Tribe*."[60] This was a project foreshadowed in embryonic form in at least two other texts that he wrote shortly after concluding his second trip to the Basque Country. The first of these was a note on the Basque language that he published as part of Christian August Fischer's book *Voyage en Espagne* (1801, translated into English as *Travels in Spain*, 1802).[61] The second can be found in Humboldt's "Fragmente der Monographie über die Basken"

---

58. Humboldt, "Über die Verschiedenheiten des menschlichen Sprachbaues" (1827–1829), *Gesammelte Schriften*, vol. 6, 138.

59. Humboldt, "Cantabrica" (1800), *Gesammelte Schriften*, vol. 3, 118.

60. Humboldt, "c über die Vaskische Sprach und Nation" (1812), *Gesammelte Schriften*, vol. 3, 291–92.

61. See Humboldt's note on Euskara in French in Fischer, *Voyage en Espagne*, vol. 1, 139–44 and in English in Fischer, *Travels in Spain*, 103–7. For example, Humboldt remarks that, "the language of Biscay deserves the particular attention of philologists, though it has hitherto been too much neglected" (103 in the English-language edition).

(Fragments of the monograph on the Basques, 1801–1802).[62] In the 1812 text, Humboldt wrote that "the Basques" constituted "a very interesting object of study." Specifically, he proposed a three-part investigation that would provide a comprehensive description of the Basque people as a nation. He wrote that the first part would "provide the reader a clear portrait of the country and its inhabitants." The form that this part of the project took turned out to be *The Basques*, with its observations on the Spanish and French components of the Basque Country.[63] Humboldt wrote that the more extensive second part of his projected monograph would offer a rigorous and systematic "explanation of the Basque language," namely "a clear idea" of both its grammatical and lexical structure.[64] The third and final part, which would be based on the first two segments, was conceived as the presentation of a series of "historical and philosophical investigations into the Basque nation and language," which would define their place within the family of nations and languages.[65] Humboldt never finished the Basque monograph in the way he had projected. However, he did complete the first part and, in addition, conducted in-depth research on the topics projected for parts two and three regarding both the language and history of the Basque people.

Between 1810 and 1814, Humboldt wrote a number of texts in which he provided an analysis of the Basque language. One of these was *Announcement of a Publication*. Another was titled "Berichtigungen und Zusätze zum ersten Abschnitte des zweiten Bandes des Mithridates über die Cantabrische oder baskische Sprache" (1811, Correction and Additions to the First Section of the Second Volume of the Untitled Work of Mithridates Regarding the Cantabrian or Basque Language).[66] In general, one could say that, of the two parts into which his observations on the Basque language are divided, the first corresponds to the study of its "lexical formation." Humboldt's most important proposal in this regard is that of reversing Manuel de Larramendi's Spanish-Basque diction-

---

62. In *Gesammelte Schriften*, vol. 7, 593–603.

63. Humboldt, "Ankündigung einer Schrift über die Vaskische Sprach und Nation" (1812), *Gesammelte Schriften*, vol. 3, 294.

64. Ibid.

65. Ibid., 299.

66. In *Gesammelte Schriften*, vol. 3, 222–87. In this text Humboldt presents a series of complementary notes to an article about Basque, an article that forms a part of a four-volume work called *Mithridates oder allgemeine Sprachkunde*, edited J. C. Adelung y J. S. Vater. See the bibliography.

ary, thereby creating a Basque-Spanish dictionary in which words would be presented in terms of their "phonetic relationships" rather than in terms of "semantic affinity."[67] Similarly, and in reference to the analysis of Basque words, Humboldt wrote that, "the Basque language scholar I used the most [Astarloa] has created his own system in this matter, which, correct or false, must be mentioned and reviewed in any case."[68] The second part of his linguistic observations can best be seen within the framework of Humboldt's investigation of the "grammatical formation" of the Basque language. Here as elsewhere, he relies on Astarloa's studies as a fundamental source. Although Humboldt criticizes him for his "many strange and exaggerated ideas," he also gives Astarloa credit for having utilized the correct "principle" of acknowledging "the need to reduce the confusing quantity of specific examples of use to general and simple rules."[69] Specifically, Humboldt studied the formation of sentences in Euskara, noting their "agglutinative tendency."[70] Thereafter, he analyzed those grammatical aspects of the language that he felt were fundamentally important: the declination of nouns and the conjugation of verbs.[71] These considerations allow us to confidently conclude that, in accordance with his proposal for the second part of his projected monograph, Humboldt's interest in the Basque language received detailed and varied expression in his writings.

Years later, Humboldt wrote "Prüfung der Untersuchungen über die Urbewohner Hispaniens vermittelst der vaskischen Sprache" (An examination of studies of the ancient inhabitants of Hispania by means of the Basque language, 1821).[72] Humboldt himself described this work in a letter to Goethe as growing out of his project of "uniting historical

---

67. Humboldt, "Berichtigungen und Zusätze zum ersten Abschnitte des zweiten Bandes des Mithridates über die Cantabrische oder baskische Sprache" (1811), *Gesammelte Schriften*, vol. 3, 267, 252. On Larramendi, see Madariaga Orbea, ed., *Anthology of Apologists and Detractors of the Basque Language*, 322–52.

68. Humboldt, "Ankündigung einer Schrift über die vaskische Sprache und Nation" (1812), *Gesammelte Schriften*, vol. 3, 298.

69. Humboldt, "Berichtigungen und Zusätze zum ersten Abschnitte des zweiten Bandes des Mithridates über die Cantabrische oder baskische Sprache" (1811), *Gesammelte Schriften*, vol. 3, 268.

70. Cf. Humboldt, "Ueber die Verschiedenheit des menschlichen Sprachbaues und ihren Einfluss auf die geistige Entwicklung des Menschengeschlechts, Gesammelte Schriften" (1830–1835), vol. 7, 150.

71. Cf. Gárate, *Guillermo de Humboldt*, 164.

72. In Humboldt, *Gesammelte Schriften*, vol. 4, 57–232.

and linguistic research" on the Basques. This work could justly be characterized as marking the height of popularity of the so-called Basque-Iberianist theory;[73] a theory that had been initially proposed more than two centuries previously by Esteban de Garibay in *Los XL libros d'el Compendio historial de las Chronicas y universal historia de todos los Reynos de España* (The forty books of the historical compendium of the chronicles and universal history of all the kingdoms of Spain, 1571) and which would later be amplified by Hugo Schuchardt's *Die iberische Deklination* (Iberian declination, 1907).[74] In Humboldt's words, this theory held that "the ancient Iberians were the ancestors of today's Basques, and that the former could thus be said to have constituted "a nation that populated the entire peninsula, and that spoke a single language" (that is, an archaic form of Euskara).[75] In this way, Humboldt gave scholarly expression to the assertions of his predecessors regarding this subject. He also undoubtedly saw a number of Basque toponyms and old names as supporting his particular view. Thus, after explaining the "etymological principles" of his research, Humboldt demonstrates the strong resemblance between "the Iberian and Basque phonetic systems," concluding that "Basque was a local language" in ancient Iberia.[76] Humboldt in fact had two different but related goals: "to establish a new foundation for the known history of the nation and its people, and the clarification of the origin, extent, and relatives of the Basque language."[77] In this regard, it is important to point out that, while it is true that Humboldt applied a certain scholarly veneer to the Basque-Iberianist theory, it is no less true that the deciphering of Iberian conducted by Manuel Gómez-Moreno beginning in 1922 led to the discrediting of that selfsame theory.[78] Be that as it may, it seems reasonable to conclude that the "Prüfung" contains material that Humboldt had planned to include in the third part of his projected monograph.

---

73. On this see Caro Baroja, *Sobre la lengua vasca y el vasco-iberismo*.

74. Basque courtier and historian, 1525–1599, see biographical entry in Madariaga Orbea, *Anthology of Apologists and Detractors of the Basque Language*, 187–89.

75. Humboldt, "Prüfung der Untersuchungen über die Urbewohner Hispaniens vermittelst der vaskischen Sprache" (1821), *Gesammelte Schriften*, vol. 4, 174–75.

76. Ibid., 67, 76, 128.

77. Ibid., 64–65.

78. Caro Baroja, *Sobre la lengua vasca y el vasco-iberismo*, 130.

Humboldt's Basque Research as a Watershed

The importance of Humboldt's travels among and research on the Basques resides first and foremost in the fact that this activity led him to reformulate his anthropological theory, and to shift its emphasis in the direction of linguistic research. His encounter with the Basques marked a watershed in his career because it led him to fully appreciate the implications of something that he had hitherto only dimly perceived: Nation and language are not simply concommitant elements but instead constitute inextricably related phenomena. In the words of his biographer Paul Sweet:

> From the beginning of his researches on the Basques, Humboldt approached the problem on a broad front. He was interested, of course, in the language per se; but since he did not conceive of language [as] distinct from its cultural setting, he was at pains also to accumulate, by observation and study, concrete details about the Basque way of life, with the object of reaching philosophical conclusions about the relation of the nation to language in general.[79]

Another way of expressing this is that his visits to the Basque Country provided him the opportunity to determine, with a greater degree of precision and from a fresh perspective, the general purpose of a new comparative anthropology with a greater linguistic emphasis. Humboldt himself wrote the following to Madame de Staël on June 7, 1801 (just four days after concluding his second visit to the Basque Country):

> The task before us will consist of nothing more than finding easy and reliable ways to obtain knowledge regarding many different nations, their languages, and their literatures, without wasting precious time on the mechanical study of words and rules. It seems to me that it is possible to do this if we go back to the sources to lay the foundations of an analytical history of nations and their languages. This is the task to which I have been dedicated for the last few years.

In practical terms, Humboldt's new emphasis on linguistics was due in large part to his having discovered a language like Euskara, which he himself characterized as a "vernacular."[80] Humboldt specifically meant here that Basque is essentially a spoken language that has remained in its

---

79. Sweet, *Wilhelm von Humboldt: A Biography*, vol. 1, 241.

80. Humboldt, "Die Vasken" (1805), *Gesammelte Schriften*, vol. 13, 11.

natural state and thus preserved its unique structure. It is therefore not in the least surprising that this particular language became an interesting subject of anthropological study for him. As Jürgen Trabant writes, "Humboldt 'the anthropologist' was so struck by the spiritual aspect of Euskara that it began to absorb more and more of his energies."[81] Until he took up the study of Euskara, Humboldt had exclusively studied languages—whether classical or modern—that had formidable literary traditions. It is for this reason that his encounter with Euskara posed a challenge for him that enabled him to come to the realization that all languages were of both anthropological and linguistic importance. In this regard, Koldo Mitxelena (also known as Luis Michelena) writes the following: "Humboldt was all too aware of the negative consequences for the development of general linguistics of an overemphasis (for a number of different reasons) on the most 'important' languages and their relatives."[82] Thus, Humboldt began to take a stronger interest in the Basque language itself rather than in its literature. As Georg Bossong notes, "He would no longer be especially concerned with what 'poets do' with the language, but rather with its natural and largely subconcious development in the speech of common people."[83] Moreover, Andreas Flitner and Klaus Giel also add that, from that point forward, Humboldt sought to "understand the language 'as a language' in its own terms, and not as a raw material for artistic and literary creation."[84] Consequently, Humboldt acknowledged that there was a general problem regading the study of language thanks to and as a result of his engagment with Euskara.

"The Basque problem," writes Friedrich Schaffstein, "shifted Humboldt's emphasis toward linguistic research."[85] The main goals of his comparative anthropology remained in place. However, after his engagement with the Basques, language became the primary focus of all of his research. Tilman Borsche, for example, notes that, "Living among the Basque people and their language served as the primary catalyst to dedicate the rest of his life to research on 'the diversity and structure

---

81. Trabant, *Traditionen Humboldts*, 45–46.

82. Michelena, "Guillaume de Humboldt et la langue basque," 109.

83. Bossong, "Wilhelm von Humboldt y Hugo Schuchardt," 174.

84. Flitner and Giel, in *Wilhelm von Humboldt: Werke in fünf Bänden*, vol. 5, 636.

85. Schaffstein, *Wilhelm von Humboldt: Ein Lebensbild*, 152.

of human language.'"[86] Before he became acquainted with the Basques, language had nothing more than a secondary role in Humboldt's work in terms of characterizing individuals and nations. And as Borsche points out: "It was only the two trips from Paris to the Basque Country in 1799 and 1801—and the study of the Basque language that began with those journeys—that steered him in a different direction."[87] Through his research on Euskara, Humboldt came to realize that all languages—over and apart from their literary and scientific use—are capable of developing the most diverse linguistic functions, and this led him to a deeper engagement with language generally. As Flitner and Giel put it, he would no longer ask "if" a particular language is or is not "capable of" but instead "how" or "according to what organizational models" a language "manages to order its elements in a way that allows it to either construct particular forms or to dispense with them."[88] Thus, Humboldt understands that the main challenge in his future linguistic studies would be capturing the internal order of each language. The crucial importance of Humboldt's Basque experience in the development of his thought is summed up by Sweet in the following words: "In Humboldt's intellectual development, his experience of the Basques was to be the most significant thing that had happened to him during the years he was away from Germany between 1797 and 1801."[89]

Development of a Theory of Language

Humboldt's research on the Basques coincides with his political activity, which began (shortly after the conclusion of his second trip to the Basque Country) in Rome on May 25, 1802 and ended on December 31, 1819 in Berlin (just before publishing his final work on the Basques). The importance of this research—which was frequently interrupted and never definitively completed—resides in the fact that it reflects the need to transform his comparative anthropology into comparative linguistics. In this regard, and with a view to properly contextualizing this research on the Basques, I will now examine some of the general aspects of the anthropological theory of language developed by Humboldt for the most part from 1820 to 1835. His most important work in this context is *Ueber die*

---

86. Borsche, *Wilhelm von Humboldt*, 26.

87. Ibid., 138.

88. Flitner and Giel, in *Wilhelm von Humboldt: Werke in fünf Bänden*, vol. 5, 637.

89. Sweet, *Wilhelm von Humboldt: A Biography*, vol. 1, 231.

*Verschiedenheit des menschlichen Sprachbaues und ihren Einfluss auf die
geistige Entwicklung des Menschengeschlechts* (The heterogeneity of language and its influence on the intellectual development of mankind).⁹⁰

From the entirety of Humboldt's theory of language, I would like
to note three key ideas of a markedly anthropolgoical and philosophical
nature that seem to underlie his linguistic thinking. The first of these is
that the question of the "origin of language" is in effect the same as the
question of the "human origin" and therefore cannot possibly yield a
"genetic" answer. In line with Herder, Humboldt believed that "a human
being is a human being only because of language" and also that "language emerges as a necessity from every human being.⁹¹ The discussion
regarding the "origin of language" therefore becomes for Humboldt a
kind of excuse for posing the problem of the meaning and role of language in the context of "the inherent constitution of human beings."

Second is Humboldt's idea that we can only approximate and never
attain a satisfactory conceptualization of the "essence of language," thus
mirroring the same phenomenon with respect to human nature. Humboldt places supreme emphasis on the dynamic rather than the static
features of language: "Language itself is not a work (*ergon*) but rather
an activity (*energeia*)."⁹² He similarly underscores the idea that language
does not merely serve as a transmitter of thought: "Language is the organ
that shapes thought."⁹³ These are the premises underlying Humboldt's
quest to determine the nature and importance of language.

Third and final is his assertion that language constitutes an "intermediate space" between humans and the world that, through its historical and cultural reality, exercises an influence on both individuals and
nations. "The word is situated between the world of external reality and
the world of our own inner reality."⁹⁴ But this language is only real in
actual human languages and, for this reason, its influence actually mani-
fests itself in various "linguistic images of the world." This represents an

---

90. In *Gesammelte Schriften*, vol. 7, 1–344.

91. Humboldt, "Über das vergleichende Sprachstudium in Beziehung auf die verschie-
denen Epochen der Sprachentwicklung" (1820), *Gesammelte Schriften*, vol. 4, 15.

92. Humboldt, "Ueber die Verschiedenheit des menschlichen Sprachbaues und ihren
Einfluss auf die geistige Entwicklung des Menschengeschlechts" (1830–1835), *Gesammelte Schriften*, vol. 7, 45–46.

93. Ibid., 53–55.

94. Humboldt, "Latium und Hellas oder Betrachtungen über das klassische Altertum"
(1806), *Gesammelte Schriften*, vol. 3, 167.

embryonic formulation of what would later become known as "linguistic relativism."

Humboldt's theory of language also poses other anthropological and pedagogical questions, three of which seem to be of special importance. The first of these is his reflection on the real "social character of language," which leads to his bold contention that the "act of speaking" and the "act of understanding" occur at one and the same time, and that therefore both of these acts "are nothing more than different effects of the same linguistic force."[95] In essence, human understanding is only possible because all human beings share the same basic nature. But Humboldt clearly realizes that this also implies a "possibility of *mis*-understanding*.*" This is why Humboldt emphasizes the hermeneutic importance of "dialogue."

Second is his contention that language only becomes real in historical languages spoken by linguistic communities that each has its own cultural history. This contention is the basis of Humboldt's concept of a "national character of language." In line with his realization of the genetic inseparability of humanness and human language, Humboldt here emphasizes the idea that the nation does not precede its language, or vice versa. He therefore writes: "The distribution of the human race among nations is nothing more than their distribution according to language."[96] In other words, the nation is synonymous with the linguistic community.

Third is the assertion that language is not only human but humanizing. What this means is that we can and must speak of the "educational character of language" in the sense that it plays "the most important role" in the "process" by which "individuality" approximates "universality."[97] According to Humboldt, human education takes concrete form in a process of ongoing cognitive and moral refining that is only possible via the mediation of language, which allows us to not only expand our knowledge, but also to learn to coexist.

---

95. Humboldt, "Ueber die Verschiedenheit des menschlichen Sprachbaues und ihren Einfluss auf die geistige Entwicklung des Menschengeschlechts" (1830–1835), *Gesammelte Schriften*, vol. 7, 56.

96. Humboldt, "Über die Verschiedenheiten des menschlichen Sprachbaues" (1827–1829), *Gesammelte Schriften*, vol. 6, 126.

97. Ibid., 124, 126.

I conclude this summary of Humboldt's theory of language by recalling once more that his encounter with the Basque people and their language occurred when he began stressing the importance of language within his anthropology. One of the most important Humboldt scholars, Clemens Menze, explains this change as follows: "It was during the second trip to Spain (in 1801), which was exclusively devoted to the study of the Basque language, that linguistic issues began to completely consume Humboldt. It was at that time that his reflections on national character became inextricably intertwined with the question of language."[98] Sweet is similarly certain of the crucial role of Humboldt's Basque experience in the development of his linguistic thought: "Humboldt's place of honor in the history of linguistics is chiefly due to his general theory and method. In his work on the Basques, he laid a significant part of the groundwork for that theory."[99] Looking back more than twenty years later on his research on the Basque language, Humboldt wrote: "This initial experience within the arena of linguistic studies established the mold for those experiences that followed."[100]

Some Observations Regarding the Texts in This Book

In terms of formal training, one must acknowledge that Humboldt was an amateur in the fields of anthropological-philosophical and anthropological-linguistic research. This helps us understand not only why so little of his work was published during his lifetime, but also why his work is so wide ranging and, at times, even fragmentary. Yet these issues do not gainsay the fact that the entirety of his work, irrespective of its apparent diversity, has a constant center of gravity, and that is the human being— not only what he is, but what he might become. This remained the case when his anthropology took a linguistic turn. Specifically, the Basque experience of Humboldt marks an important turning point in his anthropological thinking. That is why we are presenting two of his seminal works here regarding the Basque people and their language.

The complete title of the first text presented in this book is as follows: *Die Vasken, oder Bemerkungen auf einer Reise durch Biscaya und das französische Basquenland im Frühling des Jahrs 1801, nebst Unter-*

---

98. Menze, *Wilhelm von Humboldts Lehre und Bild vom Menschen*, 213.

99. Sweet, *Wilhelm von Humboldt: A Biography*, vol. 1, 241.

100. Humboldt, "Über die Verschiedenheiten des menschlichen Sprachbaues" (1827–1829), *Gesammelte Schriften*, vol. 6, 139.

suchungen über die Vaskische Sprache und Nation, und einer kurzen Darstellung ihrer Grammatik und ihres Wörtervorraths (The Basques, or Observations on a Journey through Biscay and the French Basque Country in the Spring of 1801 Amid Studies on the Basque Language and Nation, and a Brief Demonstration of Its Grammar and Vocabulary). Humboldt began to write this text in Berlin in 1802 and completed it in Rome in 1805. However, for a variety of reasons, the manuscript was lost until Albert Leitzmann found it and published it in 1920 in volume 13 of Humboldt's *Gesammelte Schriften* (Complete Works). What is important for our purposes is that *The Basques* resulted from a "firm decision" (as Humboldt wrote on June 28, 1802 to the linguist Joachim Heinrich Campe) to give up the project of providing a complete account of his trip to Spain and to concentrate instead on his trip to the Basque Country. In fact, as a result of his initial trip of 1799, he had already produced a number of texts on different regions of Spain, such as "Der Montserrat bei Barcelona" (On Montserrat, near Barcelona, 1800), "Über das antike Theater in Sagunt" (On the old theater in Sagunt, 1800-1801), and "Cantabrica" (1800). Following this decision, a portion of "Cantabrica" (which was initially titled "Reiseskizzen aus Biscaya" or "Travel notes from Biscay") was included in *The Basques*.

Humboldt's purpose was to characterize the Basque nation and, in fact, *The Basques*, which for the most part consists of an account of his second trip to the Basque Country in 1801, was (as noted) planned as the first part of a much larger project that he never completed. We also need to recognize that this work (which he dedicated to his traveling companion Bockelmann) does not deliver what it promises in its long title. Specifically, it does not offer linguistic research studies of Euskara.

The second text presented in this book, which Humboldt published in 1812, bears the title *Announcement of a Publication Regarding the Basque Language and the Basque Nation*. It seems that, after having taken up and abandoned his research on the Basques a number of different times (his frenetic political activity made sustained involvement in such a pursuit well-nigh impossible) he at that point felt strong enough to make the public aware of his project. It is important to note that, by then, Humboldt had already spent a good many years preparing a monograph study on the Basques that he had publicly referred to on a number of occasions. There is abundant evidence of this project: a "Note on Euskara" published in French in 1801 and English in 1802; the previously mentioned "Fragments of a Monograph on the Basques" (1801–1802); and various letters written between 1801 and 1807 in which he describes his plans to a number of different friends. During his stay in Rome (1802–1808), Humboldt also prepared detailed outlines of work projects aimed at analyzing the Basque language.[101] However, after completing the final draft of *The Basques* in 1805, he felt tired and, although he continued to compile material for his Basque monograph, he never actually completed any important work. Humboldt even gave expression to being somewhat "fed up" with his studies about the Basques in a letter written on July 18, 1807 to Johann Gottfried Schweighäuser. Following his transfer to Vienna in 1810, Humboldt took up his research on texts on the Basque language with renewed energy, and in 1811 he completed the previously mentioned "Berichtigungen und Zusätze." It was within this context that the second text of this book, the *Announcement of a Publication*, was published in 1812.

Nearly another decade elapsed before Humboldt would, after abandoning politics, once again seriously concern himself with matters pertaining to the Basques (and with other research interests as well). In 1821, he published the aforementioned "Prüfung," which contained part of the material that he had projected for his monograph. It is important in this regard to point out that Humboldt's research on the Basques, however satisfactory or unsatisfactory its results, is not insignificant within the contexts of his anthropological and linguistic thought as a whole. On the contrary, it could well be said that the development of Humboldt's thought can only be explained by fully appreciating the importance of his research on the Basques. Conversely, it is no less true that this research can only be fully understood within the frame of reference of his thought in general. Bringing together both his specific interest in the Basques and a general tenet of Humboldt's anthropology, I will conclude by hoping that the texts presented here will help the reader not only understand better who the Basques *are*, but also what they might be capable of *becoming*.

---

101. Cf. Humboldt, "Fragmente der Monographie über die Basken" (1801–1802), *Gesammelte Schriften*, vol. 7, 604–5.

Bibliography

General Editions of the Works of Wilhelm von Humboldt

Wilhelm von Humboldt. Gesammelte Schriften, edited by Albert Leitzmann. 18 volumes. Berlin: Behr, 1903–1936.

Wilhelm von Humboldt. Werke in fünf Bänden, edited by Andreas Flitner and Klaus Giel. 4 volumes. Darmstadt: Wissenschaftliche Buchgesellschaft, 1960–1981.

Wilhelm von Humboldt. Schriften zur Anthropologie der Basken, edited by Bernhard Hurch. Paderborn: Ferdinand Schöning, 2010.

Wilhelm von Humboldt. Baskische Wortstudien und Grammatik, edited by Bernhard Hurch. Paderborn: Ferdinand Schöning, 2012.

In English

Essays on Language. Edited by T. Harden and D. Farrelly. Translated by John Wieczorek and Ian Roe. Frankfurt am Main and New York: P. Lang, 1997.

Humanist Without Portfolio: An Anthology of the Writings of Wilhelm von Humboldt. Translated from the German with an introduction by Marianne Cowan. Detroit: Wayne State University Press, 1963.

The Limits of State Action. Edited by J.W. Burrow. Indianapolis: Liberty Fund, 1993.

Linguistic Variability and Intellectual Development. Translated by George C. Buck and Frithjof A. Raven. Philadelphia: University of Pennsylvania Press, 1971.

On Language: On the Diversity of Human Language Construction and Its Influence on the Mental Development of the Human Species. Edited by Michael Losonsky. Translated by Peter Heath. Cambridge and New York: Cambridge University Press, 1999.

"On the Task of the Historian." Translated by Linda DeMichiel. In *The Hermeneutics Reader*, edited by Kurt Mueller-Vollmer. New York: Continuum, 2000.

Religious Thoughts and Opinions. Boston: W. Crosby and H.P. Nichols, 1851.

The Spheres and Duties of Government. Translated by Joseph Coulthard Jr. London: J. Chapman, 1854. Reprint: Bristol: Thoemmes Press, 1994.

Thoughts and Opinions of a Statesman. London: W. Pickering, 1850.

Letters Written by Humboldt That Are Cited in This Book (Ordered by Correspondent's Name)

Campe, Joachim Heinrich: In *Briefe von Wilhelm von Humboldt* (Abhandlungen der Deutschen Akademie der Wissenschaften zu Berlin, Philosophisch-historische Klasse, Jg. 1948, Nr.3), edited by Albert Leitzmann. Berlin: Akademie Verlag, 1949.

Diede, Charlotte: In Wilhelm Freiherr von Humboldt. *Wilhelm von Humboldts Briefe an eine Freundin,* edited by Albert Leitzmann. Leipzig: Insel, 1909.

Goethe, Johann Wolfgang von: In Johann Wolfgang von Goethe. *Goethes Briefwechsel mit Wilhelm und Alexander von Humboldt,* edited by Ludwig Geiger. Berlin: Bondy, 1909.

Humboldt, Caroline von: In Wilhelm Freiherr von Humboldt. *Wilhelm und Caroline von Humboldt in ihren Briefen,* edited by Anna von Sydow. Berlin: Mittler, 1906–1916. Reprint, Osnabrück: Neudruck, 1968.

Schiller, Friedrich: In *Der Briefwechsel zwischen Friedrich Schiller und Wilhelm von Humboldt,* edited by Siegfried Seidel. Berlin: Aufbau, 1962.

Schweighäuser, Johann Gottfried: In *Wilhelm von Humboldts Briefe an Johann Gottfried Schweighäuser. Zum ersten Male nach den Originalen,* edited by Albert Leitzmann, Jena: Frommann-Biedermann, 1934.

Staël, Madame de: In *W. v. Humboldt und Frau von Staël,* Deutsche Rundschau, 169, 170, 171, edited by Albert Leitzmann, 1916–1917.

Wolf, Friedrich August: In Wilhelm von Humboldt. *Wilhelm von Humboldt: Briefe an Friedrich August Wolf,* edited by Philip Mattson. Berlin and New York: Walter de Gruyter, 1990.

Cited Secondary Literature and Other Recommended Reading

Adelung, Johann Christoph, and Johann Severin Vater, *Mithridates oder allgemeine Sprachkunde mit dem Vater Unser als Sprachprobe bey nae fünfhundert Sprachen und Mundarten,* 4 Bände [1806, 1809, 1812, 1817]. Berlin: Vossische Buchhandlung, 1806–1817.

Agirreazkuenaga, Joseba. *The Making of the Basque Question: Experiencing Self-Government, 1793–1877.* Reno: Center for Basque Studies, 2011.

Agirreazkuenaga, Joseba, and Joxe Azurmendi, eds. "Wilhelm von Humboldt: Un puente entre dos pueblos." Special issue, *RIEV* 41, no. 2 (1996).

———. "Wilhelm von Humboldt: Euskal Herria arakatzen, 1801; investiga en Vasconia, 1801; Untersuchungen im Baskenland, 1801." Special issue, *RIEV* 48, no. 1 (2003).

Ahedo Gurrutxaga, Igor. *The Transformation of National Identity in the Basque Country of France, 1789–2006.* Translated by Cameron J. Watson. Reno: Center for Basque Studies, 2008.

Bikandi, Sabin. *Alejandro Aldekoa: Master of the Pipe and Tabor Dance Music in the Basque Country.* Reno: Center for Basque Studies, 2009.

Borsche, Tilman. *Wilhelm von Humboldt.* München: C. H. Beck, 1990.

Bossong, Georg. "Wilhelm von Humboldt y Hugo Schuchardt: Dos eminentes vascólogos alemanes." *Arbor* 467–468 (1984): 163–81.

Brown, Roger Langham. *Wilhelm von Humboldt's Conception of Linguistic Relativity.* The Hague and Paris: Mouton, 1967.

Caro Baroja, Julio. *Sobre la lengua vasca y el vasco-iberismo.* Donostia-San Sebastián: Txertoa, 1988.

Fischer, Christian August. *Voyage en Espagne, aux années 1797 et 1798; faisant suite au Voyage en Espagne, du citoyen Bourgoing.* Translated by Charles Friedrich Kramer. 2 volumes. Paris: Duchesne, 1801. In English: *Travels in Spain in 1797 and 1798.* Translated from the German. London: T.N. Longman and O. Rees, 1802.

Gárate, Justo. *Guillermo de Humboldt: Estudio de sus trabajos sobre Vasconia.* Bilbao: Imprenta Provincial de Vizcaya, 1933.

González Abrisketa, Olatz. *Basque Pelota: A Ritual, An Aesthetic.* Reno: Center for Basque Studies, 2012.

Hurch, Bernhard. *Die baskischen Materialien aus dem Nachlass Wilhelm von Humboldts.* Paderborn: Ferdinand Schöning, 2002.

Ibarra Güell, Pedro, and Xabier Irujo Ametzaga, eds. *Basque Political Systems.* Reno: Center for Basque Studies, 2012.

Jacob, James E. *Hills of Conflict: Basque Nationalism in France.* Reno: University of Nevada Press, 1994.

Joseph, John E. "A Matter of Consequence: Humboldt, Race and the Genius of the Chinese Language." *Historiographia Linguistica* 26, nos. 1–2 (1999): 89–148.

Madariaga Orbea, Juan, ed. "Wilhelm Freiherr von Humboldt." In *Anthology of Apologists and Detractors of the Basque Language.* Translated by Frederick H. Fornoff, María Cristina Saavedra, Amaia Gabantxo, and Cameron J. Watson. Reno: Center for Basque Studies, 2006.

Manchester, Martin L. *The Philosophical Foundations of Humboldt's Linguistic Doctrines.* Amsterdam and Philadelphia: J. Benjamins, 1985.

Menze, Clemens. *Wilhelm von Humboldts Lehre und Bild vom Menschen.* Ratingen: Henn, 1965.

Michelena, Luis. "Guillaume de Humboldtt et la langue basque." *Lingua e stile* 1 (1973): 107–25.

Miller, Robert L. *The Linguistic Relativity Principle and Humboldtian Ethnolinguistics.* The Hague and Paris: Mouton, 1968.

———. "From Poetics to Linguistics: Wilhelm von Humboldt and the Romantic Idea of Language." *Le Groupe de Coppet.* Actes et Documents du deuxième Colloque de Coppet, edited by Simone Balayé and Jean-Daniel Candaux. Geneva and Paris: M. Slatkin and H. Champion, 1977.

Monreal Zia, Gregorio. *The Old Law of Bizkaia (1452).* Translated by William A. Douglass and Linda White. Reno: Center for Basque Studies, 2005.

Mueller-Volmer, Kurt. *Wilhelm von Humboldts Sprachwissenschaft: Ein kommentiertes Verzeichnis des sprachwissenschaftlichen Nachlasses.* Paderborn: F. Schöning, 1993.

Olson, Kenneth Russell. "Wilhelm von Humboldt's Philosophy of Language." PhD diss., Stanford University, 1978.

Quillien, Jean. *L'Anthropologie philosophique de Guillaume de Humboldt.* Lille: Presses Universitaires de Lille, 1991.

Roberts, John. *Wilhelm von Humboldt and German Liberalism: A Reassessment.* Oakville, ON and Niagra Falls, NY: Mosaic Press, 2009.

Schaffstein, Friedrich. *Wilhelm von Humboldt: Ein Lebensbild.* Frankfurt am Main: V. Klostermann, 1952.

Stubbs, Elsina. *Wilhelm von Humboldt's Philosophy of Language, Its Sources and Influence.* Lewiston, NY: E. Mellen Press, 2002.

Sweet, Paul. *Wilhelm von Humboldt: A Biography.* 2 volumes. Columbus: Ohio State University Press, 1978–1980.

Trabant, Jürgen. *Traditionen Humboldts*. Frankfurt am Main: Suhrkamp, 1990.

Underhill, James W. *Humboldt, Worldview and Language*. Edinburgh: Edinburgh University Press, 2009.

Veyrin, Philippe. *The Basques of Zuberoa, Lapurdi, and Lower Navarre: Their History and Their Traditions*. Translated by Andrew Brown. Reno: Center for Basque Studies, 2011.

Vick, Brian. "Of Basques, Greeks, and Germans: Liberalism, Nationalism, and the Ancient Republican Tradition in the Thought of Wilhelm von Humboldt." *Central European History* 40 (2007): 653–81.

Zabaleta Gorrotxategi, Iñaki. *Wilhelm von Humboldt: Hezkuntza eta hizkuntza*. Donostia-San Sebastián: Jakin, 2005.

———. *Wilhelm von Humboldts Forschungen über die baskische Nation und Sprache und ihre Bedeutung für seine Anthropologie*. Bilbao: UPV-EHU, 2006.

The Basques

or Observations on a Journey
through Biscay and the French Basque Country
in the Spring of 1801
Amid
Studies on the Basque Language and Nation,
and a Brief Demonstration of Its Grammar and Vocabulary

Wilhelm von Humboldt

Dedicated to Mr. Bockelmann from Hamburg
At the Bay of Biscay's solitary flooded coasts,
I lingered, dear, with you once in the days of May.
May the flame of longing swirl about your bosom
as your friend devotes to thee this reminiscing page.

Hidden behind mountains, a tribe lives on both sides of the Western Pyrenees that has retained its original language, and, in large part, its former constitution and customs. In addition, the tribe of the Basques, or Biscayans, has, according to the felicitous expression of a contemporary author, eluded both the eye of the beholder and the sword of the conqueror.[1] Just as the high mountains with their wooded slopes had saved themselves from the revolutions of the Earth, this little flock of people had saved themselves from the mighty storms that have haunted southwestern France and Spain ever since the demise of Roman dominance. Even if today they are torn into two very uneven parts and subordinate to two great and powerful nations, the Basques have nonetheless never given up their liberty and independence. Not mixing with their neigh-

---

1. One is at a loss should one want to apply one name to the whole tribe of the 'biscayische' nation. One searches in vain for a name that has been accepted uniformly by the Spanish, French, and Germans. The French do not have a universal term. They say: *Biscayens* when they speak of the Spanish and *Basques* when they mean the French Basques and, when needed, resort to the old name: *Cantabres* [Cantabrians]. The Spaniards limit the name *Vizcaya* [Bizkaia] to the actual lordship, the Seigniory [*el Señorío*]. By the way, they refer to the country as *las provincias Bascongadas* [the Basque provinces] and to the language as *el Bascuence*. The people are referred to according to their respective province as *Vizcainos* [Bizkaians], *Guipuzcoanos* [Gipuzkoans], *Alaveses* [Arabans]. So this unfortunate tribe has even lost the unity of its name. To be frank and clear, I will draw on the following terms taking into account the various names that are used among these various nations. When speaking of the whole tribe scattered across the Basque Country, Biscay, and Navarre: Basques; when I speak of the Spanish part of the country: Biscay; when I speak of the Basques who are subjugated by the French Republic: French Basques; when I specifically mean the so-called Seigniory: Bizkaia—Given the variance of Basque dialects, I will always write the names of individuals and places in the way that is customary in the dialect of which they are a part.

Publisher's note: Such terminological difficulties remain to this day. For the purposes of this work, the terms "Basques"/"Basque Country" will be used to refer to the people and geographical area as a whole. Where Humboldt draws a distinction between the provinces and inhabitants of Araba (Álava), Bizkaia (Vizcaya), and Gipuzkoa (Guipúzcoa), on the one hand, and (Higher) Navarre on the other—all forming part of the Southern Basque Country—the terms "Biscayans"/"Biscay" and "Navarrese"/"Navarre" will be used respectively. Humboldt uses the term *Basquen* to refer to Basques in France; here, the term "French Basques" will be used.

bors and resilient to the advancement of luxury and refinement, they have preserved a state of original simplicity regarding their customs, have ceaselessly retained the idiosyncrasies of their national character, and, moreover, have kept the old spirit of freedom and independence for which already Greek and Roman authors had praised them.

There are countless people in other parts of Europe, too, who have been driven back into secluded valleys or to barren and unworkable coasts by the momentum of violent revolutions, who have displayed a defiance that effectively renders their misfortunes honorable, who have rescued their paternal language and customs from the floods of destruction, who now, partly out of habit, partly out of national pride—which is the more noble—refuse obstinately any melting together with their foreign neighbors. The Lower Britons [Bretons] in France and their brothers in England [the Cornish], the occupants of Wales, the Highlanders in Scotland, the Wend tribes scattered around certain parts of Southern and Northern Germany, the brave Dalecarlians in Sweden, the Estonians and Livonians, and other more insignificant tribes in Italy and on the Italian islands, all of whom, and some of them for not much longer, have come to exist as the living ruins of formerly powerful and far-reaching nations. But compared to the Basques, not one of these nations has managed to acquire an independent political constitution and flourishing wealth, not one of them has succeeded more than the Basques in transplanting many of the Enlightenment's most beneficial fruitions right into their wildest of lands; all without forfeiting their uniqueness and original simplicity. It seems as though they owe this privilege to their location between the Pyrenees and the ocean. One side protects them from hostile invasions and too much traffic with their neighbors. The other, however, gives them an opening to the community of nations and commerce with every part of the world. It is in this, their geographical position, that one must look for the key to their whole history—especially to their earlier history.

The fate of Spain's southern and northern coasts was formed above all by the two seas that wash against their shores. Only along the coasts of the Mediterranean did the more beautiful blossoms of early culture prosper. As Phoenicians, Carthaginians, Greeks, and foreigners from the refined Orient sailed to the blessed *Baetica* [*Hispania*] as far back as most ancient times, today's Andalusia, Valencia, and Catalonia, from Gades [Cádiz] to Emporium [Empúries, in Catalonia], came to teem with various peoples' plantations. But Hercules's feared columns rose up behind Gades and marked the beginnings of the realm of fables and crazes. One believed that the sun would dive into the sea with a sizzle, that the brightness of day was instantly followed by darkness of night with no twilight. Thus superstitious delusion and inept navigation prevented the traveler from taking the short route through the Straits of Gibraltar and beyond toward Portugal's and Spain's western coasts. Some merchant ships undoubtedly went much farther and all the way up to Brittany, but their lucre tended to shield the secrets of their course so as to keep their advantage. So it happened that Galicia and the Bay of Biscay only came to witness its first Roman fleet under Caesar and Augustus respectively. Yes the former had not even fully sailed Spain's northern coast as he had only come from Aquitania.[2] Thus, the people of the region lived with hardly any interaction with other foreigners until the end of the Cantabrian War (the 734th Roman Year [19 CE]), some even beyond that, and so preserved their rough and irrepressible savageness—that is inherently tied to their specific seclusion. What adds to this is the particular character of the terrain, cold, mountainous, and infertile, which no one would have been tempted to visit—even if one subtracted the dangers of a sea voyage or the toil of overland travel.[3] So what Spain used to have in terms of ancient inhabitants—one can either hold these to be the original Iberian tribes or ones that got mixed with Celts and other outsiders in the most ancient times—are to be found solely in this area: at the coast of this secluded and unvisited ocean. The more the south of the country was, time and again, ravaged or conquered by Carthaginians and Romans, the more the original inhabitants that were unwilling to be yoked, flocked close to the ocean and the Pyrenees.

During the great migration, when Spain became the stomping ground to many quarreling nations, the Pyrenees did see some foreign tribes marching through. But they either opted for the better known southern coast via Roussillon [Rosselló in Catalan] and Catalonia, or, being bounty-coveting barbarians with an eye on the promising riches of Spain, would have had no desire to delay while besieging this poor yet courageous folk at the outset, and so the Basques remained, again, detached and independent. Not even the Moors encroached upon the country deeply as they only carried out minor explorations to Araba. Thus the remnants of the Basque tribe gradually settled within the natural borders they still have today, with the sea to the north, the range of the Pyrenees to the east and mountains to the west and south, separat-

---

2. Orosius. l. 6. C. 21 *(Mann. 255)*.

3. Strabo. l. 3. p. 200, 234. *(ed. Almeloveenii)*.

ing Bizkaia, Araba, and Navarre on the left banks of the Ebro from Old Castile. On the French side of the Pyrenees, they extend only very little into the country, and only the small towns that lie at the immediate foot of the mountains belong to them.

No likely violent commotion lies ahead of them today though; in fact, the Basque provinces in Spain and France can expect a rise in population and affluence. But it is the slow influences that, given the reciprocal contacts between almost all points in Europe, will surely augur the demise of their national peculiarities just as these days any lesser folk is forced to give up their exclusive character. These influences more and more drive out their language and so, inevitably, their national character is lost at the same time. Even now the language, being persecuted from all sides and neglected, above all, by the most enlightened parts of the nation, has decade by decade to withdraw deeper into the mountains and it is foreseeable that its decay will occur at an even faster pace from now on. The fast decline of the Provençal and Toulouse vernacular in the south of France ever since the beginnings of the Revolution is a warning and instructive example. Basque will possibly have vanished from the list of living languages in less than a century; there have been similar developments even in our modern age. At the beginning of the eighteenth century, the Old Prussian language died out this way with a handful of old men in a remote corner of Samland;[4] moreover, in our own day we have seen the demise of one of the Cymric [Welsh] vernaculars in Cornwall [a reference to the Cornish language].[5]

It seems to be irrevocably determined in the course of human culture that the differences that separate the minor tribes from each other must necessarily fade away with a certain level of education, and that only greater groups of people are able to survive effectively as a society. It takes great political measures to move whole nations toward significant intellectual progress and, moreover, to ensure that they do not fall back into barbarianism and ignorance. The diversity that emerges from these new circumstances induces a plurality and innovation of opinions and ideas; and the human spirit might never have achieved its most sublime findings without the rousing spectacle of a heavy and almost universal friction of human powers. But the other question, and surely a not unimportant

---

4. Praetorii Nachricht von der Preussischen Sprache in *Actis Boruss.* V.2, *p.* 900 (Schlözers Nord. Gesch. p. 9. 34).

5. This is, if I am not mistaken, in the *Origines Gauloises.* p. 114.

one, is whether or not this should have its limits; whether or not education can come to a point at which, in order to preserve society's warmth and strength without which it will bear no inner fruit, it becomes just as necessary to keep the imagination and sentiment within a tight circle as it is to lead reason toward a broader sphere.

Without wanting to ponder on this subject, too, but the demise of a people—even if as a sacrifice to the beneficial destiny of human kind—always stirs up a melancholic sensation and even more so when it is faced with the demise of a whole language. We are used to thinking of humans as transient beings; thus, when even their surviving language also falls silent, when the mold breaks apart into which a single tribe has casted its thoughts and feelings, their demise appears twice woeful, for then every connection between them and their future ceases to exist. Even if a language that has not yet been refined by literature is merely the pure expression of a rough people's thinking, its loss should not be met with indifference. Even within highest culture there is an undeniable point at which even the most delicate impulses of a most refined sentiment returns to the simple flow of natural feeling; where the most carefully educated individuals of a truly cultivated nation maintain continuous and reciprocal contact with the simple, but healthy, parts of society.

It is precisely because the Basque language is a vernacular, and because one must look among the Basques for sound judgment rather than any scientific education, for natural, warm and lively feeling rather than refined sensibility, that this language and this nation becomes for us highly interesting. As soon as language is formed by literacy and science, it is wrested out of the hands of the people, and only seldom does it ever again recover its energy or abundance. In contrast with its writers, a language always receives a more sensual and varied imprint when used by the people. Before language can be put to the highest intellectual use by later and more refined generations through its vibrancy, power, and depth, language must have stood the test of giving voice to a powerful and widespread people (it is their natural property), expressing their most immediate needs, their most natural sensations, most childish fantasies, even the rawest of their passions. After all, man is born to be formed as a social being; an individual must always become part of a mass of people, and all that is human converges in the simplicity of nature and in the full bloom of education at the same time. Without a decisive, steady, and robust national character one waits in vain for truth, power, and demeanor even amid the finest cultural spheres of a nation. The more unfathomable the gap between a nation's people and its educated classes becomes, the rarer the occurrence of national characters. Thus, if one still wants to see the latter in brisk and lively action, one has to do just that, one must avoid higher culture and go to areas that have been less altered by it. With the Basques, however, there are additional factors that merge together making this phenomenon even more so striking and instructive.

The Basques, in particular those of the Spanish side, are not simply poor mountain shepherds or even oppressed serfs. They are a people who pursue agriculture, shipping, and commerce; they do not lack physical wealth without which no ethical improvement would be possible. They have a free constitution and public debates, which are mainly held in their own vernacular, and thus have a common interest that affects everyone and to which everyone can contribute. The Basques are taken with an enthusiasm for their country and nation—which may appear slightly odd to the foreigner—to such an extent that even the more wealthy Basques, including those who receive honors and titles in Castile or hold prestigious offices, remain devoted to their home country. Here they live in very close relation with the vast masses of the people as they cannot cut themselves off from the prevailing customs and language. In this way, parts of the newer Enlightenment and education flows into the people's vernacular and their terminology, and dissociation between the classes is less obvious; in fact, in the eyes of a true Basque these differences are entirely negligible. Furthermore, the physiognomy of the country and the people makes it clear to the traveler that people in the Basque provinces have more natural education and their nobler breed enjoy a greater popularity than in neighboring Spain or France. In this, one can only compare them to the small cantons in Switzerland, but their political independence gives them a different exterior aspect and their marginal detachment, given that they hardly constitute a distinct nation, makes for a different internal situation as well. What qualifies the Basques as a pure and separate national tribe is their language, constitution, custom, physiognomy, in short, everything that surrounds them, the scenery of the country not excluded. Their singularity, deeply unified internally, is quite independent of external and accidental influences; yes, they do not know any related tribe, whether close or far away, as they exist alone like an island, in their region between the mountains and the ocean. Thus, what a pure tribal character might mean and how this comes into existence can nowhere better be examined than here. Obviously, the strong contrasts of national characters have to be whittled away during the process of formation and, therefore, such a study might seem to be the mere object of idle curiosity. But to the careful preservation and nourishment of parts of these characteristics and to the process of leading them toward refined culture and to the giving of currency, must surely belong the hardly ever recognized measures that are required to maintain a nation's power and its character; the lack of which is justifiably admonished very often. For every attempt to lead toward educational formation is ill guided, if the influence of pure nature is to be kept alive as much as possible.

The unique tribal characteristics of the Basques point back toward centuries far distant, to the times before Roman and Carthaginian dominion, and toward the first inhabitants of Spain. Obviously, these peculiarities diminish over time on account of increased commerce with their neighbors, but no matter how they will eventually merge or fashion themselves in the future, a part of these idiosyncrasies will remain for a long time to come. This poses two important questions, one historical and one political: Where do the Basques and their language originate and with which other tribes and languages are they related? And how should the Spanish Monarchy treat the Basque nation for the purpose of putting their force and industriousness to the best possible uses for Spain? (France's Basque districts must surely be of very little importance to the French Republic.)

Although the first question has been raised often, it has never been answered thoroughly. All the given answers are less the result of an elaborate study than rather arbitrary judgments resulting from a craze for categorization and a partisan ideology. In addition, it would seem that no foreigner has ever written about this matter—native writers are suspicious for different reasons—who might possess any extensive knowledge of the language.

The second question is of a more practical interest, especially today as it is increasingly the case that different peoples are unified within the same state. One has to admit though that, hitherto, more thought has been put into removing the problems that came with these differences than using the good that these peculiarities have to offer.

It is on account of these and other observations that the Basque nation and language became for me a desirable object of study ever since I had made the decision to travel through Spain. I studied Basque grammar and looked for information on the country, but I lacked the necessary aids, in particular a certain very rare dictionary that none of the various public libraries in Paris (I was living there at the time) owned. The first time I went to Spain, it was in the fall of 1799, I did not have the time to visit each of the Basque provinces. Furthermore, I was too unaccustomed to Spain itself as to profit extensively from such a journey. Just like anyone else who travels from Baiona [Bayonne] to Madrid, I only drove through the less spectacular parts of the country. But even then the wonderful alternation between pleasantly covered hills and sweetly cultivated valleys, the lush freshness of growing trees, the prudent layout of the land, much of which was parceled into small gardens often hemmed in with hedges, the cleanliness of the villages and cities, and, above all, the vivacious and appealing physiognomy of the inhabitants, had instilled in me a great desire to dwell in this area for a longer time. On my return to Paris in the summer of 1800 I resumed my interrupted studies of Basque, I got hold of the necessary aids, the published dictionary as well as a handwritten one belonging to the National Library. I read what the travel writers had to say about this little country and nation, especially the treatise of the Englishman [William] Bowles,[6] which is, though not of great importance, written with such empathy for the subject that it captivates the reader, too. In addition I fraternized with a number of natives, Frenchmen and Spaniards, who thus generously offered me very valuable information. Altogether, this greatly heightened my desire to journey through this country. Moreover, it became clear to me that a language that is only spoken cannot be learned anywhere else but in situ.

Around this time, it was the beginning of April last year, my friend Mr. B traveled from Baiona to Cádiz. He suggested that I accompanied him to the borders of Castile; I quickly accepted his proposal as I had acquired enough knowledge to fill this journey with purpose and also, because my acquaintances in Paris would get me access to the most interesting persons in the country. We departed twenty four hours later; I spent two happy months partly in the Spanish, partly in the French Basque countries; and I will always think of this spring at the shores of the Bay of Biscay as one of the loveliest of my life.

My main focus during this trip was on language; I knew from my preparations that I was going to meet some people there who had already ventured deeply into this matter; most noticeably, a cleric in Durango, D. Pedro de Astarloa. The following pages will show how much I owe to this erudite and venerable man and his friendship. If the one single outcome of this trip had been what I had gained from him, I would have

---

6. *Introduccion à la hist. Natural y à la Geografia fisica de Espana por D. Guillermo Bowles*. Madrid 1775. kl. 4. P. 281.

felt perfectly rewarded. But how many more and manifold delights did I encounter in the sweet coastal valleys of Gipuzkoa and Bizkaia, among hospitable and worthy Biscayans, among the jovial and worthy Basques!

My friends' kindness, far more than my own efforts, accounted for the fact that I obtained a remarkable magnitude of published and hand-written resources collecting more material than any other foreigner before had done. And thus I understand it as my duty not to let these materials go unused, but to do my part in providing better and more accurate terms and definitions regarding the Basque nation and language than those that currently prevail. It is my main intention to hoist the linguist and historian up to a position from which he can decide for himself. While my predecessors limited their linguistic samples to proving their own private system, I wish to submit to the reader as much material as to overthrow every preexisting system including possibly even my own assessments.

But above all it is important to me to describe the Basques' customs and their way of life, and toward this end I will attempt to demonstrate their language as a living image of their way of thinking and feeling. To do so, I paid special attention to their proverbs, their national dances, their music and poetry, and I hope to communicate to the reader samples from each of these items. But for the same reason, he will allow me to submit a brief and simple account of my wanderings. In order to give the reader a more vivid idea of the land and its inhabitants, the easiest way will be to allow him follow this thread. Once this is done, he will be in a better place to follow and to judge my scientific study regarding the lineage of the Basque nation and the origins of their language that will mark the end of these pages.

I will not flatter myself into thinking that I will succeed in giving an account of the Basque nation that is anything even like the image of it that is forever engraved on my soul. But should I have accomplished this even in part, I would feel doubly rewarded for all the toils I had to combat, particularly while studying the language. Furthermore, because then I would have succeeded in setting up a monument in its honor, which, even if not in the least worthy of it, would however correspond to all the feelings of respect and love that the Basques have instilled in me!

* * *

We traveled from Paris to Baiona in nine days. We had glided past the fertile banks of the Loire, we fleetingly glanced at the formerly renowned, now mostly forgotten walls of Blois, Amboise, Tours, Poitiers, and Angoulême;

we stayed in Bordeaux for three days, and then we continued through sparsely cultivated and meager lands until we finally reached Baiona.

Once we had crossed nearly the whole width of France in haste, we took to traveling the small Basque Country step by step. We did not, however, leave Baiona without visiting Biarritz first, which is the common coastal resort of the people of Baiona and a most lovely area.

The houses of the city are scattered along the cliffs, and the sea washes directly below them. The rock that forms these cliffs is very loose, and the sea has carved out a number of caves; single mighty pieces of stone have detached themselves, some in considerable distance from the shore and loom out of the sea where the waves break against them in a majestic roar. Whatever you might expect from a marvelous view of the sea comes together here: picturesque figures of a rocky coast close by combined with an undisturbed view of an enormous space. We looked to our right to see the areas that we would soon be getting to know in more detail, Donibane Lohizune [Saint-Jean-de-Luz], the Spanish Biscay, the mountains of Hondarribia [Fuenterrabía] and Lezo, to our left the lower French banks of the Atturi's [Adour] outlet and the dreaded Barre—a dangerous sandbank off the coast.

We followed the shoreline to this side a bit farther while making our way back to the city. We found the same kind of coastline everywhere, low cliffs, consisting of the same porous rock, extending into the sea in flat layers, piled on top of each other they create wonderful windy and perforated figures whose dark gray color resembles hardened silt.

At one point we were surprised by a peculiar spectacle. About two hundred feet from the coast there stood a single rock that opened up into a wide circle below. The tide had just withdrawn and the rock was swarming with people—men, women, and half-grown boys—who were busying themselves with fishing by low tide. Most of them were angling, some were searching for mussels, and a couple of men were swimming out to the deeper waters beyond, climbing to the flatly polished rocks with remarkable skill in order to rob the birds' nests above. The alarmed mother birds fluttered anxiously around their ruined nests and the crowds below took lively interest in how the egg hunters fared.

The actual aim of our walk, though, had been to see a grotto called the Grotto of Love (La Grotte d'Amour). We were meagerly rewarded for our efforts, however, as, moreover, it had been a very hot day. The grotto has really nothing remarkable to offer, aside from its name and the legend that escaping lovers had once sought refuge there.

Donibane Lohizune

The way from Baiona to Donibane Lohizune lacks trees and shade. If it were any different, the views of the Pyrenees and the sea and of the endearing houses between Bidarte [Bidart] and Getaria [Guéthary], scattered loosely around small hills and typically surrounded by gardens and agriculture, would all be equally charming and picturesque.

The inhabitants of Bidarte engage in continuous yet minor trade and transport between Donostia-San Sebastián and Baiona. For this they rely on very small yet lively strong horses. The entire business, however, is left to the women and girls, while the men are occupied with shipping and fishing. The women of Bidarte whom you encounter daily in great numbers on the streets of Baiona offer an easy and safe opportunity to any traveler who wishes to carry out a small excursion to the neighboring areas of Gipuzkoa. They take him over the Spanish border without further ado, and their *cacaulet* is not only an extremely comfortable, but also a very sociable means to travel as two persons ride on the same horse. A small straw chair with backrest and footstool is affixed to either side of a common packsaddle, though not crossways but straight just as in normal riding. One sits on these as snuggly as if in one's parlor because, being out of synchrony, one hardly feels the immediate movements of the animal, and one can enjoy both the area and the conversations in full comfort. Yes, at times I even saw travelers who played cards between the chairs while riding. The only negative side to this is the inseparability that binds the two travelers. Obviously, neither can descend without toppling the other.

Regarding industriousness, it seems as if the sexes in the Basque Country, specifically in the French Basque lands, have switched roles. I have never seen as much and wearisome work carried out by women as here. In the Spanish part, they often break the harshest and hardest of soil while hunching over the abrasive *laya*, an implement for tilling that I will describe later. In Bilbao, they unload the ships, carrying the heaviest of weights on their heads, especially the much-traded iron rods, from the river to the storehouses. I even saw them hammering away on the anvil in the smithies. The most remarkable thing is, however, that their unusual strength is equally matched by their quickness and agility.

I grew accustomed to admire this especially among the *sardinières* or sardine carriers of whom I encountered many on my way to Donibane Lohizune. It is a weird sight to see a row of five or six, sometimes even ten or twenty mostly tall and scanty female bodies trotting toward you, one by one popping up behind a hill, each carrying big, round, covered baskets of fish on their heads while keeping their bodies motionless and stiff. Each one hurries to be the first to market their sardines in Baiona, and so they jog the whole way, slowing down only where the terrain ascends. I was assured that during the fishing season they carry their load to the market even twice a day. Thus they cover the distance of about three French miles four times on the very same day in spite of a road without shade and the sun burning down on them.

Their clothing is very light as one would suspect, their feet completely bare; their arms are merely covered by their shirt sleeves, their gowns are gathered up half way down their thighs so that they only reach their knees or just a little more. The lightness of their walking reveals itself in their steady, skillful step but it also finds its expression in their bodies' physique. Nearly all have well-formed even graceful legs, a delicate bone structure and neatly defined muscles; no awkward knuckles can be seen sticking out, nor do they have clumsy or depressed calves. In contrast, the unfortunate amount of work seems to have cut away any excess growth, and inasmuch as one often sees all the generations together, it is seldom that one finds a true beauty among them although most are tall, slim, and with good proportions. Naturally, the heavy carrying on their heads gives the upper part of their body an inevitable stiffness, and their laborious efforts are vivid in the look of their faces.

I have dwelled on this description a bit longer because it also entails an outline of the basic national physiognomy of the Basque female. Nearly always, she airs an expression of character rather than appeal; she has fine and profoundly elaborate features conserved in old age, she bears a seriousness in the narrowness of the face, in a long, straight descending nose, black, strong, narrowly positioned eyebrows, a seriousness that tends toward severity—but it always remains distant from Castilian gloominess and sorrowful melancholia.

The particular situation of the opposite sex on the coast, specifically in Donibane Lohizune, has a noticeable effect on their physiognomy. Almost all the men in this area are seamen and thus the majority of them are absent. At the time of my journey, many men from Donibane Lohizune were in English captivity. The women not only had to maintain the house during their absence, but often send them money abroad, too. The poor sardine carriers make only very little profit in their exhausting business; and then they even lose profit when there is large competition among the sellers. Bearing the burden of keeping house alone and constantly worrying about her continuously endangered husband gives the woman austere, almost male facial features that over time takes a toll on the national physiognomy of an industrious coastal people.

Generally it is this industriousness of the female sex that is one of the numerous traits that Strabo mentions as the common similarities preserved along the northern coast of Spain, and the one feature that differs from the inner parts of the country, especially the center. In the mountains of Pas, close to the Carriedo Valley, in the North of Old Castile, the women carry butter and cheese on their backs for twenty Spanish miles and come back with goods in return. In his substantial treatise on the people's education, [Pedro Rodríguez de] Campomanes compares them to the women of earlier times—Juvenal[1] sets them against the slacking women of his day—whose raw strength, according to him, superseded even that of their own savage men. By the way, these so-called *pasiegas* are known for exactly the opposite of what is noticeable among the women of Biscay, that is, their clumsy, cloddish size and abundance of body. The question is, however, whether the difference between carrying on one's back or on one's head would suffice to bring about these transformations. The former seems to press down on the body ignobly, while the latter, should it succeed, presupposes an easiness and steadiness in the walk and a certain skillfulness of posture. In Galicia, I have been told this by observant witnesses, the differences of intellect between the sexes in the lower working classes, their cunning in doing business,

---

1. *silvestrem montana torum cum sterneret uxor*
   frondibus et culmo vicinarumque ferarum pellibus—
   sed potanda ferens infantibus ubera magnis
   et saepe horridior glandem ructante marito. Juvenal, Satirae 6.

   when the hill-bred wife spread her silvan bed with leaves and straw
   and the skins of her neighbours the wild beasts—
   but one whose breasts gave suck to lusty babes, often more unkempt herself
   than her acorn-belching husband.
   [Juvenal, *Satires*, trans. G.G. Ramsay (1918)]

become instantly obvious. The men carry out the hauling of goods—especially water—across all of Spain. They become raw and dulled on account of this monotonous, purely physical work. The *aguadores gallegos* [Galician water-carriers] have become laughingstock of the Spanish people's humor to an excessive degree, whereas the women gain an unusual amount of insight and dexterity while caring for the multifarious aspects of keeping house. You encounter this form of business-cunningness (which by the way is generally greater in France than in Germany) to a higher degree in the Basque Country, too. In Bilbao it is not uncommon that women not only support their husband merchants in the management of the business, even if this entails major speculation, but they preside over them with regard to all aspects, big and small; and they do this successfully.

In contrast, the women in Castile, as in the whole central part of the kingdom, and the southern provinces—as long as you exclude Catalonia and, in a sense, also Valencia—lead quite an otiose and passive life. Campomanes[2] holds this to be a remnant of what was so common among the Moors: the other sex was locked away, which inevitably leads to idleness and feebleness. Yet it is peculiar that it is in the areas where the Moors had settled for the longest time—lower Andalusia, Granada, and particularly Málaga—that the women, even those with a lower education among the common people, possess a vivaciousness and elegance of the spirit, a rich and refined sense of wit—surpassing that of the men by far. This, in conjunction with their, in the main, charming formation, gives them such a unique kind of amiability that the foreigner is almost insufficiently equipped to pick up on it. Should one want to seek traces of Moorish habits in all of this, one should not be unreceptive to these influences indeed. If there is, however, a part of Spain where the common women reveal neither strength, which emerges from work, nor facial expression, which comes with a cheerful and busy temper, it is the inner provinces—Old Castile in particular. I find it a lot more probable that the numerous unfortunate influences that Old Castile has been haunted with over the centuries and that have condemned the Castilian—being not in the least equal to his neighbors in terms of inner chivalry—to the idleness and poverty against his own intentions (the story of which I reserve to develop elsewhere) in fact hit the female sex twice as hard and suppressed it twice as deeply.

---

2. p. 86.

I left the road just behind Getaria and chose a lonelier path that closely followed the coastline. It was a beautiful spring morning and the gently rippled waves glittered in infinite brilliance. As I was riding on the flank of a hill, I came upon a natural spring where the girls from the neighboring village would fetch the water bearing great earthen vessels on their heads. I saw Biarritz behind me with its scattered cliffs that extend deep into the sea, in front of me was Donibane Lohizune and in its background laid the mountains of Hondarribia.

The Pyrenees' highest summit lies right at their center, in the area of Barèges and Gavarnie, in a group that surrounds the Mont Perdu. With a height of 1,763 *toises*,[3] it dominates the whole eastern and western range. It is from there that it cuts toward both seas, however differently in proportion, though. The west side descends gently and dwindles down into insignificant hills on the coast of the ocean; the east side is steep, however, and poses some cragged foothills against the Mediterranean. The way from Perpignan [Perpinyà in Catalan] to Spain had to be cut through stone with great effort while the way from Baiona runs gently through minor hills.

[Louis] Ramond begins his text, which is abundant with detailed and crafted portrayals of the Pyrenees's natural aspects, with the remark that no other mountain range can offer the natural explorer such a regularity of shape, as evidenced in the evenly figured descent of the western part of the range. This mountain range boasts similarly shaped steps, almost each one with a drop of two hundred *toises*,[4] descending all the

---

3. *Observations faites dans les Pyrénées (par Ramond)*, p. 126. Publisher's note: 1 toise (former French measurement) = 1.9043 m, since conversion into metric system (between 1812–1840) one toise = 2 m.

4. I take this remark from *Mémoires sur la derniere guerre entre la France et l'Espagne*, Paris and Strasbourg, 1801. The author identifies nine mountain tops that make eight such steps.

Vignemale	1,728 *toises* (Ramond, p. 126, 1,722 *toises*)
La Somme de Soule	1,607
Le pic de Midi de Pau ou d'Ossau	1,472

On p. 127 Ramond cites a different measurement according to which the latter would be 1,557 *toises* high, but he admits that this figure might be exaggerated.

Until here the mountains are covered in snow for the most part of the year. But from this point onward their appearance becomes milder—For the snowline in the Pyrenees is set at 1200 *toises* (100 *toises* higher than in the Alps). Ramond, p. 302.

Le pic d'Anie, the French Basques 1,280 *toises* (Ramond, p. 127 1269 *toises*) call it Ahagua, the Spaniards call it Cenia-Larra [known today in Basque as Auñamendi—ed.].

way from Vignemale at the end of the Cauterets Valley (from whence in passing the most beautiful waterfalls of Gave you come to Lake Gaube, rising up like an enormous snow pyramid beyond the dark blue waters of the lake) to the last hilltops at the coast, so that around Baiona you are no longer faced with any of the higher Pyrenees.

The most beautiful mountains viewed from there are Larrun [La Rhune][5] and the crown Mountain, Montagne Couronnée [Aiako Harria in Basque—ed.]. The former appears to be stretched out in length, slowly ascending to one side; on the other the slope falls off abruptly; the three pinnacle-shaped elevations gave the latter mountain its other name, the Three-Column-Mountain. It is difficult for the approaching traveler to recognize it. From what I could gather, this mountain is the same one that is called La Haya de Oyarzun in Biscay; and it did decide the outcome of the military campaign of 1794. The Generals Moncey and Delaborde drove off the Spaniards from their entrenched camp on the 14 Thermidor of the aforementioned year once their troops had climbed the mountain with incredible effort and daringness; it is only then that Freyville was able to circumvent and eventually take over the emplacement of St Martial known to be impenetrable if attacked directly. It was impossible to enter Spain via the Bidasoa River as long as the enemy continued to make this claim.[6]

The mentioned mountains that join the set of Lezo and Hondarribia at the sea are set in a conjoined circle, only interrupted where the Behobia [Behobie] Pass cuts into Spain. From this graceful mountain crest a gulf of fertile land descends toward the sea. The mountains phase out

---

Orhi	1,031 *toises*
Ortzantzurieta	801 *toises*
Auza, above the Baztan Valley	667 *toises*
Larrun (not La Rhune)	462 *toises*
Jaizkibel	278 *toises*

5. It is a common error in Spain and France to switch around the first syllable of Basque names and make them into Spanish and French propositions. Larrun, for instance, (derived from *larrea*, meadow, and *ona*, good, or good pasture ground) is commonly referred to in Baiona as La Rhune, Elorrio, Elantxobe [Elanchove] on Spanish maps as *el Orrio, el Anchove*. The most remarkable mutilation of this kind is the disfigured name of the well-known du Halde, who in terms of lineage was a Basque regardless of having been born in Paris; actually, he was called Uhalde (d'Uhalde), though. In fact, Uhalde (the one living on the water side, just as Larralde means living aside the meadows) is a common family name in Biscay.

6. *Mèm. sur la guerre etc.* p. 100–112.

into lower hills, and these hills dwindle away into a plain, and at the end of this plain, right on the sea and carved in by it, lays Donibane Lohizune. A wonderful amphitheater enclosed by the ocean and an incredible mass of mountain.

A small river divides Donibane Lohizune in two parts, Ziburu [Ciboure] and Donibane Lohizune. They gave this small and nameless water the name Nivelle [Urdazuri in Basque], presumably in contrast to the Nive [Errobi in Basque] in Baiona. But the waters that stream in with every tide make this rather insignificant creek an arm of the sea confined by ashlar-built quays that surround the bay. The bay is small but picturesque; a near perfect curve, stuck between Fort Socoa[7] on the left and Fort Ste. Barbe on the right. The harbor of Ziburu is close to Zokoa, in fact it is the main port of the town. Upon the hill of Bordagaina,[8] right behind the little town, stands a lighthouse and next to it is a balcony that serves the seamen as a meeting point. Donibane Lohizune has its own harbor in the town itself, although it is of dangerous entry.

One can best see how Donibane Lohizune is situated from Ste. Barbe. Prompted by Vauban's recommendation, Louis XIV intended to enclose the whole bay by erecting a wall all the way from the sea ground in order to provide ships with a safe haven that could only be entered through an opening in the middle. The realization of this almost gigantic endeavor was postponed like so many. In more recent times, the Intendant of the Province, Dupré de St. Maur, took up this almost forgotten plan and it was at his behest that there are two pieces of stone wall that extend a few hundred paces into the sea; these are built with an audacious greatness that defies the centuries and steadfastly resists the advances of the roaring sea. Alone, Dupré was unable to finish this site and so it remained as it is.

At Ste. Barbe, should one climb the crumbly foliated rock all the way down to the beginnings of the aforementioned wall and turn toward Baiona, you will enjoy an overwhelming view of the sea. The shoreline recedes, a steep cliff obstructs your view of the land, the sky and the sea are just everywhere. The waves smash against the shore with a tremendous force even when the sea is calm; the white foam sprays up high above the stone wall and the waves shoot into the caves of the perforated rocks. One can hear them scream under one's feet as the waves erode the

---

7. *Socoa*, the Spanish Basques refer to it as *Zocoa*, the angle, the corner.

8. Farm upon the hill. *Borda*, farm, *gaina*, Gip. *gaña*, height, summit.

foundations of the cliff often ripping off pieces that plunge into the sea. I suppose that the massive rocks in the sea at Biarritz came about this way. On the left, there is the view of the enchanting, enclosed bay, the fertile lands of the town, opposite is the corner of Zokoa, the hill of the lighthouse clad with greenery, and beyond that in the distance is the blue mountain range that extends way into the sea ending in a narrow land tongue, Higer Point,[9] which from here just glimmers as a single point in the sea.

There are many signs of the destruction caused by the ravaging advances of the sea on the way from Ste. Barbe to the mouth of the Urdazubi. Entering from this side, the place really looks like a fishing town. Single stone houses with flat roofs have been erected sporadically here and there without any sense of order. The sea used to be a lot farther from the town; old people have transmitted that less than two hundred years ago there were still gardens within the bay, and people aged fifty still remember playing in places at the sea in their childhood, places that the sea today would never leave uncovered. One sees ruins of abandoned houses everywhere, farther away, the walls of the houses are covered in sand a few feet high, sand that the sea tends to send ahead before it comes crashing in. The locals use these abandoned ruins as gardens and have withdrawn their houses toward the hill. And yet, this is where the morass is, so they are also crowded in from this side as well.

Close by the mouth of the river used to be an Ursuline monastery. In big storms, the sea's spray used to shoot right into the nuns' roof. About fifteen years ago, the bishop moved them to a new monastery, and now one can take an unhindered look into its formerly holy interiors as the crippled walls make for a marvelous ruin.

The river's stone quay used to extend farther into the bay; now it is very damaged and fallen into disrepair. I can remember vividly how I stood in the very same place two years before with my family on a stormy autumn day. We had to wait for low tide in order to cross the river (because the bridge had just gone to pieces) so we walked down to the harbor and sat down at the very end of the quay. There were a few fishermen angling right next to us; the rags, under which their strong naked limbs transpired, confirmed the meagerness of their catch, and reminded us vividly of how Theocrit depicts the paltriness of a fisherman's life.

---

9. *La pointe du figuier* or *la punta del Higuer* in Hondarribia.

We sat there for a long time while we gloated over the incredible spectacle of the storm driven sea. The waves rolled majestically toward us from the horizon, other waves from the river mouth crashed against them, and hindered by this resistance, their dark-mounted tops broke apart in white foam, and they ran from their center, just like a suddenly ignited fire, to both sides in infinite rows; then the waves broke with twice the force and collapsed clamorously roaring into the river between the quays. The same tide, however, that here in front of us, crushed in by the incoming and outgoing stream, raged wildly, poured out as swift as an arrow onto the smoothly jetted shoreline in charming snakelike movements and—this is how fast it went—when the second wave met the returning first wave one could observe, just as if in a transparent crystal, two conjoined reflecting surfaces that on top of each other glided in opposite directions. One heard a muffled rage in the distance, the confused turmoil of the waves; emerging from the dark tides foam shoots against the protruding cliffs, and once in a while in the most distant horizons, the shimmering sails of a ship would dither across.

Never before had I been so overwhelmed by the dead and raw mass of Creation, never have I deemed the seed of life in nature as weaker and hopeless than here between the Pyrenees and the ocean. In the mountains, those tremendous masses of rock, not even encircled with attenuating greenery, the image of a never inactive calmness, weight that always presses down on the center of its gravity, and dares to crumble down only to suffocate every possible game of life by cleaving together even closer. One enjoys the view of the land and of the mountains while going along the river toward the city. There is a former monastery of the Recollects on a small peninsula in the river right between Ziburu and Donibane Lohizune. Both towns had extensive commerce between each other in former times. This usually erupted on the occasion of ceremonial processions. First they hit each other with the crosses, followed by stone throwing and other weapons. Finally, in the previous century, they agreed to erect this monastery at shared cost as a sign of restored concord, never again to be disturbed. Other parts of the Basque Country also contributed toward it and a reformatory was linked to it as well. There stand a few poplars around this reconciliation monastery. Beyond, the view is very nice. A hill behind the town at the foot of Larrun is wreathed with delightful green woods, and a friendly country house emerges from the bushes, with a splendid green foreground of the gray mountains behind.

Ziburu[10] is, as mentioned, separated from Donibane Lohizune merely by a bridge. At the beginning of the Revolution, Ziburu was less receptive toward the changes compared to Donibane Lohizune. The nickname *oltrapontains*[11] alone, which was given to the inhabitants of Ziburu, changed the minds of many.

Both places were far more prosperous in past times than they are today. They derived their main nourishment from whale hunting and stock fishing. The former ceased a long time ago, and the latter is far less significant today than it used to be. In the year 1730 about thirty ships were sent out to that end; today it is only six. In 1675, the government requested sailors from Ziburu (this information, as I have been told, can be found in the Ziburu archives) but the town responded that they had already submitted three thousand men for various expeditions and could not come up with any more. Today one cannot count more than 1,400 souls, in Donibane Lohizune it is about 2,000.

Donibane Lohizune has become notable in several political events given that it is the last significant French border town against the Spaniards. They point out the house in which Charles V lived when he came through on his way to Spain, as well as the one that housed Louis XIV when he came to meet his Spanish bride in 1660. It is in the marketplace and has four small doors at the corners, the house of the *infanta* was diagonally across and a wooden canopied aisle was erected across the marketplace, so that one could get to the other directly.

---

10. The name is even delineated from it. *zubia*, bridge, *burua*, head; bridgehead.

11. Publisher's note: Although *oltrapontain* is the word in the original German, this seems likely to be a typographical error and the word should be *ultrapontain* (implying "beyond the bridge"), although why this would have "changed the minds of many" is still somewhat unclear.

Hendaia and Hondarribia

We left Donibane Lohizune when the day had barely begun to dawn. The moon still shone dun-colored from the skies, and threw a divine magical light on the many scenic groups of small and big trees and the ivy-covered walls of the scattered country houses. The dulcet riches of this so infinitely diverse landscape, in which the curling road behind every new corner reveals a new scene, groups of luscious trees that become entangled, upon which from the dense green arises the walling of an old castle with its petite towers, upon which an amicable piece of field cornered in by rows of hedges, a fertile plain, or a richly water soaked meadow that spreads its green carpet that replicates itself in a delightful manner in the shady shimmering of the nocturnal lighting, and the dark mass of mountains ahead to the west casted its gloomy shadow on this enchanting picture.

Just when we left Urruña [Urrugne], the day broke. We turned our horses and saw the most glorious sunrise in front of us. Thick clouds of fog covered the east. The first rays broke through in places and gilded the dark edges. First, the radiance hit the distant clouds; they broke away from the gloomy masses and swam like golden flakes in the pure air. Then the luminousness descended closer and closer toward the horizon and only above the east rested a black cloud. From blazing crimson to a tender rosy red, all the fire-yellow nuances floated into each other, and as if the outburst of light had amid luminousness also poured out movement, it flooded the heavy and dormant mass of cloud into a heaving shimmering that went to and fro. But soon the uneven fight came to an end, the magnificent plentiful of color got lost in a blinding light, and the sun emerged behind the shadowy mountains.

In memory of this divine morning, I cannot refrain from quoting a passage of Apollonius of Rhodes in which this joyful leap, with which the mountain and the forest seems to tremble toward the emerging light each time there is a clear sunrise, is depicted in a truly great way. The Argonauts land on a desert island at dawn after a toilsome nocturnal voyage. The day breaks and the sun is shining.

And to them the son of Leto, as he passed from Lycia far away to the
countless folk of the Hyperboreans, appeared; and about his cheeks on
both sides his golden locks flowed in clusters as he moved; in his left
hand he held a silver bow, and on his back was slung a quiver hanging
from his shoulders; and beneath his feet all the island quaked, and the
waves surged high on the beach. Helpless amazement seized them as
they looked; and no one dared to gaze face to face into the fair eyes of
the god. And they stood with heads bowed to the ground; but he, far
off, passed on to the sea through the air.[1]

Urruña[2] is the last French town on the main road to Madrid. Beyond
you will only find the custom house on the Behobia[3] Pass, from where
you cross the Bidasoa.

We left the road not far beyond this spot and chose a way that took
us over the hills that were closer to the sea. A Basque, who was riding to
Hendaia [Hendaye] on his little horse, joined us. He had been in the last
war against Spain[4] and pointed out to us the various emplacements of
both armies. Already the way there had shown us more than a mere trail
of destruction in half-demolished walls and deserted houses; here one
could still see the trenches of the time, but the walls and ditches were
covered with grass, flowers and brush, and served, just as in former times,
as a peaceful pasture ground.

The area between the Behobia Pass, Hendaia, and Ziburu was the
main place of warfare during the campaign of 1793, that is before Spain
was attacked on its own land, as the French occupied all the hills in this
zone, above all the hill of Louis XIV on the Bidasoa.

---

1. Argon. II, 674. Publisher's note: this passage is found in *Appolonius Rhodius, Argonautica*, Book 2, 669, not 674 as is noted by Humboldt. Taken from *Apollonius Rhodius.
Argonautica*. Translated by Seaton, R. C. Loeb Classical Library volume 1 (London: William Heinemann Ltd, 1912).

2. It derives its name from its position on a small hill next to a stream. *Ura*, water,
oina, *oña*, elevation and thus the foot. It actually means the upper part of the foot, the
instep, and the Basque use of the word is thus based on the same image that *Rist* (related
to *Riese* [giant]) refers to in German. You can find the same syllable in other names, e.g.
Oñati, Oña, etc.

3. It is not, as some travelogues have it, *Beobid*. It means cavern, a depression down
there. Indeed, the customs house is in a cavern and you descend to it from either side.

4. Publisher's note: Probably the War of the First Coalition, 1792–1797, invasion of
Spain in 1794.

On April 23, the Spaniards attacked the enemy's positions on the mountain and Hendaia with a hail of bombs, cannonballs, and howitzers. The frightened inhabitants fled with the women and children and in spite of the fact that the Spaniards did return to beyond the Bidasoa, this expedition had compelled the enemy to leave his previous positions and retreat all the way to the *Croix des bouquets*.

The main strike however would have to be carried out against their camp at Sara [Sare] and the Spaniards turned their full attention toward it. They descended on the French on the morning of May 1. They were shocked to see that they were shot at from the mountain's abysses even before they could spot an enemy against whom they could defend themselves. They fled as well as they could, and the Spaniards, bursting out from their ambuscade, advanced on the camp. The brave Théophile Malo Corret de la Tourd'Auvergne, who had earned the Basques' gratitude both as a warrior and as a writer, attempted to muster a last bit of resistance again them. He positioned himself with one hundred men on the hill of Saint Barbara, and—while being surrounded by confusion and fright, flight and persecution—he calmly awaited the attack of the five-hundred-men strong Spanish cavalry. He allowed them to advance until they were twenty paces away when he received them with a tremendous musket fire that luckily blasted them apart. But alas his cohort was too small, and he too had to retreat shortly thereafter, he reached the camp at Sara only with a few remaining Grenadiers. Yet he came upon nothing but chaos and confusion there and thus the whole army withdrew to Uztaritze [Ustaritz].

Hendaia could not be held after they had abandoned their positions at Sara. Thus General [Joseph] Servan gave orders to abandon camp on May 2. The enemy made not even the slightest move at this however, but the panicky fright that had beset the French was so great that this retreat appeared to be a full-blown flight. Only the camp tools were saved; a lot of provisions and military supply including a number of heavy guns stayed behind at the fort. All this fell into Spanish hands; they hauled the lot to the other side of the Bidasoa, destroyed the fortresses at Hendaia, and set up several smaller camps along the shoreline of the sea and on the mountain of Louis XIV.

If one's fantasy were to stir up an image of wasteland, a void of people, and destruction, the current condition of Hendaia would be a true depiction. The small town is scattered around a wide area, as it once seems to have had a clean and pleasant appearance. Now all the houses are destroyed, with the exception of a few; the empty walls stand there half caved in, the floors on which people used to live are covered with wild scrubs and thorns, ivy entwines up and around the inner walls, one looks straight through the demolished windows and through the house onto the wild sea. Here and there, you still find bombs lying around on the streets, but you hardly ever meet a person. Most of the population died owing to the dangers and misery of the flight or are scattered elsewhere; now not even fifty families live in this whole town, and the thing that most irritates is that new arrivers, incapable of restoring the old, have extended miserable huts within the wide walls of the old houses, thus merely leaning against the former wealth.

We hurried to leave this wailful sight and climbed the ruins of the fortress, which are beneath the town on a nicely overgrown hill close to the bay, and which had brought about the town's unhappy fate. We climbed across the stones and the decrepit walls and enjoyed a beautiful view of Hondarribia ahead, of the shores of the Bidasoa extending into the lands to our left, and of the fields and meadows behind us, enclosed picturesquely by the higher mountains.

Hondarribia and Hendaia are situated straight across from each other, at the bay that is created by the sea's rising tide in the Bidasoa Estuary. The bay is long, narrow, and contorted along its various twists. Two almost sickle shaped sandbanks narrow it even more just leaving a curved straight that would really only serve the fisherman and his barge as an exit to the sea. Hendaia's houses, as mentioned, are village-less scattered around. Hondarribia, reflecting in the sea with its high church and tower on the round foothill, has, closely built, a more citylike, yet gloomy and sad appearance. The hills behind Hendaia are covered densely with grass and trees, a pleasant ground surface, behind which the Pyrenees, above all the top of Larrun, emerge. The mountains behind Hondarribia toward the sea are higher; a conjoined range, the extension of Jaizkibel, spans to the top of Higer Point, but these are barren meadows, treeless and bleak. The sound of the bells came across from Hondarribia calling to mass; in Hendaia the drums signaled the in fact somewhat belated announcement (on April 30) of the Treaty of Lunéville; it was only when we assured the poor inhabitants of its verity—so incredulous had they become upon this catastrophe—did they cease to doubt it. So differently did Spain and France present themselves.

The inhabitants of Hondarribia and Hendaia live naturally in a quotidian community. Belonging to the same tribe, sharing the same language, and speaking with only minor differences of dialect on the border, they must be connected to each other much more than other border people of differing kingdoms. It is a little noticed cruelty that our wars—which are rather scarcely intertwined with the interests of the people who have to carry them out—suddenly cut through these communities and set up a dividing wall of hatred and hostility between them, which is equally against their interest and inclination.

In the more distant mountain valleys, it cost the Basques' uneducated and simple sense of nature a lot of effort to comprehend that a war between two states, which they only belonged to coincidentally, would wrench them from their common setting and come to dominate their feelings. Right at the outset of the first campaign in the year 1793, there was a remarkable example in Higher Navarre [in other words, Navarre —ed].

The valleys of Maule [Mauléon, in Zuberoa] and Barétous [Varetons in Occitan, a valley in Bearn] used to pay the Spanish valleys of Erronkari [Roncal] and Zaraitzu [Salazar] three young cows in toll annually. As if war had never broken out between the two countries, or as if a dispute between the King of Spain and the French Republic could ever disturb the mutual friendship between them and their neighbors, the inhabitants of the Spanish valleys wandered to the usual place at the usual time in order to receive their toll. However, since no one appeared, they went across the border, chose three young cows from the first herd they could find, and returned calmly to their homes, unaware of having done anything that would provoke an act of retaliation. The French, however, did not deem this affair to be so harmless. They descended on the Spanish valleys, drove out a great number of herds and even set fire to some of the houses. Now that one had forced the peaceful people of Navarre into treating their neighbors with hostility, the feeling of suffered injustice crept up inside them, too. In turn, the inhabitants of the valleys in question advanced on France and set fire to the town of Urdatx [also known as Santa Grazi in Basque and Sainte-Engrâce in French].[5] How much misery could have been avoided if only one would have left these valleys, which nature had isolated from the rest of the world by enormous mountains, in the blissful ignorance of the crimes and foolishness that were committed beyond!

Hondarribia got its name from the shoaled river mouth it is at. It is named On- or Undarribia in thirteenth-century documents, and today's

---

5. This anecdote is so peculiar that some may request a witness. It is mentioned in the *Mém. sur la dernière guerre*, p. 14, already cited above.

Basques call it Hondarribia, both from *Ondarr-ibaya*, sandy river.[6] Ondarroa, another small coastal town in Biscay, has the same origin of name. The Spanish and French[7] name derived from a later contortion of Hondarribia.

Should you ferry across the bay you will find a way that leads land inward along the river. We followed it without visiting the town itself. It runs along a row of steep cliffs, yet densely covered with scrubs, on which small steps in the rocks lead up to vegetable gardens. There is a an avenue of alders and ash trees on the left and you can see through them to the river banks made up of lots of narrow, carefully cultivated vegetable gardens divided by water-filled ditches. Viewing the gloomy town with its fortifications being damaged on this side from this lavish and dense green makes for a peculiar contrast. The fortifications still lay there, reduced to rubble and in horror, just as when the mine had detonated, while behind them, the high and unscathed church and its tower rises.

Hondarribia fell into the hands of the French in August 1794. The town had suffered a lot during a six-day shelling and since the occupants consisted of a mere six hundred men as reserves for various regiments, their commander, D. Vicente de los Reyes, an aged officer, should be excused for capitulating at first demand. The fortresses were blown up only later and only a minor part remained, and a mine had already been placed underneath this part as well. The Higer Fort had capitulated during the same time.[8]

We turned right toward Donostia-San Sebastián at the mountain's edge next to the Capuchin monastery.

---

6. Oihenart in his *Notitia utriusque Vasconiae*, p. 168 translates *Ondarribaya* as last river, since the Bidasoa is the last river coming from Spain. *Ondoa*, however (related to *fundus*), actually means ground, the deepest part of something and thus only in this sense the end, the last; *ondarra* comes from *ondoa*, that what settles on the ground, the silt, with the additional meaning of sand. The true delineation dawns on you when you compare the meaning of the word with the geography of the town and the name of the similarly situated Ondarroa.

7. Risco in his sequel to *España sagrada*. v. 32, p. 153 believes the Basque name to be more recent than the Spanish one [Fuenterrabía]—without any sufficient explanation though. Authors who write in Latin have twisted the true name more elegantly to *fons rapidus* or *rabidus*.

8. *Mém. sur la dernière guerre etc.* p. 114.

Pasaia

With the exception of a few highways that are fit for carriage use, you can only get ahead by horse in the inner parts of Biscay, and some roads are nonetheless dangerous or uncomfortable for riding. Usually there are narrow, badly cobbled roads that at least confirm a lively business between the towns.

One of these roads led us along the riverbed of Jaizkibel, to our left we saw the nicely laid out plain, which is cut through everywhere by hills and lovely fields. We became tired of just facing the dreary Jaizkibel[1] and being bereft of an unobstructed view of the sea on account of it; we left our horses and, in spite of the midday heat, climbed to the top of the mountain.

It is covered with woods for about the first third; after that come bare and stony heather. The ascent is cumbersome even for the walker because of the steepness; nonetheless, they even take an ox-cart up the mountain, this way at least one understands the reason for their small size.

Above, the immensity of the sea view took us by surprise. The unfathomable ocean lay before us without any objects disrupting it; completely calm and waveless in the heat of the midday hour, the outermost seam appeared to ascend like wafts of scent on the horizon; the bare mountain's solitude corresponded to the look of the sea and land, sky and water completed the image of a tremendous, gloom evoking wasteland. What sort of an impression must this appearance have made on the Roman, when his fleet ventured into this lonesome bay from the much-traveled Mediterranean at a time when impenetrable woods were likely to have covered this inhospitable coast, when no beneficial culture had yet broken the climate's roughness, where not a trace of human effort smiles at

---

1. Jaizkibel gets its name from its position. *Quibela* or *guibela* [today *gibela* —ed.] means the back of something, *guibelean*, behind. Apparently, the first syllable comes from *itsasoa*, the sea, hence behind the sea, the back of the sea.

him, and the crudeness of the inhabitants and the barbarian ring of their sounds—his mollycoddled ear would even shy away from stowing a few place names[2]—would spawn the fearfulness of area even more.

We wandered along the summit some distance. The mountain's moorland descends toward the sea over a number of hills, scattered cattle graze above. New mountains lay ahead, among which we noticed above all two sisterly rising peaks of similar shape and height. We then entered a new mountain area and the familiar peaks, which we had greeted every morning, started to fade in the distance.

The plain one overlooks from Jaizkibel is the Oiartzun [Oyarzun] Valley. This valley can be found mentioned a lot in the records from the Middle Ages: at the time it extended from Donostia-San Sebastián to the Bidasoa, and comprised of, next to the market town Oiartzun, Hondarribia, Errenteria [Rentería], and Irun; in fact, Pasaia [Pasajes] only referred to the harbor of Oiartzun. The Spanish writers praise the courage and the physical strength of the inhabitants, and the Kings of Spain granted them several privileges. But beginning in the thirteenth century, a number of the appertaining towns have received special liberties and their own jurisdiction, and ever since, the name of Oiartzun is limited to the surrounding area of the town that carries this name.

When Pliny in his geographical survey of Europe turns from Gallia to Spain, he begins with the Pyrenees that rise from the ocean: the Basque wooded mountain range Olarso.[3] The same place, if with different versions of the name, Iarso, Oeaso, Eason, can be found among the old geographical remains. Here today's place name can be easily rediscovered—in the documents of the Middle Ages Oyarzo—which can be viewed as proving the age of the Basque language. For Oiartzun is a pure Basque word denoting stony elevation. In reality this market town is built on such and the whole valley is parceled by such hills.

The promontory Oeaso is presumably Jaizkibel or its most outward peak, Higer Point, and the town bearing the same name was probably farther inland above Pasaia;[4] for there also the sea could bare its bosom

---

2. The ancient writers complain of the tremendous harshness regarding the names of Spain's northern coast.

3. IV. 34. *Vasconum saltus, Olarso*.

4. Risco explains its position in his *España sagrada*, vol. XXXII, p. 186, he situates it (possibly too accurately) on an elevation, that is called Basanoaga (perhaps from *basoa*, *anoa*, and *aga*, wood spinney place.)

washing ashore, given that in former times the sea went farther inland on this side, and one still knows that there used to be shipyards at Errenteria where there are gardens today. Of the forests that Pliny records, one would not find as many today. But there were times when the market town Errenteria owned twenty-nine mercantile marine ships that had been built from their own woodlands.

Descending from Jaizkibel we found the way more rock strewn, and our view of the lowland was blocked by many emerging hills, most of them garlanded by trees, which would let us only look into the craterlike potholes that they created. The character of the area is almost the same everywhere along the coast. Coming down from the more distant mountains smaller and bigger streams burst out into the sea. The tide rises into them and leaves its silt behind. Thus ever so often leaving narrow valleys between the mountains, deep river beds, and often sandy ravines. At these heights we had once again a view of a beautiful bay. Two cliffs standing out made a narrow water mouth, a fishing boat was swimming on the calm, green-shadowy face of the lovely bay covered with overhanging brush and you could see the high seas through the narrow opening between the rocks.

Jaizkibel is 278 French fathoms high,[5] we had descended considerably when we saw a fine oak forest below us in the depth. Just as an altar formed by nature, there lay a great piece of rock in front of an old, mighty oak—unusual to come across in the southern countries—and, in some distance, there was a circle with another, smaller one. We remained here for a few moments; as we were resting mellow from the tiring ascent, it did not dawn on us however that we were only separated a few paces from possibly the most lovely place kissed by the sea along the French and Spanish coast. How great was our surprise, having got up and drawn closer to the flank of the hill, when we saw the tops of ships' masts, then a new bay, the most picturesque group of cliffs, and whitely shimmering houses between them and the sea. We rushed down the small rocky steps next to us in great haste, and all at once we found ourselves on the streets of Pasaia.

We dismissed our escort, a farm boy, whom we had taken off the field to guide us over the mountains. He did not know a word of Spanish. We tried to muster all our Basque, but we managed only rarely to elicit a comprehensible answer from him. Mostly we had to make do with his

---

5. *Mém. sur la dernier guerre etc.* p. 12.

sad *eztaquit* ("I do not understand," *ez dakit* in modern unified Basque
—ed.).

The beauty and security of Pasaia's harbor has been long known
from other accounts. Solely its entrance is extraordinarily narrow, the
entry and exit thus not without peril.

The sea forms a long and narrow passage into the land between high
and steep cliffs; viewed from this side of the bank, three cliffs stand out,
the middle one more than the others, and, in turn, form their own two
little bays. At the outward entrance stands the Saint Isabelle Fort, at the
inner the Saint Sebastian Fort. At the end of this rocky passage this narrow arm of the sea, threatened from both sides by tremendous faces of
the rock, expands into calm and pleasant bays. The actual inner harbor
is in the town itself from where the tide turns to the left and extends
toward Donostia-San Sebastián into a lake surrounded by vineyards and
gardens. Another part of the waters reach Lezo, and smaller arms still
today Errenteria, whereas in former times even bigger ships got thus far.

This mild transition from tremendous cliffs to lower, pleasantly cultivated hills, and the deep calmness of the harbor right behind the raging
waves of the ocean, give this place a unique and matchless magical spell.
Secluded from the rest of the world, one feels as if deeply rooted to this
exquisite coastal valley, rushing back and forth from the dark depths of
the harbor to the glittering reflection of the wide lake, one cannot get
enough of indulging in this kind solitude in which it seems that the tremendous mass's sole purpose is to function as a protective barrier against
the sea, so that nothing will disturb the heavenly peace behind. Whichever mountain top you climb, the heights above the bay or the marvelous
oak forest on the slope, or the chapel of Saint Anne's close by, the rocks
are laden with lush coppice and multifarious greens, the hills are carefully cultivated and planted. The bold crest of Jaizkibel is too far back
to disturb the magnificent appearance, and no lovelier transition to the
barren mountain ridge could possibly be.

Whoever yearns for nature's indulgence should never take a different
road to Pasaia than the one that chance made us find. It is the easiest for
those that travel from Baiona to Madrid and do not wish to leave their
carriage for long, to get there from Oiartzun. For Oiartzun lies so close
to Errenteria that it used to be its suburb[6] and the sea arm at Pasaia

---

6. *Errenteria* means leasehold, it is a general name for additional smaller places that are close
to major ones. There exists, among others, an Errenteria in Ondarroa and in Gernika.

reaches all the way to Errenteria. You could thus leave your carriage in Oiartzun, which is a short way to ride or to walk.

The houses of Pasaia were built partly on the side of the lake[7] toward Donostia-San Sebastián, partly around the harbor. Steep cliffs rise up immediately behind them, and from the inn in which we stopped one could walk out to a terrace on the same level made by the mountain. The houses are often flooded with water in front. Amid the density, the inhabitants are forced to change houses often, but this happens without much shuffling given of the minuteness of the houses. We saw desolated ruins in many places.

Just a few days before our arrival, a French frigate, *l'Egiptienne*, coming from Isle de France had moored in Pasaia. The inn was filled with passengers who were amazingly curious to find out about everything that had happened in France in the months during their absence.

Right at the moment the frigate entered the harbor, a French privateer-captain shot himself in his ship. He had captured eight ships, yet had lost all of them again, save two insignificant ones. This had only been his second campaign and now he was mooring idly and full of desperation in Pasaia. Upon seeing *l'Egiptienne* coming into the harbor he asked, what ship is this? He was informed, adding that she had had an unusually fast and successful voyage. "*Ah! qu'ils sont heureux ceux-là!*"[8] he exclaimed, left the deck for his cabin, and shot himself.

Another unfortunate event occurred during that time. The Spanish government had imposed a ban on all ships intending to sail to sea with immediate effect. One French ship destined for Guadeloupe, which had been harboring for a long time, had the boldness to leave the harbor in a very stormy night in order to evade the ban. It ran ashore, eleven people died, yet the captain and his three brothers (all of whom were officers on the ship) rescued themselves. Among the deceased was a woman with her child who had wanted to follow her husband already living in Guadeloupe. The unfortunate woman seems to have had a premonition of her subsequent fate. While in Pasaia, she never stopped talking about it with anyone she knew. "*Je m'embarque*," she often said, "*mais je sais que je vais me perdre.*"[9]

---

7. More properly an arm of the bay. —ed.

8. "Ah! Those are the happy ones!" —ed.

9. "I'll embark." "But I know I'll be lost." —ed.

We ferried across the lake [*sic*] to Donostia-San Sebastián late in the evening. It is always girls that take over the rowers' part; they surround the foreigner as soon as he approaches the water, and compete with each other in incomprehensible Basque for the honor of transporting him across. We found our horses on the other side and rode to Donostia-San Sebastián. At the lake, we were received by a lot of children, mostly girls, with tambourines and they accompanied us, playing and dancing, to the city with awful clamor. This way of begging is customary only during the month of May, though.

Donostia-San Sebastián

The little land of Gipuzkoa, of which Donostia-San Sebastián is the prime marketplace, extends from Bidasoa to the little river that flows into the sea at Ondarroa [Bizkaia]. It borders on Navarre and Araba in the south. It is, just as all the Basque provinces, very mountainous, and yet very fertile especially in certain areas, and the most populated among them. The size of the population in the census of 1787 was 120,716. Regarding language this province has its own dialect, which is more pleasant to the foreigner's ear than the actual Bizkaian, yet still not as enchanting as the French (Lapurdian) dialect. Many fantastical conjectures regarding the origin of the name Gipuzkoa[1] have been made; even though the sounds are apparently Basque, it would prove difficult to detect anything probable; the land is usually called Ipuscua,[2] Ypuscua, in the older documents and Donostia-San Sebastián is just called S. Sebastian de Puzico[3] in one of the year 980. Every man knows the liberties that the Basque provinces enjoy. As they were incorporated neither through conquest nor inheritance, but by voluntary transfer of the crown, it was for them to set the conditions. As is well known, the incorporation occurred in the year 1200 under Alfonso VIII. Araba and Gipuzkoa had been until that day—with minor interruptions—under the dominion of the crown of Navarre. But when Alfonso VIII (actually the III of Castile) was at war with Sancho of Navarre and laid siege to Vitoria-Gasteiz, the Gipuzkoans

---

1. Oihenart's delineation from *Biturigibus Ubiscis* or *Viuiscis* is just as invalid as the others. *Not. Vascon.* p. 163. In addition, the *Viuisci* were foreign tribes in Aquitania and have their origins in Northern Gallia. Strabo. IV. p.131.

2. Oihenart l.c. asserts that the original inhabitants always resorted to this name; but I always only find Guipuzcoa in the printed Basque books, even as early as in Axular's *Gueroco guero*, among others.

3. Marca *Hist. de Bearne.* l. I. c.4 [Larram. *Dicc.* I. LXXI] If the *Paesici* (*Paesici. Plin. ed. Bip.* IV. 34. *Cellarii not. Orb. Ant.* I. 86 § 56) had not lived farther west, even beyond the Cantabrians, one could think of them for the delineation of the name.

who were unsatisfied with Sancho called him in, seceded from Navarre, and submitted themselves to him. It appears as if Gipuzkoa had subjected itself to Castile completely and irrevocably, for one does not find a second documented subjugation—in contrast to Araba. Yet, the details of the circumstances for this transition are not known. More generally, it is regrettable that the history of Biscay has been so little examined to this day. The frugal fragments one can find have to be cumbersomely gathered from the general histories of Spain and Navarre; the only ones that have focused solely on the Basque Country, as far as I know, are [Arnaud] Oihenart[4] and Henao. The latter's Cantabrian antiquarianism remains unsatisfactory in many regards and the former writes only about the French Basque Country and Navarre. It would be thus most desirable that a native author were to fill this important lacuna. For sure, he would not be lacking extensive material. There are few countries that are as rich in sources, both in public and private archives, for a native history as is Spain; only few have a comparable zest for explorations of this kind and a certain skillfulness in the reading and copying of documents as widely disseminated, and the person who would commit to the task of writing this history would surely find older manuscripts, works that were written for the same purpose, that he could draw on.

I remember, without searching for it specifically, to have seen an unpublished history of Gipuzkoa at a scholar's and in the house of the Mazarredos in Bilbao a history of the Salazar family, one of the most ancient and renowned families of Spain, which through an heiress passed into the Mazarredo family with its main ancestral seat in Bizkaia.

The history of Gipuzkoa remains the most opaque. We do not even know whether it had its own counts, as in Bizkaia, or not. In the documents we only find single examples of the title 'Lord of Ipuscua'; anyway, it is likely that this province, just as the others, chose its own protectors, be it on a continual basis, be it only from time to time. It was only under Henry IV that they were privileged to become immediate subjects of the king and under no circumstance could he sell them off or hand them over to others.[5]

One can easily leave it to the future historian to describe all the petty feuds and internal riots that all of Biscay endured uninterruptedly before

---

4. *Notitia utriusque Vasconiae tum Ibericae, tum Aquitanicae etc. Authore Arnaldo Oihenarto Mauleosolensi* (Maule in the Province of Zuberoa) *Parisiis*, 1638, 4.

5. Oihenart, p. 170.

Spain attained its inner political consistency. But how interesting it would be to shed light on the fortunate circumstances under which this small mountain folk succeeded to impose their own constitution—in times of general suppression and violence—that, equally far from anarchy and despotism, breathes the noble spirit of liberty while its beneficial ramifications are still distinctive in their customs and character.

The privileges that distinguish Biscay are generally shared by all three provinces. But each of their constitutions diverges considerably from each other. Gipuzkoa's is less entangled than that of Bizkaia, and both are more purely democratic than Araba's.

All deciding powers regarding the administration of matters concerned with the province lay with the assembly of the town councils in Gipuzkoa. It is here that both the chief delegate and the delegates of the district are elected, and not only must they abide by the assembly's decisions, they also have to summon it anew in matters of great importance and await its decision.

The town councils do not assemble personally, though, but come together by way of delegates; and these are always elected newly for the assembly, and the foundations according to which they vote is based on the notion that each elector votes solely for himself and must appear in person. When this constitution was devised for the first time, each town was granted a certain number of votes according to the number of heads of families (*vecinos*), and the weight that comes to bear on the decision depends on that number of votes and not on the number of delegates dispatched. Beacuse this number is arbitrary, each town also tends to send only one or two delegates. Obviously, this election method has the disadvantage that solely the major towns carry the decision in their own hands. Should eight or ten of them favor a cause the weight of their votes will beat the other seventy, should they unanimously be of a different opinion. For the overall number of delegates tends to amount to eighty.

This general assembly circulates among the eighteen towns of Gipuzkoa. Its function is to appoint the chief—and the district—delegates, to decide on the province's general matters, and to determine the points that should be discussed in the next following assembly. The meeting takes part in a closed room, not open to the public, and the speeches are kept to Spanish. Whatever is said is only explained to those who do not understand Spanish in Basque for important matters. The delegates are the true representatives of their power base in a most literal sense. In matters of interest to them, the town councils instruct the delegates clearly on what opinion they should voice and the positions of one town are so much regarded as one collective voice that when two delegates of the same borough voice disparate opinions, they are not allowed to vote on that particular matter of dissent.

Thus one cannot suppose of a representative system here; it is a pure and utter democracy. No one lets his will be represented by someone more capable; everybody decides every matter for himself, and the delegate is merely the vehicle for the majority of votes in the borough.

The case that delegates of the same town do not concur happens only rarely, as they never fail to ask their commissioners for their opinions on this or that matter. Thus it could occur only if the matter discussed is not important to the place that sends them off, and the debate finds them unprepared. The appointment comes about in a special meeting of each borough. The *alcalde* [mayor] has the floor and he is usually elected. Neither here nor at the general assembly is there an order of priority. Every Gipuzkoan is aristocratic by birth; everyone, irrespective of wealth and trade, can be elected to the office of chief delegate; but everyone who desires the right to vote must be a freeholder. In some places, the political constitution has been connected to the culture of the land in a most beneficial way in this regard. I saw a remarkable example of this during a stroll in Donostia-San Sebastián. There is a mountain next to the village of Astigarraga,[6] called Santiago by way of its cappella, which is well maintained all the way up to its top. I wondered about this extraordinary effort, but I was told later that according to an old tradition, no one in town would be able to enjoy the right as a voting citizen, if he did not own a piece of a field on this particular mountain, regardless of however much he owned in the valley. In this way there is a seemingly wonderful phenomenon of a once barren heath that was turned into fertile farmland and gardens. The chief delegate stands at the top of the administration regarding all matters of the land and holds his office for two years.[7] He has an adjunct at his side, and he confers with the district delegates whenever he deems it necessary or he calls for an extraordinary general assembly meeting. The district delegates (*diputados de partido*) are eight in number, and the chief delegate holds two regular meetings with them per year, one in July, the other in November, in order to render an account

---

6. Place of linden trees.

7. Josef de Beovide writes to Hervas on 15 May 1784: "the province holds an annual assembly . . . at each of these a chief delegate is appointed." At the time he would have been elected every year.

of his administration. He is nothing more than their chairman and, as we see, cannot decide according to his own capriciousness on any matter of greater consequence.

The seat of the chief delegate, just as that of the royal *corregidor*[8] as the highest level of jurisdiction in the country, circulated between the four cities of Tolosa, Donostia-San Sebastián, Azkoitia, and Azpeitia, and the chief delegate had to be taken from one of these four cities. For some time there had been the wish to change this. But the mentioned predominance of the four bigger cities, whose interests were at play here, foiled all attempts in the process. Finally, it was pushed through that the matter would be decided by a commission. Today the permanent seat of the chief delegate and the *corregidor* is in Tolosa, which is suited best given its size and position on the road to Madrid and its location almost right in the center of the land, and the election of the former is no longer limited to a particular town.

It is another oddity that no attorney, nor any other jurist, is allowed to be present during the time and in the town where the general assembly is being held, including a farther surrounding sector beyond. The town itself appoints merely a few jurists that the assembly can lean on for consultancy if need be. It seems as though one carefully sought to let the simple, but sound sense of the country people—among which most of the delegates tended to come from—unfold and to keep them free from the influences of captious jurisprudence.[9]

As is known, the king cannot excise taxes on the Basques; he can solely solicit, if the circumstances afford it, voluntary donations. These are distributed in Gipuzkoa according to the proportion of votes that every town enjoys, and in order to procure it, the town councils put a small tax on the sales of meat, wine, and so on. Throughout Spain this is the common way to raise the required sums for municipal expenditures. These charges are called *arbitrios*, while the income gained from the boroughs' assets is called *proprios*. Both the *proprios* and the *arbitrios* are directly under the supervision of Council of Castile. Commons are likewise in Biscay, just as in the rest of Spain, subjugated to land cultivation.

---

8. Publisher's note: The main royal representative in a province. Excellent explanations of this office can be found in both Monreal, ed., *The Old Law of Bizkaia* and Barahona, *Vizcaya on the Eve of Carlism*.

9. According to the ordinance of Henry IV of 1463, no advocate was allowed to be present during the assembly of the *hermandades* of Araba, too—except for a few special cases. Landazuri *Hist. de Alava*. I, 264.

The forests in particular suffer. A lot of wood is sold whenever the needs become more pressing; little or none is replanted, and, moreover, lack of surveillance promotes thieving of all sorts. [Gaspar Melchor de] Jovellanos in his felicitous, although abroad not nearly well enough known, book on the reform of Spanish farming law,[10] which sheds such a bright light on the whole condition of Spanish farming, complains about this malpractice. The late director of the Seminary of Bergara, D.[José de] Iturriaga, had devised a plan for Gipuzkoa whereby the town councils could ameliorate their shattered finances through a limited divestiture of their commodities, and yet return a considerable amount of the now almost fully relinquished land to the country's original landscape. However, he was met with too many difficulties as to persevere with it.

I deemed it necessary to begin with these general descriptions about this little country, where we will remain with our wanderings for a few more moments. I will return to these now.

We went and saw the castle right after our arrival in the morning in order to relish the view of the sea below from this altitude, something we longed for time and again. The way up runs along the sides of the mountains and there are many points from where one can view the area very well. The castle is called after its French constructor La Mota.

The sea creates small bays to both sides of the mountain on which the fort stands, which only leave room for a narrow tongue of land. The town is built right there at the foot of the castle's mountain. Both of the bays are curbed by bleak and barren mountains. On that of the western side of the town, Mendiotza (Spanish *Monte Frio*, cold mountain),[11] stands the lighthouse of the harbor; the one on the eastside is called Ulia. The island of Saint Clara lies before the western bay; it is a small rocky island and the waves' foam splashes up against its shores covered with shrubbery—the most picturesque view in this otherwise barren and desolate landscape. Moreover, the harbor lies on this side, a small and partly dried basin when the tide goes out.

There was no ship there when we were there. Just a few in the docks. Trade in Donostia-San Sebastián was more insignificant than that of

---

10. *Informe de la Sociedad Economica de esta corte al Consejo de Castilla en el Expediente de Ley Agraria, extendido por D. Gaspar Melchor de Jovellanos*, Madrid 1795, 4. § 55, p. 17.

11. Publisher's note: Today this mountain is known as Mendizorrotz, which means something completely different: pointed, acute, or even demanding mountain.

other Spanish coastal cities during this time. During the first part of the French War, Donostia-San Sebastián did good business as it served as a transfer site between the Americas and France as long as the United States was not on clear and good terms with France. Sometimes, French privateers found it advantageous to make prize here rather than in French ports. It is stated that the number of the city's inhabitants is eight thousand and fourteen thousand in the district.

The view of the high sea is less beautiful here than in Donibane Lohizune or farther down the coast. The mountains come forward too close, but one can still see the most exposed headland of Getaria [Guetaria].

The view of the city from the land side is remarkable, but only in the sense of odd, not endearing. It looks like an equal sided square, fixed on all corners. The streets are narrow, although the houses are high and some are built with splendor; the amount of balconies, the regular-shaped nature of the marketplace, the opulently gilded city hall (*casa de ayuntamiento*), all kept according to truly Spanish taste. As you look down into the streets from up above, nowhere greater does the smallness of the town strike your eyes, and the height and style of the buildings and the positioning of the alleys give it its dark and dejected appearance. There are two monasteries on either side of the town, on the west side that of Carmelite nuns, on the east side that of Dominicans. Never have I seen anything more melancholic than that view into the monastery's courtyard, which is surrounded by a gothic cross-coat and eclipsed by a large cypress at its center. The city's surrounding area keeps in line with this appearance. The sea has sanded up the coastline everywhere. But only a short distance away one sees green brush and fields again, and the background is made up of a ridge of high mountains in Navarre and Biscay.

Deprived of the full and direct view of the sea by the mountain on which the castle stands, and surrounded by bare hills and sandy stretches, it becomes vivid that Donostia-San Sebastián does not revel in a pleasant location. The climate is harsh and the rain tends to often and persistently dominate two thirds of the year so that the Spaniards' common wit rendered it with a less honorable by-name.[12] One might thus think that the Basque proverb "To the God-fearing, Donostia-San Sebastián and Biriatu [Biriatou] (a village close by) are an equally delightful mansion" could easily find a more general application, also to the less pious.

---

12. It is ironically referred to as *el orinal del cielo* [heaven's urinal —ed.].

Yet how pleasantly surprised one is by the area, if one looks around just a bit farther away. Whichever among the numerous walks around the city one pleases to choose, one finds a most lovely variety of forested hills and fertile valleys and it would be difficult to find any other Biscayan city lying in the center of such delightful scenery. One needs to see this beautiful coastland for oneself in order to conceive its so particular mellifluence and the vegetation's freshness.

If one would temper the wildness and the terrific size of a mountain area to the graceful and surprising alternation of mountains and valleys, the harshness of the northern climate to the rejuvenating coolness and strengthening freshness; if one would lend a quicker and more invigorating growth to the more inertial vegetation of the north, to mingle the cold, at times gloomy earnestness of its inhabitants with a bit of the southerner's vivaciousness and serenity, you would attain a true image of Biscay, and especially of that of the most populated and fertile parts of Gipuzkoa. One feels being in the north, the air in the spring and in the fall cannot be referred to as mild, the produce of our homeland and that of northern France can also be found here, the more delicate of the south, oranges, palm trees, almonds, even olive trees are lacking. But this north is the North of Spain, and the vegetation is sufficiently compensated for the persistently rough climate by the abundant irrigation of the land.

Valley and mountains are far more gracefully linked to each other and entangled than in any other country. The scenery changes with every moment; there is a closed view almost everywhere, the eye oversees only small yet always picturesquely confined parts. Quickly gushing streams plummet from the heights, cut through the village greens with calm, numerous turns or wheel mills and smelting works by ferociously swooshing through narrow stream beds. Seldom does one see bare summits, the mountains are covered in green all the way to the top, and naked beaks of rocks emerge solely from tangly scrubs. The fields are fenced in by living hedgerows, they are followed by meadows and woodlands that mostly consist of two types of oak (*robles* and *encinas*) predominant throughout Spain.

No longer does one find such amplitude of vegetation as on the shores of the Garonne, it is no longer heavy laden vines that stretch out and entwine around high and slender elm trees; neither is it the lush, cow-covered grass of our marshlands; yet the stout growth of the trees, the thick, curly, for the eyes impervious foliage; the ubiquitously hefty, sprouting of the grass and sowing have a masculine beauty that befits the mountainous character of the area.

You seldom find the dignified figure of our oak that defies the centuries in Biscay. It remains a specific enchantment of our northern landscape that is solely because of habit not sufficiently recognized. As rich and opulent as the vegetation of the south, as subtle and tender the formation of the plants that leave us enchanted right at first sight, as gorgeous as the glittering mix of their colors may be, it cannot be denied that the north imprints its forests with a character of greatness and dignity that unsettles the force of imagination much deeper and more seriously. I admit it freely that I, at least, had often yearned for them with desire during my entire stay in France and Spain and had welcomed the first that I encountered on German soil with incredible joy.

In Gipuzkoa and Bizkaia, the trees are generally decapitated, partly because the wood is needed as charcoal for the ironworks, partly for political reasons. Heretofore the royal navy had the right to cut the strong wood in the districts of their respective departments for shipbuilding. From that moment on it no longer belonged to the owner, who only received a certain statutory compensation, but to the king. Instead of benefitting from the growth of his trees, the owner could only expect constraints with regard to his own property. This scheme has been recently abolished as it was detrimental both to the forests and thus the royal navy. The cutting of the trees has stopped; once again the owner enjoys the right to sell his wood freely with no difference to the size and the king has merely reserved his preemption right.

Among all the Spanish provinces it is the Basque provinces that deserve to be recognized as the most carefully cultivated. Even though Gipuzkoa is more suitable for cultivation than the tougher and hillier Bizkaia, the soil is not very fertile, nonetheless, and only the areas of Azpeitia, Azkoitia, Oñati [Oñate], and Arrasate-Mondragón, where it is not unusual to harvest the thirtieth and thirty-sixth grain, are the exception here. It is thus only on account of the people's diligence and incredible industriousness that this small country can feed such a great number of inhabitants. I had much desired to attain trustworthy information regarding both size and population of all the three provinces. Nowhere—according to the Spaniards' own admission—is it as difficult to get reliable statistical information, than in Spain. Not out of reticence, but because this point no longer gains much attention. With regard to population one still need to rely on the census of 1787, which in itself is not free of error. According to these figures all of Biscay comprises 250 square miles.[13] The largest third by far is the province of Araba, poorly inhabited, while Gipuzkoa amounts most of the population with yet the smallest surface area. If one estimates, even if only roughly, the relation of all three provinces to each other in size, it is not exaggerated to figure two thousand people per square mile in Gipuzkoa, which means that the population outnumbers that of Switzerland.[14] However, one must not forget that Gipuzkoa has not one square mile of soil that is completely flat and not cut through by mountains.

All the major landowning families lease their lands to others. By this they make only insignificant earnings from them and for the most part would not even receive half of the real profits. However, they do provide the country with a lot of well-to-do and content tenant families in this way. Moreover, these tenancies come very close to being true ownership. They are handed down from father to son, and remain in the same family for 150 to 200 years. For even though the landlord can exchange the tenants at his leisure, he would deem it disgraceful to do so without having good cause.[15] The tenant puts in all the labor and defrays all the costs, though he usually carries out all the toilsome farming solely with the help of his family and his workmen. Seldom do they hire day laborers; during harvest or whenever else the tasks becomes pressing, the different tenants help each other and provide each other with food. In the event that the tenant has no sons but a daughter, he would indicate to the landlord to whom he wishes to have her married. He, then, would inquire about the young man's state of affairs and comportment; by consenting to the marriage he at the same time tacitly declares that he would leave the farm to his future son-in-law.

This arrangement could scarcely be considered the best for the country's agriculture. The tenants farm their fields according to their once adopted pattern; they are hardly moved to innovation, and it still requires a great effort to get them to seed potatoes and make butter; and given that the conditions of their tenancy are so little cumbersome, there is nothing to give them cause to conceive of great improvements. The more wealthy landlords on the other hand often lead too much of an idle life—if they are not at the service of the crown that is—and, amid their

---

13. *Neuere Staatskunde von Spanien*, I, 101.

14. We reckoned about sixty square miles for Gipuzkoa.

15. The same goes for many parts in England. For this see Mr. D. Thaer's *Einleitung zur Kenntniss der Englischen Landwirtschaft*, I, 22.

ambition, a most considerable amount of capital is lost by not engaging in more intensive farming. However one must also bear in mind that this small mountain country must not be compared to greater states, like for instance France or England. The possessions encompass too little and are too scattered; one could hardly introduce a major agricultural system there. Moreover, a country in which power, reputation, yes even its self-determined existence is based only to a minor degree on the produce of the soil and the profits from trade and industry, but almost entirely on the character, the effort and national diligence of its inhabitants, as it is so obviously the case in Biscay, requires that, wherever possible, every single person remains in a state of independent affluence.

In these cases, however, in which the profit returns will always remain relative in regard to national wealth and in which a most respectable self-reliance becomes vivid in the people's character, it is necessary to subordinate the fundamentals of advanced political economics under the last-mentioned maxims at least for so long until both can be married without disadvantage. For only if the results are great enough to effectuate such a vital transformation of all human forces, so that all purposes of pursuit are suddenly expanded and all means multiplied, will they be able to continue to lead a nation on its intellectual and moral trajectory. In Biscay the current constitution has a most fortunate influence on the state of formation and ethics that in a most honorable way bears witness to the character of the people, the temperate and equitable disposition of the wealthy, and the diligence of the lower class. In the communion in which both live with each other on a continuous basis, it is always possible to introduce improvements, even if slowly and time after time, and such is truly the case indeed.

I did not linger long enough in Donostia-San Sebastián to undertake even the more exquisite among the city's walks. All by myself on a beautiful spring evening, on the banks of the small Urumea River,[16] which runs into the sea on the east side of the castle, toward Hernani, I refound the truly dulcet character of the Biscayan lands, which were still so vivid in my memories of my first journey to Spain, in the enchanting vacillation of nature's picturesque scenery.

---

16. Small water, *eau mince*, from *ura*, water, and *mea*, fine, thin.

Zarautz and Getaria

The mountains of Igeldo [Igueldo], over which the road behind the lighthouse of Monte Frio from Donostia-San Sebastián to Orio leads, resemble the barren ridges of Jaizkibel. We came across only few places up there that bear fields and coppice, mostly just heather on which some herds were grazing. It was only on land inward that we saw wooden hills and carefully cultivated valleys, and it is this mix of wild appearance and diligent agriculture that are not the worst of Biscay's charms. From this altitude we could clearly see the character of this area. Between the highest mountains, which surround the horizon and for the most part belong to Navarre, and the lower mountains, which make for the back of the sea just as a parapet, numerous diagonally inclining higher and lower mountain ranges run across leaving deep valleys between them like mighty gorges dug deeply by time, but ornamented by the hand's cultivation with fields, meadows, and charming hedges. Creating such valleys and coming down from the water-shedding and border-marking mountains of Gipuzkoa, Araba, and Navarre, five predominant rivers run along the coast of Gipuzkoa toward the sea and divide the country in just as many natural sections. At their estuaries lie small harbors. We had left the river of Pasaia and the Urumea behind us. Now we were passing the Orio while the Urola and the Deba remained in front of us.

We found nothing on this secluded mountain top but a church with many crosses that were erected around it. Moreover, we met only one single Franciscan monk; he was an aged man with intensely worn, meaningful features from which you could tell that the ravages of time and experience had carved these revealing forms.

Tired by the bare mountain heather our gaze rested pleasantly on the Orio's fertile banks. We again admired the Biscayans' assiduity in cultivating their land. They use as much care for the tilling of a field for wheat and corn here as we would when planting flowers at home.

Orio is a badly built, insignificant market town of about one hundred families. Even in the smallest Biscayan towns does one always find a certain cleanliness and daintiness, and at least some bigger, in parts even opulent buildings. It is always the church, the town hall and—something that never goes lacking in Biscay—the pelota court that stand out, which is usually surrounded by a wall and equipped with seats of stone. The costs for these buildings are paid from the revenues gained from the public goods (*propios*).

We noticed coats of arms above the doors of many houses in Orio, mostly shields that were held by eagles, lions, and wild men and carved in stone, which showed us that these were *casas solariegas*[1] (the ancestral homes) of the families living in them. One often finds these ancestral homes in the country villages as well. The pride of a *hidalgo de aldea* (squire) is often mocked in the comical and satirical writings of the Spaniards. He is described "as how he gravely walks around the squalid marketplace of a miserable town, enwrapped by an inferior coat, eying the coat of arms above the door of a half derelict house, and thanking God and His providence pathetically for having him being born as Don So-and-So[2] of N.N. Never. He will never take off his hat," continues said description "nor will he greet the stranger entering the tavern, even if this were the governor of the province or the president of the High Court. All he would possibly condescend to do is ask whether the stranger stems from an ancestral home recognized by Castilian law? Which coat of arms would he bear? And whether he has known relatives in the neighborhood? (Although it is the city nobility that is usually associated with this ridiculousness) for as highborn as the stranger's family could possibly be, he will always retain the inexcusable stain that he was not born in the very town he is currently traveling through, for the nobility there is of a

---

1. *Solar* or *casa solariega* from the Latin *solum*. These ancestral homes are very important because they serve as proof for the oldest nobility even if the house no longer stands.

2. The Spaniards have their own name for what we signify as "so-and-so" (see Adelung's *Wörterbuch*, III, 355.), it is: *fulano*, here for instance "Don Fulano de Tal." According to D. Thomas Antonio Sanchez (*Coleccion de Poesias Castellanas anteriores al siglo 15*, II., 513) the word comes from the Arabs, who say *falan*. They supposedly took it from the Hebrew *pheloni*. The Spaniards however add *zutano* when they wish to speak of two nameless persons, something that Sanchez does not explain. *Zut* means erect (*debout*) in Basque and hence *zutano* possibly someone upright, a "somebody." If *fulano* were possibly not of Arabic origin, one could delineate if from *fullare*, *fouler* (in today's Spanish *holler*), someone who treads, and thus both words express analogous terms, which, as so often, would have been connected by rhyme in the vernacular. In Romanic *fular*, to churn.

kind that has become extinct elsewhere in the kingdom."[3] The original figures of this tale, should they still be hidden somewhere in a remote corner of Spain, which I do not believe, did not cross my path anywhere, although I did make it my purpose during this journey to seek out those very classes of the nation that had the least changed their customs while exposed to foreigners. Never, however, will the foreigner be confronted with proud contempt in guest-void Biscay. I will always remember with heartfelt and thankful joy how friendly I was welcomed, at times without any recommendation, to these country estates, at times spending several days with the family, and with how much obliging kindness they would introduce me to the curiosities of the land. The way these houses are built is usually quite simple, but with a certain solid opulence. They are mostly rectangular, erected completely with ashlar rocks, and laid out with four small towers on each corner. Inside, one clearly misses what is referred to as nice *ameublement* [furnishings] in France and with us. Even among the rich you come across mere straw chairs and a white wall with one upholstered baseboard, but generally there is great cleanliness; there are fine *esteras* (footmats),[4] and nice paintings by Spanish and foreign masters. Also, it would be in vain to expect the residents to wear luxurious clothes. There is a lot of quiet and humble public spirit that come to the fore in all the Spanish provinces, but especially in Biscay, where even in a lordly home you will recognize the lady of the house rather by the flock of children that surround her than by her attire.

Zarautz is a small town with only fifteen hundred souls, but it boasts a great parish church and a new city hall that has a high-columned entrance. The back end of the town leans on Mount Santa Barbara at a high and steep face, covered with brush above, which limits the view on the way coming from Orio in a romantic way.

Upon climbing the top of the hill that divides the small distance between Zarautz and Getaria, we overlooked the greatest part of the Bay of Biscay; the blue tide oscillated through the green leaves of the vine-

---

3. *Cartas Marruecas del Coronel D. Joseph Cadahalso.* (Moroccan letters by Colonel etc.) 1796, p. 99.

4. The name of these footmats, which are usually made out of woven straw or *spartum*, is also of Basque origin. *Estutu* means to pull together, to compress, from which comes the adverb *estera*, congested; these matts are obviously very densely interwoven. One has two kinds, smooth ones to walk on throughout the parlor, and shaggy ones (*felpados*) to be put under the feet for warmth.

yards that cover the slopes and the foot hills of the mountain, and the marvelous rock of Getaria lay at our feet.

Amid all the towns I visited in this part of Spain, Getaria is the most vivacious example of Basque patriotism. Originally, this town had been a shabby fishing harbor that one can still tell from the old, badly built houses. It now boasts several grand houses, entirely built of stone, and is adorned with stony quays, magnificently designed fountains, and a statue of a sea hero in its midst. All this is the work of some private persons who have become wealthy in the Americas, they are customarily called *Indianos* here.

For Gipuzkoa is too populated so as not to have a considerable amount of its population having to find its keep elsewhere. Since the Basques are generally accustomed to hard work and order, and for the most part display good penmanship, they are sought after in companies throughout Spain, and are willingly taken in to the royal offices. Possibly no other province in comparison accounts for as many persons in lower and higher public service. Another group goes to the Americas, and finally, many work as artisans or manufacturers in the rest of Spain.

Now, it is remarkable, what warm and unwavering devotion all these people from such diverse classes and with so many occupations have retained toward their homeland. Not only do they seize every chance to put their possibilities to use for it, they also hold whatever they can achieve in this respect as the greatest and most honorable opportunity. Nothing adulates their pride as much as the remembrance of their ancestry; only recently there was a minister, whose enlightened love for his homeland could have been even more advantageous for Biscay if he had been left in his post for longer, at the center of all affairs, in the highest favor of the king and endowed with the prime dignitary positions, carried out a tenacious legal dispute about half a house in Araba merely to prove his civil autochthonous affiliation with it and that he originated there.

Wherever they meet abroad, they stick together so firmly and infrangibly even if little acquainted with each other, that this often gives cause to jealousy among the other Spaniards; thus, the Basque provinces and Navarre are called the United Provinces of Spain[5] in jest.

---

5. *Las Provincias unidas de España. Cartas Marruecas*, p. 70.

It is only seldom that they lose their desire to return to their place of origin. Even if they spend thirty or forty years in the Americas, they do tend to return to their place of birth, and they then put a part of their wealth toward embellishing it. You find traces of this patriotic beautification effort throughout Biscay; apparently this is especially the case for the market town of Elorrio, where I did not come through, however. The love for the national customs and entertainment is so strong that only few of the many carpenters, that is, those that work far away, even if as far as twenty or twenty-five miles, fail to return to their place of birth for the sole purpose of dining with their wives, children, and friends on Christmas Eve and to fill the town with music for a part of the night.

The *Indiano*, D. Francisco Echabe, whom Mr. Fischer commemorates in his travels, was no longer alive when we visited Getaria. Now someone else, D. Manuel Agote, must be credited for eternalizing the memory of the renowned Elcano with a statue.

Juan Sebastian Elcano accompanied Magellan on his round the world sail and embarked with him in Seville as the steersman of the fourth ship *Concepción*. The Spaniards and foreigners usually call him Cano or el Cano. It is only on the inscription of the statue that he is referred to as Elcano, this, and not Cano, is the actual Basque name; the first syllable is frequently turned into the French or Spanish article, as mentioned above. When upon Magellan's assassination on the island Cebu in April 1521 his successor also died, someone else, however, chose to return with his ship via Panama, Elcano was given the command and he sailed back to Seville on September 6, 1522,[6] with the only remaining ship, the *Victoria*, and with only 18 of the original 237[7] seamen that had set off at the same time. He was thus the first to have really circumnavigated the world and Charles V gave him a coat of arms of a globe with the known engraving: "You are the first to have circled me" (*Primus me circumdedisti*). The *Victoria* was kept as a holy remnant of this voyage until it fully disintegrated of age. Elcano carried out a second voyage to the South Seas with a small fleet of seven ships that was headed by the Knight of Malta, [Francisco José] Jofré de Loaysa. Elcano was given the command once more when the latter died during the voyage, but he only retained it for four days as he himself died on August 4, 1526. His alleged

---

6. According to Pigafetta, p. 236. On the 7th or 8th according to others.

7. Anton Pigafetta's *Beschr. D. v. Magellan unternommenen ersten Reise um die Welt. Aus dem Französischen übers. v. Jacobs und Kries.* Gotha, Perthes. 1801. p. XLVIII.

birth house is still displayed in Getaria. It is painted yellow and it is close by the gate one enters from the direction of Zarautz.[8]

It is precisely there where his statue stands in a rectangular square. It is made of sandstone, made in Madrid, but the work is very mediocre only; it supposedly cost 22,000 *reales de vellon* (about 1,500 Thaler in our currency), and has a Latin, Spanish, and Basque engraving on three sides of the pedestal.

Where national spirit derives from national feeling, it is first of all confined to the circles that directly surround the individual; indeed, it features by taking hold of a relative while distancing the stranger; just as in any natural force, love emerges amid repugnance in humans, and every magnetic pole knows its repulsive one. It is reserved to reason alone to encompass everything comprehensible at once in the highest; and it is reserved to the idealized feeling to spark invigorating and animating warmth from elements that are merely alike. Common sentiment requires friction with diverse substances, and even the hatred of the most hate-worthy of all, moral evil, is, in terms of hatred, stronger in common nature than in that of sublime nature.

I had reason to make this observation on many occasions in Biscay. While traveling through the inner parts of the land and having familiarized myself with the customs there, the whole country seemed to me as cut out into a lot of small circles of which their mutually excluding borders showed glaring demarcations. These, however, faded into greater circles time and again; and I found such a natural relationship in the mutual to and fro of these diverse masses, partly in political, but particularly in ethical terms, which finds its balance in its own wavering. It is only then that I vividly recognized that no true national character can come about without such an ever-active interplay, and, in turn, that without this national character a land that, apart from its position by

---

8. It is extremely peculiar that Pigafetta does not refer to Elcano at all, indeed he does not even mention his name, given that he lists all the other commanders and, more than once, even the steersmen as well. The reasons for this can only really be private enmity that must have been between them. For when Carvajo, the second commander after Magellan's demise, remained on Tidore with his ship *Trinidad*, Pigafetta neglects to mention who commanded the *Vitoria* sailing back on its own, but continues his account by keeping to the second person plural, we sailed, we did, we carried out and so on, and thus it seems that he omitted Elcano's name on purpose. Remarking on their passage through the Strait of Magellan, he mentions the name of the steersman of the *Concepción*, Juan Serano. *l.c.* p. 50. Elcano had perhaps been given a different post on this or a different ship at the time.

the sea, is so meagerly blessed by nature, could never have achieved such a degree of prosperity, general affluence, and enlightenment by the sheer power of its people alone.

One cannot deny that the Biscayans' love and devotedness to their birth land and their birthplace has something exclusive about it. There is a certain jealousy between all the neighboring towns, and even abroad the Biscayans are reproached—I do not know if with good reason—for nuancing their love for their compatriots according to the distance that lies between their respective birthplaces, regardless of the general unity and these minor provocations between neighboring towns extend even to public amusements. But one can say with good reason that they come to an end right there. I have never heard of an example in which these small, insignificant rivalries dropped silent the instant it came to matters of general interest; conversely, I have more than once observed how they would incite useful and stimulating competition.

The game of pelota offers the most common opportunity to put these in motion. It is the Biscayans' greatest enjoyment. Not only does every town have its own more or less luxuriously designed court, but everyone takes part in the game as well. Just as in everything in Biscay, but especially when it comes to playing ball, there is no difference in class, and on Sundays a great number of both sexes of the towns are present, the *alcaldes* and the clergy not excluded, watch the players and follow them amid vivid interest by applauding or by showing their disapproval. Whole towns challenge each other to ceremonious games. Allegedly, the Gipuzkoans are the best players of the Biscayan provinces. At times, a higher national interest meddles in as well. At least in former times, the Navarrese (who equally speak Basque) challenged the French and vice versa; in these cases the whole general area is full of participation. The greatest part of the Spaniards would even root for the French. The patriotic muse does not hold still at these challenges. Bards perform in their national language, taunt the beaten opponent, or accuse them in advance of their presumption to challenge such skilled contenders. A song I once came across by chance on the occasion of a challenge between Markina [Marquina] and Mutriku [Motrico] commenced with the following stanza:

> *Have you made a challenge,*
> *but to do what? Oh, how presumptious!*
> *Toward the noble game of pelota,*
> *toward all of Markina here at our side!*

How arrogant are such challenges.
Ha! People of Mutriku, be my witness!
Have you not always been stricken down
by Markina in flying victory?

Another occasion for envious rivalry, at times even for real altercations, are the rural festivities when one village comes to visit another, or when a town invites all the surrounding country inhabitants to the dance with a few skins of wine. It does occur during these occasions that someone or other believes his honor to have suffered injury on grounds of some newly introduced matter of etiquette, and then the entire town's young people make this insult their own. They fly in their faces and what follows is a brawl, and it is seldom that a year passes without someone being killed or badly wounded this way. The Biscayans' true national weapon is a long and thick mountain cane without which he never or seldom wanders. When both insulted parties encounter each other they challenge each other with the word[9] "*aup!*" which signifies in an expressive way a sudden eruption, a mustering of all forces. Should they pause or hesitate to attack, you would hear: "*biderdia!*" ("To the middle of the street!"). Combat begins instantly. The club is held by both hands, and this form of fencing knows its rules just as well as we do ours. The skilled fighter knows how to swiftly hold off his opponent's stroke and how to immediately follow it with his own. The parry depends on how the strike is carried out, either horizontally in front of the face, or else to both sides further down. If the striking proves unsuccessful, the end of the cane can also serve for stabbing. When one of them is stricken down, his followers go before him, and cover him with their clubs, just as Homer's heroes with their lances and shields for their fallen warriors, and while fighting and retreating, attempt to pull him away from the battle. It would be impossible to intend to anticipate each eruption of passion among this excitable and courageous mountain people and the resulting misfortune that follows from time to time is less of a detriment than if an anxious police were to try to suppress the joyous and exuberant temperament of the people. At least, the mountain cane is a forthright and honest type of weapon and gives testament to the courage and directness of a people.

---

9. Thus the verb *aupatatu*. Both terms seem to pertain to the Bizkaian dialect. Obviously, this whole custom can only take part in the more mountainous parts of the nation.

It is wonderful that these local rivalries, if you want to use such a term, also have great bearing on the language. It is only natural that the Basque is attached to his language in direct relation to the degree with which it is illegitimately being persecuted, that he rejoices when the stranger shows interest and makes the effort to try and smatter a few words, that he wishes to explain to him all its idiosyncrasies and oddities, and especially to reveal the significance and decode the etymology of what is so ever present in Basque words. But even more striking is the rivaling dispute over where the best and purest Basque is spoken. Markina in Gipuzkoa[10] and Durango in Bizkaia mutually claim primacy.[11] Both lie in the heart of the land, as close to each other as they are merely separated by Mount Oiz, both well inhabited, affluent more as a result of farming and industry than by trade and thus scarcely visited by foreigners, and finally, both are surrounded by mountain inhabitants that in their scattered and isolated houses have retained the oldest, purest, and unchanged Basque, which at times even ceases to be understood[12] by the city dwellers, in good part remained untouched by the entanglement with Castilian words and idioms. Moreover, both enjoy the advantage of having two so very learned and thorough linguists: Markina has D. Juan de Moguel; Durango has D. Pablo de Astarloa. And even if the latter has explored the structure and nature of his language more deeply, even the expert would not be comfortable having to judge between them. The point of contestation, however, is to know which of the two towns outranks the other, and I frequently heard persistent and heated debate about this.

---

10. Publisher's Note: This is an errata on Humbolt's part, Markina is actually in the province of Bizkaia as well.

11. I do not know just how the author of the recent *Staatskunde von Spanien*, I, 102, comes to mention Bilbao and Urduña [Orduña] in this respect. It is general knowledge that Basque is spoken especially badly in Bilbao and that one can hardly expect to find a pure dialect in a border town, such as Urduña. The same goes for this statement that "the Bizkaian language" is very different to "the Basque that is spoken in French Navarre," I, 302.

12. The following anecdote lends credence to this observation. A mountain shepherd confessed to a city priest that he had committed a crime that he called *biganderia*. The confused priest, who could not understand the word and could not get anything out of him by means of further questioning, absolved that person. Only later upon some more research did he find out that the term was a combination of the words *bigaya*, young cow, *andrea*, woman, and *eria*, illness, vice, and thus indicated a misfortunate aberration that is almost without parallel in Biscay—but for which perhaps a lonely shepherd should be judged less harshly.

The following phenomenon is even more peculiar and it bears heavily on language acquisition. Just as any language that is aboriginal, rich, and used to be spoken much wider afield, Basque has a lot of synonymous words. *Zaldia* and *zamaria* mean horse, *erhia* and *atza* mean finger, *goracoa* and *arbasoa* the forefather, and so on. The dialect of each area has either adopted one of these words, is ignorant of them, or just finds them to be uncommon. As insightful observers assured me, it is on account of the rivalry between these small towns that one is disinclined to use words that are typically common to the other, in spite of the fact that personal names show that they were formerly more widespread. In Durango one says *batu* to express the act of collecting, in Gipuzkoa *bildu*. Here, however, the names of several country homes are put together by including the former word. It is thus not uncommon to find such single local expressions in more distant towns rather than in those that lie in the proximity. This has no greater consequence for the language's general comprehension, however, as only a small number of expressions are concerned. But it does impede on the act of gathering the complete vocabulary, and it also points out the general tendency of every national character to cut each other off into smaller masses before they join into a greater one.

By chance, we came across an interesting example of the lively rivalry that flares up whenever one town attempts to gain the advantage over the next on our way from Zumaia to Deba. We encountered two women, an older one and a younger one, her niece, who were going to their neighboring town. The aunt had vowed to visit the Virgin of Itziar, and her niece, a quick, young, and pretty girl, accompanied her. Upon our request to sing to us and explain some *zortzicos*—this is what the eight-lined Basque national songs are called, from *zortzi*, eight—she did. I dotted down one, inasmuch as I could follow; and even though she refused to sing at first, when I got tired of all the many verses, she pressed another one on me claiming this would be a particularly nice one. The poetics of the song were not very significant as one could expect, but the contents amused us a lot. They told us that Zarautz and Getaria fought for the honor of being Elcano's birthplace. Supposedly there were still persons of that name in Zarautz, yet not in Getaria. A seaman in Zarautz, who according to himself could neither write nor did he have any Castilian, took this feeble piece of proof and composed a song about it. He hereby saved his birthplace's honor and at the same time taunted the poor *Indiano* in Getaria; a little later, a few Zumaians (Zumaia is nearby Getaria) sang this song when they went aboard a ship in Getaria.

They intended to forbid it and even threatened them with castigation, but our resolute heroine, who was part of it, polished off the threats with a brief reply: *un cantar es para cantar* (a song is made for singing).

Elcano's statue is not the only monument of the Basque's maritime glory we encountered in Getaria. We saw in many gardens how large whale bones supported the grapevines. A year rarely passes without whales going astray in the Bay of Biscay; and they had captured one just a few weeks before our arrival at Zarautz. They tend to be thirty-six cubits in length and eight in height.

It seems to be settled that Europe owes this whole business of whaling to the courage and skill of the Basques. Moreover, it is specifically the Baiona fishermen who are credited with being the first. They noticed that the whales they caught each year at their coasts regularly appeared and cleared away again at certain particular times and they sought to follow them when they left the southern waters; they were thus lured all the way to Greenland and Iceland. They used to rig small fleets of fifty to sixty fishing-boats to go there,[13] and they knew how to win the affection of the Icelanders to such an extent that they were given preference. They hunted in many areas and moved whenever the returns of an area diminished. They would commence around Greenland and Iceland, turn toward Finland, and end up in the Davis Strait.

They could not call it their own for long though; they were even driven out of the northern waters by the Dutch for a period. The Dutch began their endeavors of this kind in 1612, but they could not do without the Basques so that they always sought to engage several of them in their service. They made up a considerable part of their crew and were used especially as harpooners. They had unlimited authority on the ships during the catch, and even the captain would have to obey them. Only when additional nations joined the Dutch in this type of fishing as well, did the Basques take it up again too. The bays around Spitsbergen were formally allocated: the English took away the most southern one, they were followed by the Dutch, and the most northern bay fell to the Basques and

---

13. Cf. for this subject the article *Pêche de Baleine* in the *Grosse Encyclopädie*, and the *histoire des pêches, des découvertes et des établissements des Hollandais dans les mers du Nord*, T. I, p. XXII and also p. 2, 4, 13, 17, 132 ff., translated by Bernard de Reste from Dutch into French. This, as the most recent writing on the subject that I am aware of, mentions the same number of ships as I have. The *Encyclopédie* speaks only of thirty, each one at 250 tons and with fifty men and Sprengel (*Geschichte der Europaeer in Nordamerika*, Vol. I. p. 35.) reckons with the same for the mid-sixteenth century.

Spaniards at Red Bay where the Biscayan headlands are still known today.
More recently, the Basques have replaced whaling with stock fishing, but
they will always keep the fame for having acquainted Europe with the
most useful, and yet most dangerous kind of fishing, nonetheless, and for
having put their name on one the most northern peaks of the earth.

Most of the procedures in whaling and most of the preparations of
whales are Basque innovations. A citizen of Ziburu, François Soupite,
has been recognized as having come up with one of the most important:
the treatment of blubber on the ships themselves at open sea because it
turns out much better this way compared to the Dutch way of just dump-
ing the blubber into barrels and leaving it there until having returned to
land. He designed a stove for this purpose made out of bricks on which
one puts the kettle; it is placed on the second deck. One keeps barrels full
of water next to it in order to avoid the dangers of fire.

What is more questionable than whether they were the first to dis-
cover whaling is whether the pursuance of these residents of the North
Pole led the Basques to Newfoundland and Canada prior to Columbus's
sea crossing. The indigenous people claim it, and even link this discovery
closely to that of Columbus's. Basques, they claim, had settled in Newfoundland already one hundred years before Columbus; their descendants, however, were forced to return as they could no longer withstand
the climate. Sick of scurvy and unable to continue sailing, they landed on
one of the Canary Islands just at the time when Columbus also arrived
there on his expedition. They informed him of their voyage and of the
land where they had lived, and thereby determined America's real discovery. But since they died of scurvy before reaching their homeland, all they
were left with was their glory and the rumors of their voyage darkened.
It would be difficult to prove this in a precise and historically acceptable
way; it is solely a Basque seaman Derazu that has supposedly penned
a manuscript about it based on oral histories, and it is this that Garat
draws on whenever, in the French *Mercure*, he promises to prove that
America was in fact first discovered by the Basques.[14]

---

14. Cf. the treatise *Sur la découverte de l'Amérique adressée au docteur Franklin* in the
Mémoires de la société philosophique d'Amérique. (Excerpts of it in *Moniteur.* 3. Brum.
An 13, 25. Oct. 1804, No. 33.) This treatise is based on a passage about the history of Peru
by Garcilaso de la Vega, in which it is said that Columbus, after having been informed
about the existence of another part of the world by Alonso Sánchez de Huelva, "while on
route to the Canaries had been blown off course to the Caribbean, had benefited greatly
from the information of a famous geographer, Martin Behenira." The author of this

Getaria's location is sufficiently discussed in Mr. Fischer's *Travels in Spain*. We stayed in the same house that the surgeon had lived in for a few days, and we found the small book collection that he so exhaustively describes in the same condition. The carvings in the choir of the church, which has a high and extravagantly ornamented tower, are renowned. In the larger and older Catholic churches prevails a certain mischief of the artist's fancy in this kind of work. Whereas one beholds only serious and religious images throughout the building, it is within the bars of the chancel and on the colorful chancel seats that the force of imagination roams freely without any regard for the function and holiness of the place. In Burgos the archbishop on his chancel seat leans against Europe, whom Jupiter abducts by taking the form of a bull, and I remember how I saw a priest in Auch, whom two apes had chained to their either side. Here too were most diverse arabesques and capriccio figures, riders on monsters that are numerously interlocked within each other, Centaurs, lion hunts, and so on. But the finesse of the work does not even remotely come close to that in the Cathedral of Auch. It is virtually impossible to think of carvings that are richer, freer, and more delicate in its conception and finer and more assertive in its realization than the carvings in the chancel of this latter church. It is fortunate that this remarkable building had not suffered from the destructions of the Revolution, which generally had come down rather more sparingly on worship in the southwestern parts of France compared to the northern provinces; it is regrettable that she is not visited more often by artists. The Raphaelite loggias aside, I do not know of anything in the arabesque genre that is comparable to it in taste and grace apart from the ornaments in a manuscript of Quintilian in the monastery San Miguel de los Reyes in Valencia, which was

---

report understands this name as Martin Behaim. "These syllables *ira*," he adds, "are due to a particular circumstance: the circumstance, I find, in the trust he was bestowed by John II, King of Portugal." (How does he link the syllables *ira* and this trust? Behenira could quite easily be a Basque surname). With all this in mind, the fact that Columbus received word in the Canary Islands appears to refer to a passage in the *géographie reformée* by Riccioli, book III, p. 90. "Christopher Columbus," it says there, "thought about undertaking a voyage to the West Indies through directions he had obtained in Madeira, where he was drawing up charts. This information was given him by Martin Bohem, at least according to the Spanish through Alfonso Sánchez de Huelva, a captain who had chanced upon the island that came to be known later as Dominica." Similarly, Mariana (I. XXVI. C. 3) observes that, "a certain vessel on its way to Africa had been thrown off course by a gale to an unknown land and that the sailors, following their return to Madeira, had notified Christopher Columbus of the circumstances of their journey."

endowed by Duke Ferdinand of Calabria.[15] Amid the 224 very nicely written and richly ornamented Latin manuscripts in this monastery's library it is especially this one that stands out among the others. And even if these manuscripts are, because of their short age, not very significant in philological terms, they surely deserve artistic attention, above all because these ornamentations seem to extend beyond Raphael's era.

The view from the island St. Anton, which is connected to the land by a narrow dam, is the broadest and freest one can find along this coast. As yet, this had always been the last point our eyes had reached along the coast. From here we saw Cape Matxitxako [Machichaco], and all at once we oversaw the whole Bay of Biscay from Bermeo to Donostia-San Sebastián. For Cape Matxitxako, the island St. Anton, and Higer Point are the three points that reach furthest into the sea along this coast, between them the land makes two flat bends. The island consists of two peaks divided by a valley, of which the hindmost and highest is a mere heap of cliffs piling up on top of each other, reached by a narrow footpath that runs along enormous abysses. There is a watchtower on the foremost peak, there is a hermitage on the most remote one. There are many such hermitages in Spain, they are not always inhabited by hermits, however, but frequently by peasants instead. The island is partly pasture, partly farmland. There are cows climbing around the steep hill slopes, and the men and women used to carry baskets full of manure on their heads up the endlessly exhausting path, which has steps cut into the rock in parts.

---

15. This Duke of Calabria was originally an Aragón prince and a son of Frederick of Aragón, King of Naples. He was born in Apulia [Puglia] in 1488. When his father had lost his kingdom on account of Ferdinand the Catholic and Louis XII, he defended himself for a while in Taranto, but then had to surrender to the so-called *Gran Capitán*, Gonzalo Fernández of Cordoba, and was subsequently held captive for ten years in Spain, in Xàtiva [Játiva, Valencia], now San Felipe. Finally, Charles V restored him to freedom and married him to D. Ursula Germana, widow of Ferdinand the Catholic, and made him Viceroy of Valencia. Here he resided with all the grandeur of royal privilege, and hence the monastery received its name.

Zumaia, Deba, Mutriku, Ondarroa, and Markina

This day's trip—we had ridden off from Getaria in the morning and reached Markina on that same evening—had given us an incredibly versatile change of areas. First the pleasant location of the harbor of Zumaia. The Urola streams forth from an enchantingly vegetated valley that unites with another one along its shores, and pours into the sea between rocks. The gaze that follows it inland is limited by a high mountain wall; and steep but cultivated mountains rise up behind the small market town that lies beyond the hillside. Then the lonely mountain path to Deba comes to an end at Itziar. Enclosed by two rows of mountains, and surrounded by wonderfully shaped cliffs, one feels as though transferred right into the Alps or Pyrenees; but the bare wildness of the area is softened by the sight of graceful fields and gardens, with which the inhabitants' assiduity crowned even the steepest of mountains. What follows is an unlimited view of the sea between Mutriku and Ondarroa. A narrow yet well-designed country road connects these two small harbors while always running along the slopes of the mountains above the sea. Ondarroa gets its romantic appearance from its bridge arching high above the river and its quaint church. All the churches of these small coastal towns are designed in long squares, without actual towers but with several tower-like extensions on the sides, with incredibly thick walls, flying buttresses, and vaults, equal to fortresses. This one though distinguishes itself by its size, its age, and its gothic ornaments with which it is richly decorated. Finally, down the coast the wonderful valley of the village of Berriatua leading along the banks of a small stream to Markina. Right within the manifold greens of the fields, pastures, and gardens, surrounded by pleasantly cultivated hills and dark mountain forest, Berriatua has a wild-countrified guise. The valley is a true mountain valley; bare edges of rock break free of the coppice, at the side deep below, the small yet torrential forest stream whooshes, and heaps of black cinder from the ironworks that it drives loom through the green of the trees. Time after time, we stumbled across the ancestral homes of great families; the simple design of these does not resemble either our newer, nor older castles, and they can only be recognized by their size and the carved coat of arms above the door.

From Ondarroa onward we found ourselves, properly speaking, in Bizkaia.

In Markina, a small town that was solely based on farming, we suddenly found ourselves transferred right into the midst of the land and amid real Bizkaian customs. Chance made us stay there for a few days, and I repeatedly traversed the fields and sought to converse with the peasants. By always indicating and uttering the items intended, I managed just about, but less so on account of my knowledge of the language and rather because of their untiring patience with which they came to my help amid a vivid display of joy for showing such interest in their language and customs.

The grave difficulty that cultivation in Biscay needs to overcome is the hardness and acerbity of the soil. Not only do they plow through it several times and again, but use tools of their very own making to do so. The most peculiar among them is the *laya*.[1] It consists of a long two-pronged fork with a short shaft that is not fixed to the middle, however, but to one side. Every farmworker holds two such forks in their hands, cuts into the soil horizontally, pushes it farther down by stepping on it with one or two feet at the same time, and rips out a large piece of sod each time, turning it by pressing the shaft down and back toward him. Being constantly stooped over in itself makes it extremely exhausting labor and is carried out by several people together, just as we do when digging; there is a proverb that has made it into Spanish: *son de una misma laya*,[2] they are "they are of the same *laia*."

Our single-pronged plow[3] is used only seldomly or not at all in this area, at best to mark out a single furrow in order to lead the *laya* farmworkers. In contrast, there are numerous multi-pronged plows[4] that are

---

1. Publisher's note: Today this is spelled *laia*.

2. "Two or three ladies of the same *laia* lived in the same house," etc. *Aventuras de Gil Blas de Santillana* I, 321. The meaning of this word in current Spanish dictionaries is: "type, quality." Therefore it is, according to this, merely metaphorical and derived.

3. *Goldea.*

4. Larramendi terms this plow (I have never, precisely, heard this word) *bostortza*, five teeth.

customary among which some resemble our harrows. The *nabasaia*[5] has four long hook-like forward-leaning pieces of iron, which are fastened to a horizontal block of wood, to which a pole is immediately, and without wheels, attached, and which dig deeply into the soil, especially if the farmworker is not satisfied with just pushing down on the two curved handles of the wooden block with his hands, which are made for this, but adds rocks as well. The *burdinarea*[6] is of a similar shape, but behind the four-pronged block of wood there is another smaller one with two further prongs that fit the spaces between the four in front, and these prongs fit precisely below. What most resembles our harrow is the quadrangular *area*,[7] which is normally comprised of four connected poles, each with six strong pieces of iron attached. Only when the poles are angled, in such a way that they come together in a forward-leaning way, is a handle attached on the top, with which the farmworker, when he deems it neces-

---

5. From leveling plowed up ground, perhaps also from lancing. *Nauada* or *naua* [today, *laua* —ed.], which has also passed into Spanish, means plain or level ground. This is origin, for example, of the name of the famous battle on the plains of Tolosa, in which at the beginning of the eighteenth century the Moors were defeated in Andalusia, *la batalla de las nauas*; and also Nauarra, as in the plain in the foothills of the Pyrenees. From the notion of leveling comes that of a blade. Thus, a knife is termed *nauala* [today, *labana* —ed.], and here there is perhaps some connection with the Spanish *navaja*, and even to *novacula*.

6. From *burdina*, iron, and *area*, plow or rake, since both implements have much in common with one another here.

7. It is a well-known fact that in a great number of languages the notion of plowing is represented by words that are derived from the syllable *ar*. Just compare, for example, *adelung* v. *aeren*. Yet one could add more examples to that already mentioned, for example the Basque *areatu*, the Breton *ara* (Pelletier v. *arrer*), the Welsh *aru* (Owen), the Gaelic *aradh* (MacFarlan), the Irish *araim*. It seems to me that the fundamental image is one of long straight rows (like furrows), one behind the other. This is because, as well as the sound of the syllable leading to one imagining it, in most metaphorical derivations of this family of words in still more than one language the idea of order, adaptation, is added, and in Basque in particular this is expressed with almost the same word, *aria* [today, *hari* —ed.], both thread and a long fine length, and *araua*, rule, that is, a tight rope. Nor should one rule out that the Greek *eirein*, to place in a row, the Latin *serere*, and the Basque *ereindu*, to sow, are related to all this, and also imply the planting of rows. The image of the furrow could, according to this, be transformed into that of work, force, lancing, hoeing, and as such the word passed over into the realm of the land, [meaning] what can be hoed, fertility. If one considers the root of these derivations, one admires how such a strong and noble idea is concentrated in the Greek *areté*, which, closely related to *aroura*, compares energy to earth that has been hoed, which tilling has made fruitful for any kind of production. Likewise in our way of speaking, there is so much more in "*von gutter Art sen*" than what we think, since in regard to "*Art*" we think in only one way and not in natural terms.

sary, can press it down or lift it up, and as this harrow serves at the same time to break up the soil, he increases the weight by adding rocks.

The clods of earth that still remain following such work without being completely broken up are crushed with a type of mallet, a *mazuba*,[8] still one-by-one.

As the properties are only minor, the cultivation of it, despite the amount of work, occupies the peasant only some time of the year. For the rest many go about a trade and many scatter around as carpenters in the surrounding area. Although one cannot call people in the Basque Country rich, most of them live well. Even in Markina they told me that they have meat at every lunch, always have wine in the evenings, and their midmorning snack is abundant, too. I once took part at one such family elevenses. The patron, his two sons, his menial, and a day laborer sat around a bowl with cut pieces of bread that was fried in lard; with it they had omelets and a good wheat bread given that cornbread is a worse and paltrier nourishment. The woman stood behind them and merely watched them, as she had already eaten at home. After the meal, the day laborer yoked his oxen to the four-hook-plow, and the woman sowed corn from behind. Sometimes the day laborers have their own oxen for they have their own fields as well. Working with them, they get, in addition to elevenses, bread and wine in the evening, ten *reales* for the day, fifteen gold pennies, and half that without the ox. A woman got all the food and one *real*, one gold penny, so that the day's wage is costly in relation to property. They inquired in detail about how near peace was; this is of immediate interest to them, as then they could get hold of greater and cheaper amounts of fish that they require for days of abstinence.

Deep inside the land, just as here and everywhere else where they live solely from farming and differ from the common villages merely in size and affluence, the stranger sees—and indeed not without bewilderment when compared to other countries—particularly in this part of Biscay, how the gentleman and commoner, the poor and the wealthy, converse with each other in complete equality. It occurred to us more than once that among a group of people of whom all were dressed alike and very commonly, there would be one among them who would be pointed out to us as coming from a very well-known family or one that bore a title in Castile. Just how utile it is for the richer ones, who at first glance seem to live a life of mere idleness and redundancy, to associ-

---

8. Or *mazua*. The "b" is used only in the Bizkaian dialect.

ate with their fellow countrymen shows the widespread Enlightenment among the people.

For instance, the inoculation of smallpox has become so common, especially in Markina, that even some residents in the mountains carry it out on their children as well. Its dissemination is above all owed to the unresting eagerness of the then chief delegate of Bizkaia, D. Jose Maria Murga's father, an enlightened and noble man. This by itself in addition to the education that he by and large under his own supervision had given to his son, who distinguishes himself by his plentiful knowledge and skillful management, proves amply how beneficial a seemingly small, quietly fulfilled sphere of influence can become for a country and a nation. Recently one has begun to attempt the vaccination against cowpox. Mr. D. Lope de Mazarredo in Bilbao, nephew of the well-known admiral, has translated one of the best treatises published about it in Paris and was the first to have his daughter vaccinated.[9] He has been followed by others in Bilbao and other places, for example, in Azpeitia.

It would be going too far if one were to claim that all aristocratic haughtiness has been banned from Bizkaia. Rather one has to admit that among a certain part of the nation it is still very vivid and even pervasively so. Every Bizkaian is aristocratic by birth, and must be recognized as such in other provinces of the kingdom. He has nothing else to do but to prove that his father and grandfather, in effect his ancestors by repute, truly stem from Bizkaia.[10] Wealth and poverty, indeed even the way of life and comportment, make no difference here. Only a few trades, for example that of the slaughtermen, which is mostly carried out by foreigners, are the exception. No other but this aristocracy counts at the people's assemblies in Bizkaia, whoever bares the title of a count, a marquis, or even a duke in Castile or any other province, puts it down at this point and takes on his Basque name. It is thus that many families carry double names, and given that one of them has the title and the other one belongs to the family, the title, however, strictly applied, can only be given to the one, that is, the firstborn, and it thus occurs that at times the son carries a different one to his father's. The son of the Marquis de Narros, a very well-known family, is merely called Eguia as long as his father lives, for instance. All genuine Bizkaians are thus fully equal, everyone is

---

9. It seems that in Spain it is more common to say *invacunar* than *vacunar*. The former is also more adequate language-wise.

10. *Fueros de Vizcaya, ley* 16, p. 24.

of nobility, and there is no lower or higher among them. The first point
of proud cherishment is the general prerogative of the province. Having retreated to the mountains during the invasion of the Moors, the
old population regards their aristocracy as more exceptional compared
to that of the rest of the kingdom. They frequently have to suffer the
ridicule of comical writers, and who does not remember the *Escudero
Vizcayano* in *Don Quixote*[11] and D. Rodrigo de Mondragon in Gil Blas?
In the country, the countryman regards himself as grander than the city
dweller, and, in addition, the kings' marks of favor have provoked a few
nuances by way of granting titles for some, for others the right to bear
this or that coat of arms, and so on. It is therefore that one sees the coats
of arms above the doors, or just an empty rectangular sign with the coat
of arms nailed to it; indeed sometimes the coat of arms are painted and
hung up in the parlor. It would be rare though that someone were unwise
enough as to wanting to put himself above his fellow citizens because of
it, and it is never the case that such pretensions of one should become
the subservience of another. Compared to his neighbors, a Basque is at
even greater liberty and less constrained when it comes to the common
marks of respect. Solely in the Spanish provinces, not in the French ones,
and even there only in recent times, is the unnatural form of address in
the third person, *berori*, for the Spanish *usted*, your grace, customary.
The usual form of salutation, also for the more gentlefolk, particularly in
the country and in the mountains is: *Agur adsikidea*! (good day, friend)
and it comes with a trustful handshake. This word, *agur!* has passed into
the familiar language of the Spaniards; one has to admit though that,
especially if uttered with a somewhat grumbling sound, it is not a particularly friendly, nor cultivated salute. It seems to me that it originally
came from the act of bowing; *a* is just a support, and the root syllable
gur in Basque corresponds to the Latin *curuus*, crooked.[12] In spite of this
egalitarian and confidential interaction, the standing of a well-respected
man in his town and his influence on the people is immense. His sentence
alone often suffices to hem quarrels and brawls, that for example arise
at the marketplace on Sundays; one has seen, even without having any

---

11. Publisher's note: The Basque squire, Don Sancho de Azpeitia.

12. *Agurtu*, to greet; *aguretasuna*, old age; *aguretu*, to become old; *gur-pilla*, *gur-cila*,
the wheel; *in-guruan*, all around; *gurtu*, to venerate. Upon comparison of these words
it seems that *gur* first of all signifies crookedness and roundness, and is then figuratively
transferred to veneration and the crookedly-walking old age.

legal right to issue an order, that he demanded the perpetrators to go to jail and that they obeyed; and this influence has been very beneficial regarding the popular riots as they sprang up for instance on the coast in 1720 when the government wanted to move the customs houses to Biscay. Nowhere else than here can one say that such a man:

with speech he sways their passion and soothes their breasts[13]

It seems delightful that a right, which one is accustomed to viewing as a prerogative, is supposed to be granted to all inhabitants of the province indiscriminately. Naturally, within the borders of the province this can lead to absolutely no privileges, but just the restoration of a natural balance, and thus it covers the whole of Bizkaia; it only becomes a prerogrative when the province has dealings with other provinces. Taken in this context, Bizkaia's privilege cannot possibly be a burden on the nation as the Biscayan provinces have, at any rate, their own tax and conscription systems. The constitution concerning the nobility is quite different to that in other countries and the outsider is frequently misconceived in this regard. Knowing that nobility is extensive, one concludes that the rest of the nation is languishing from its pressure, and for the same reason, one regards the attestation of nobility as being so very simple that there is a common saying that everyone in Spain is of nobility as long as he does not descend from Moors or Jews. Both things are fundamentally incorrect.

Nowhere are the legal privileges for the nobility as insignificant as they are in Spain. Exemption from a certain, inconsiderable tax that is known as *pechos*, from billeting (with the exception of the royal family visiting a town, in which case not even clerics are spared), and from mandatory military service are the actual advantages in terms of privileges, which set aside the *hidalgos*, the peers, from the *estado general* or *comun* (*tiers-état*, the commoners) and the *hombres llanos* (plain and simple people). There are a few significant offices among the magistrates to which only nobility can be appointed, but the most profitable and highest public offices solely depend on the king's favor, and many an example have recently shown that the consideration given to birth is little or none. Even the exemption from taxes cannot be listed as an exclusive privilege of nobility for there are entire municipalities that possess this right and

---

13. Virgil, *Aeneid*, I, 153.

in which the difference between nobility and the commoners is based alone on the aforementioned municipal offices. All surviving privileges are merely dignitary privileges as for example that the nobleman who is asked to give testimony can only be questioned in his own house, that he cannot be jailed for outstanding debts—although there are many exceptions to this—that he is exempt from torture, that he can only be taken to a specific jail, cannot be put to death by hanging, and so on.

Anyone who is at all noble has these privileges and it is in this sense that one can assert with the strictest integrity that all Biscayans, regardless of family and wealth, are noblemen. All commoners are recorded on a list as taxable residents (*empadronados*) in their place of residence, and to be listed on this list, or not, determines the character of whether one is noble or not. In order to free oneself from being listed one must demonstrate a title. This leads to nobility lawsuits between those wishing to rid themselves of the taxes and the town councils, whose burdens increase because of it, or even the district attorney, the result of which, should it be favorable to the person claiming immunity, provides him with a so-called *ejecutoria*[14] that represents our patent of nobility; however, it is not a document that grants ennoblement, but rather that merely certifies one that has been received and proven elsewhere. From this emerges a kind of dual nobility, the difference of which though has no legal consequence at all. It is the nobility of known ancestral seats and the nobility by judicial decision, *hijosdalgo de solar conocido* and *hijosdalgo de executorial*. The judicial decision, the *ejecutoria*, can be based on two kinds of evidence in that the person soliciting it either demonstrates that he descends in the male line from a known noble ancestral seat or by just showing that his ancestors have been exempt from taxation since time immemorial. It is only the first kind of evidence that grants him an eternal and never time-barred right, while in the latter case he can lose his privilege should he

---

14. The comical writers often speak about it. Such is the case in the jesting conversation between the nobleman D. Mendo, coming to a town with a rawboned horse and a famished dog in which soldiers are being billeted, and his groom Nuño, in Calderon's *Alcalde de Zalamea*:

NUÑO I mean the squires [*hidalguez*] sir. Ah, sir, if the soldiers aren't billeted on them, do you know why?

MENDO Well, why?

NUÑO For fear of being starved . . .

MENDO God rest my father's soul, says I, who left me a pedigree and patent all blazoned in gold and azure, that exempts me from such impositions!

or his descendants out of negligence let it happen that they are registered once more on that list of taxable citizens. Finally, the *ejecutoria* at times does not grant the privilege of nobility on the property, but the applicant is merely protected in his vested rights when he is unable to demonstrate his family's tax exemption since time immemorial, but for twenty years only. Sometimes, the necessary evidence is determined by demonstrating the holding of aristocratic magisterial offices; in this case, however, the gained right extends merely to the liberty of holding such offices in future times as well. Spanish jurists differ greatly regarding a definition of an old aristocratic ancestral seat. Some reckon that such a status is valid only for those that are situated in the mountains of León, Burgos, Bizkaia, Asturias, Galicia, Navarre, and Catalonia. Alone, such limitations are incorrect, and in fact every house and even every location of a house is anciently noble, as long as it is known to belong to an ancient noble dynasty in the province in which it lies. Evidence is thus dependent on the dynasty's repute and especially that of its male line. Usually the families carry the names of their ancestral seats as for instance do the Mendozas, Velascos, Guzmane, Sotomayores, and so on, but also because, following the expulsion of the Moors, these great families were given new ancestral seats throughout Spain and each one was thus divided into diverse branches and named after these. Now some families carry other names, though, that do not follow that of their ancestral seat, but were given to them on other special occasions, such as the Girone, Cerdas, Coellos, and so forth; they did nonetheless have ancestral seats, but their names became forgotten on account of these chance names, so that the rule that every known old nobility is derived from an ancestral seat and thus carries its name needs no exception. These chance names are called *nombres se alcuña* (lineage names) in contrast to the ancestral name (*nombres de apellido*) and they are often distinguished, though not always, by the fact that the former is not preceded by the preposition *de* that, in turn, is usually given to the latter. So one says Hernando Cortez, but Hurtado de Mendoza. They commonly derive from single events, such as for example, that of the Figueroas from the legend, that next to a fig tree (*higuera*, old Spanish *figuera*) two brothers of this dynasty had rid a king of Cordoba of twelve Christian virgins that he had been given as a tribute. Once nobility has been obtained, which occasionally is founded on an actual patent of nobility[15] granted by the king, it is handed down

---

15. *hidalgos de privilegio.*

with no interruptions to the descendants, and not even the exercise of commoners' dealings would affect it.[16]

This is the legal constitution of the nobility in Spain.[17] Accordingly, there are indeed provinces that are in fact noble. There is no difference among the nobility apart from the three distinguished classes that are merely differentiated in terms of rank, however: the *grandes* [grandee], *títulos* [titled], and the mere *hidalguía* [nobility]; and they never request an actual proof of noble ancestry, this is only the case with the actual orders of knights. Among some of them, however, it can be so strict that a delegate of an order is dispatched to the applicant's place of birth and at his expense in order to examine the validity of his claim in situ.

Naturally, the case is inevitably different when it comes to social life. Here differentiation sets in automatically according to the higher or lower age of the family, the more or less recognized name, the dignitary positions held, and the size of the estates, and to call entire provinces noble in this sense is obviously ridiculous. But one should in no way imagine the differences as great as they used to be in France and as great as they continue to be in parts of Germany. Society is definitely more mixed, nor does the government look into these class differences when filling a position, nor does the nobility enjoy any other significant advantages. The clergy, in which even the archbishop frequently comes from the lowest social stations, contributes to this equality from its side. It already helps not to have a certain prefix to a name that cuts society into two distinct classes, as is still the case at least for Northern Germany, and

16. The normally so precise and felicitous Bourgoing, *Tableau de l'Espagne modern*, I, 167, contends the opposite. It suffices to see Bernabè Moreno de Vargo's *Discursos de la nobleza de España*, Madrid 1795, 4, p. 105, in which it is clearly shown that all the existing laws for this purpose are not aimed at the nobility in general, but at the chivalrous orders. There are several inaccuracies in Bourgoing's article. He consistently places the Asturian nobility next to the Biscayan in spite of it being of a completely different kind. Asturias is unaware of such a general privilege known to the Basques; he confounds the legal and social privileges of the nobility and claims that Philip II had ennobled the Biscayans as the Biscayans would never admit to owing their privilege to a king's favor, and their *fuero*, in which their noble privilege is recognized, was already confirmed by Charles V in 1526. Philip II did nothing more than what all kings before had done, to confirm.

17. I have intentionally passed over a few classes of nobility that are today regarded almost as antiquities, such as the *caballeros pardos* in León, who enjoyed certain liberties without actually belonging to nobility, and the *caballeros quantiosos* on the border with Andalusia, who, because they had a certain quantum of estates, were obliged to keep arms and horses in order to be equipped against the Moors.

that the miscellaneous nuances blend into one another and are less easily detectable.

It is a curious custom that in Spain a widow bearing an illustrious title passes it over to her second husband as well. In this way a lieutenant, for instance, who weds a general's widow, is given the title of excellency. However, should a mere noblewoman wed a commoner, she forfeits her title, but regains it at her husband's death. In the old days, however, she had to undergo a ridiculous and indecent ceremony should she have wished to avail herself of this privilege. She had to lift a packsaddle on her shoulder, go to her late husband's grave, strike it three times with the saddle, and leave it there amid the words: "Villein, rid me of your low rank; I and my nobility leave you behind."[18]

Before I depart from Markina, I must make note of a peculiar freak of nature. There are three very large boulders at a place known as Arretxinaga [Arrechinaga]—all of which may well be forty to fifty feet in height—and two of them lie on their narrow side and are incredibly wide on top, in some distance to each other, and a very large and heavy third rests on top of them, so that they threaten to collapse at any moment, and they seem to keep erect by their own balance only. Once one could pass under the one on top; but as one has made it out to be a miracle, they placed an altar in the middle and erected a chapel, Saint Michael, above it. Yes, because only two deacons could stand in front of the altar they even had the audacity to blow away a big piece of the boulder in order to make room for a third. Moreover, the people continue to knock off pieces as they believe them to possess miraculous and healing powers.

18. The above mentioned *Discursos etc.* p. 27, which, amid Salazar de Mendoza's *Origen de las dignidades seglares*, are the most detailed works on this matter.

Vitoria-Gasteiz

The way from Markina to Vitoria-Gasteiz running from Elgoibar via Soraluze [Placencia de las Armas], where there are rifle factories, to Arrasate-Mondragon on the Deba River, offers far less beautiful sceneries than the coast, and bears nothing remarkable apart from the educational establishment of Bergara [the Royal Patriotic Seminary].

It is known that it used to have Proust (who was subsequently transferred to Segovia and today holds a teaching post in Madrid), Chabanon, and other renowned teachers; but while it was completely dissolved by the last war against France, they are working toward its reestablishment.[1]

Its benefactor was the Count of Peñaflorida, the founder of the patriotic associations. On the occasion of a feast that was celebrated in honor of the patron saint of Bergara, the most notable men of the area congregated at this location; the patriotism of this man, however, rendered a void and meaningless festivity into one of the most important beneficial deeds for Spain. For he provided the initial idea for the associations, which thereafter have become so very beneficial, and he soon added his plan for an educational establishment. His active zeal extended also to his homeland's language. He protected it in all sorts of ways: he submitted a draft of a new dictionary and wrote in it. He also produced, for the purpose of the mentioned celebration, a Basque opera and translated *Maréchal ferrant* from the French.[2] His family is truly Basque, their ancestral seat, Munibe, lies in Markina. We lived in it during our stay there upon the gracious permission of his son, the current owner, who resides in Donostia-San Sebastián.

---

1. Publisher's note: Joseph Louis Proust and Chabanon is actually Pierre-François Chavaneau.

2. Publisher's note: The Basque opera refers to *El borracho burlado* (The Drunk Tricked), a satirical opera of 1764, and *Maréchal ferrant* (The Blacksmith) an opera by Philidor (Paris, 1761).

The province of Araba, which we stepped into behind Leintz Gat-zaga [Salinas de Léniz], was the one I considered least of all for my survey. Being a border-province toward Castile and possibly also because it is mountainous only in parts, but mostly flat, it has conserved the fewest Basque peculiarities of all. In many of its districts, most notably in Vitoria-Gasteiz, one does not even speak Basque anymore. Therefore, I can only provide some general information on the character and condition of the province over all, in terms of individual towns however, I will only add a few words about Vitoria-Gasteiz.

From north to midday the province of Araba extends about sixteen, from sunrise to sunset fourteen Spanish *leguas*.[3] Within it, however, lays the Earldom of Treviño [Trebiñu in Basque], which is three *leguas* wide and four long and belongs to Castile just as a few more small pieces in the same area.

Although this province is mostly flat, three mountain ranges cross through it from east to west; firstly, to the north, the mountains de St. Adrian of which Mount Gorbeia [Gorbea] is the highest peak of the land; the second range marks almost the center of this small land, at the northern border of Treviño; and finally, the third range close to La Rioja, the mountains of Toloño.

The rivers that irrigate Araba empty into the Ebro with the exception of a few that go toward the sea on the border with Bizkaia. The Zadorra, which keeps to one's side for a long time on the way from Vitoria-Gasteiz to Madrid, is the biggest among them.

Araba can only be called fertile in parts. One cultivates mainly wheat, rye, barley, oats, corn, a lot of garden vegetables, and especially a great amount of large beans. The province supplies adjoining Gipuzkoa in part with grain, and in the year 1789, for instance, the harvest according to the tithes-register amounted to the following:

Wheat – – 490,219 *fanegas* of Castile
Barley – – 156,318 ----------------------
Oats – – 76,908 ----------------------
Corn – – 34,927 ----------------------
Rye – – 21,733 ----------------------

The Castilian *fanega* is calculated as ninety pounds, and should one, as occasioned by the new French measurements, consider the tenth part

---

3. Publisher's note: A *legua* (Spanish league) is about 4.1795 km or 2.597 miles long. North to midday refers to north to south, sunrise to sunset to east to west.

of a cubic meter as a unit to measure contents, expressed in a decimal fraction, 55.501 such units would fit the *fanega*.

The wine harvest amounted to 829,363 *cantaras* (pitchers) of Castile, which each consists of 16.133 of those units (*liters*).

Oil, too, is cultivated in the province, but only little though, and only in their part of the La Rioja area (*la Rioja Alavesa*).

The revenues from the harvests in Araba could be far more considerable, if not a shortage of hands for the cultivation of the land stood in the way and thus also a shortage of fertilizers, and if it were possible to till the land as carefully as in Rioja, and, as there, to use artificial fertilizers, lime, fern, and so on. The immense scarcity of population in relation to the surface area means that many municipalities must leave a third of their land uncultivated.

The census instigated by the Count of Floridablanca in 1786 reveals only 70,710 inhabitants for the entire province, of which 35,072 were men, 35,638 were women. Among them 39,685 not married, 26,854 married, 4,171 widowed. In the years 1793 and 1794, Mr. D. Lorenzo Prestamero, a meritorious scholar in Vitoria-Gasteiz who had collected extraordinarily precise information about his province and had devised the article on Araba in a survey of all Spanish provinces under the auspices of the Historical Academy in Madrid, sought to gather more detailed data about the number of inhabitants in Araba. As a result of his efforts he found 440 localities and 15,396 heads of household (*vecinos*) in the six districts that, under the name *cuadrillas*,[4] Araba is divided into, and that, in turn, consist of fifty-two *hermandades* [confraternities]. The number of clerics amounted to 1,401, of which 425 were priests of a religious order, 239 were monks, and 186 nuns. Should one reckon with five persons per family, the number of 76,980 souls comes about. But if one makes the comparison with a different means that they draw on in Spain in order to determine the population, this calculation also seems too remote. Any-

---

4. More detailed information as follows:

The cuadrilla of	*hermandades*	locations	*vecinos*
Vitoria-Gasteiz has	17	76	3,114
Agurain [Salvatierra]	6	71	2,061
Aiara [Ayala]	5	60	2,705
Guardia [Laguardia]	7	57	3,790
Mendotza [Mendoza]	12	84	1,942
Zuia [Zuya]	5	92	1,784
	52	440	15,396

one who is more than seven years of age obtains every year a so-called *Bula de Cruzada*, as the permission to eat dairy products during Lent depends on it.[5] In the aforementioned year in Araba, 67,553 such bulls were obtained, and if one calculates the children below seven years of age according to the commonly assumed ratios, the population would amount to 80,000 people. If one compares the state of today's population with that of former times, it turns out that it has not increased considerably since the beginning of the sixteenth century.

In 1527, it totaled 14,052 *vecinos*, whereby the valley of Orozko [Orozco] was included, though. In 1583, there were 13,469; in 1627, 14,000 *vecinos*. But in the five following years, there raged such tremendous plagues that in the census carried out yet again in 1632, one could not find more than 8,500 *vecinos*. In 1683, however, this number had risen again to 10,945.[6]

When a province devoid of people borders on one that is overpopulated, it would seem easy to alleviate the needs of the one by the other. Gipuzkoa has, as mentioned above, such a substantial amount of people that there is a yearly exodus to the rest of Spain and to the Americas. It could possibly do without forty thousand of its inhabitants and the void would still not become apparent. Araba's farming industry would already benefit considerably, if it received only ten to twelve thousand new growers, and should Gipuzkoa not suffice to provide them, Bizkaia has more inhabitants than it can feed by its own means. The advantage would fall back on both provinces as it then could obtain more corn from Araba and would not have to turn to more distant areas for it. Anyway, given the vicinity of these two little lands, the sameness of their language, privileges, and customs, no transplantation will ever again be at the mercy of such favorable circumstance. It is thus the more astonishing that it is here of all places that the political constitution is what is causing difficulties, which, despite all the efforts of patriotic statesmen, have been impossible to solve. Whoever wished to move to Araba from the northern Basque provinces, would do so obviously solely under the condition that he retained the same privileges in his new place of residence that he enjoyed in his place of birth. For this, however, he would have to prove his nobility, because otherwise (next

---

5. The purpose and history of this bull is found in detail in Bourgoing, II, 19–21.

6. D. Joaquin Josef de Landázuri y Romarate *Hist. civil de Alava*, Vitoria 1798, 4, I, 115, 116.

to the nobility, there is by law also a separate commons) they might oppose the resettlement of the newly arrived or compel him to carry out civil duties. To prove such would be easily done, given the closeness of the localities and of course the knowledge one has of all families in the land. Alas, the Spanish constitution stipulates that all procedures regarding the attestation of nobility must be addressed at one of the two major chancelleries,[7] and therefore every matter of this sort must be sent to Valladolid where it takes years and incurs great costs. Even the newer enlightened governments have not succeeded in doing away with these obstacles, although [Mariano Luis de] Urquijo's ministry has taken a step forward just very recently. It was only just that one had to undergo that very procedure of attestation in Valladolid even when a resident of Araba merely intended to move from one *hermandad* to another. This however was a blatant misfeasance; it was founded in the old privileges of the province that the attestation of nobility would be carried out before a commission of local people, and it's this right that has been returned to the province.

As incredible as it may seem, ill-conceived politics or adherence to outdated habits cause greater insurmountable partitions between neighboring provinces than nature could ever attempt even in form of the most impassable mountains; and yet these are by far not the only obstacles that hinder a better agricultural management in Araba. Another, yet similarly significant one is the majorats or substitutions (*mayorazgos ò vinculos*).[8] No other land's agriculture suffers as much from this remnant of the feudal system as does Spain. For not only can everyone found a majorat regardless of one's degree, whether noble or commoner, he is

---

7. There are two highest courts (*audiencias* and *cancillerías*) in Spain, one in Valladolid and one in Granada. While Navarre and Galicia have their own *audiencias* as well, they only have jurisdiction over their respective province, and the Galician appeals to Valladolid in some matters. The foundation of the chancellery in Valladolid is usually ascribed to the year 1442 during John II's government. But since one finds this court in Segovia as early as 1388, it seems that it was just transferred to Valladolid that year. It was relocated under Ferdinand the Catholic to Salamanca, then to Medina del Campo and Burgos, but it returned to Valladolid when the Court set up its residency in Madrid. The chancellery at Granada was endowed by Ferdinand the Catholic in Ciudad Real in 1494, but transferred there after the conquest of Granada in 1505. *Ern. De Franckenau sacra Themidis Hispanae*, ed. 2, *novis accesionibus locupletata a Francisco Cerdano et Rico. Matriti*, 1780, 8, *Sect.* XIII, p. 336–350.

8. Publisher's note: Majorat is a French term for an arrangement giving the right of succession to a specific parcel of property associated with a title of nobility to a single heir, based on male primogeniture.

also free to abet any one of his sons with one fifth of his patrimony in addition to his statutory share, and to transform this greater inheritance into a majorat (*mayorazgo por vía de mejora*). The nation, which possibly out of loyalty to the continuation of the family dynasties is inexplicably susceptible to this institution, avails of this legal privilege to the utmost. Jovellanos, therefore, calls the majorats "an incalculable abyss, into which the land's real estate sinks deeper from day to day."[9] The oldest majorats do not date from prior to the fourteenth century; and they owe their actual rise to the parliament of Toro at the beginning of the eighteenth century. From this time on, however, the nation developed an infatuation with following through with it under all circumstances, be it large or small estates, death with or without heirs, nobility or commoner, whatever, it may justly be called a true craze; one that legislature has left completely unchecked.

This parliament was, as is commonly known for all parliaments that are more political than learned, very ruinous for Spanish law. It was held in 1505 in Toro, a city in the kingdom of León on the Duero, and its actual purpose was, after Isabella's death, to pronounce her daughter Joanna queen and Ferdinand the Catholic the regent. This Joanna, the unfortunate mother of Charles V, later became insane and I could still see the rooms and galleries caged in with grids of wire in the higher part of the Alhambra (the former Moors' Palace) in Granada where she was guarded in the last years of her life. At the same time, they took advantage of the assembly of the estates to publish a collection of laws that Ferdinand and Isabella had ordered to be drawn up in advance, and that have become known as the Laws of Toro. Ever since the emergence of Roman law, its teachers had swamped the Spanish courts with a mass of opinions that ran counter to the constitution and the conditions of the land. The Laws of Toro were intended to redress the uncertainties that existed on account of them. But instead of taking them back to the old national law, they worshiped those new incoming opinions, and because they were given priority[10] among the Spanish laws, the wise laws

---

9. *esta sima insondable, donde la propiedad territorial va cayendo y sepultándose de día en día.* His *Informe en el Expediente de ley agraria,* p. 65. *nt.* It is here that one finds perhaps the most eloquent attack on this perishable institution, albeit that he still puts the case for the aristocracy. The legal precepts on the majorats are very well and briefly compiled in the *Instituciones del derecho civil de Castilla* that D. Ignacio Jordan de Asso y del Rio and D. Miguel de Manuel y Rodriguez edited in 4, p. 135–148.

10. *Sacra Themidis Hispaniae,* p. 46.

of Alfonso the Wise,[11] truly devised on home soil, were wholly subordinated. It was through the Laws of Toro that the majorats acquired their actual form. They harm the cultivation of land from more than one side. They completely close any way toward emphyteusis and thus the divestiture of at least one part of the estate that would be a great benefit for many a province; the majorat even implies that the right of the leaseholder ceases every time the respective holder of the majorat dies, which in turn renders the length of the lease uncertain forbidding even to contemplate any possible improvement for the estates; yes they even deter the real owner himself, for neither he nor his inheritors are permitted to demand compensation for the leaseholder should the majorat fall into different hands; this is a dilation of these regulations, however, that is far more the work of jurisprudents than a true reflection of the law. The greatest harm is caused because they make the selling of property as good as impossible as they cannot adjust the dimensions and boundaries according to the varying conditions of the provinces, times, and owners. The immediate effect of which is that Spain has far fewer landowners than any other country of the same size and comparative population, moreover, that the big landowners are burdened with great debts for neither do they manage their enormous estates well, nor can they help themselves by selling a piece of it; the capitalists, in turn, are confined to applying their wealth to trade; this also means that property is far too much in the hands of the great and noble (not even to mention the churches, chapters, and monasteries) and far too little in that of the middle class, which would use it with far greater skill and aptitude; what follows is that agriculture is deprived of the most substantial capital and the most industrious minds, while the nation is deprived of its prosperity and satisfaction, which would emerge from the own cultivation and improvement of sizeable, yet manageable landownerships. In no other country in the world does so much bare money lay idle and outside of essential circulation than in Spain. It is not only the inhabitants of coun-

---

11. *La ley de las siete partidas*, of the seven segments into which this book of laws is divided. This remarkable work is possibly the most complete and the most methodical book of laws and any newer nation must pride itself for possessing such a work in one's mother tongue at such an early point in time. It also contains moral-philosophical parts, for instance one about the duties of kings, and it is composed in such a precious, flowing, and pure way of writing that it is still one of the main sources for the study of old Spanish. It was begun under Ferdinand the Saint, yet finished by Alfonso X in 1258, and only under Alfonso XI did it become force of law. Although it contains many traces of Roman law, it is mainly based on the ancient laws of the kingdom and the common law of the nation.

try towns, especially drovers, that keep excessive amounts of money in closed chests, one could also list similar examples of men who devote themselves to trading and belong to the most speculative heads of their nation in this regard. There have been attempts to put a halt to the excessive foundations of majorats in recent times, though. In the year of 1789, limits were set on them by privileging one son (*por vía de mejora*). More recently—and this is probably the only wholesome effect that the often mentioned treatise of the ex-minister has ever evoked—has been the levying of a tax on the foundation of a majorat of, if I am not mistaken, 15 *p.c,* and the king has begun to permit the grandees to sell single pieces[12] of their existing land to the end of clearing their debts. Alone, these are ever just partial measures, and the obtaining of this royal dispensation, for which one has to turn to the Council of Castile, entails great circuitousness, as well.

It is not the case though that in Araba the properties are too sizable, as in Andalusia and other provinces of the empire. On the contrary, they are in fact too small and dispersed. Many are impossible to use as an outlying estate or even to erect a house, and therefore they cannot be cultivated satisfactorily from distant villages. In order to carry out farming, it would be inevitably necessary that one had utter freedom, without any recourse to the Council of Castile, to exchange these pieces of land or to sell them, so that all owners could conveniently regroup their lands and administrate them from the center.

If the provincial laws would actually facilitate the procurement of an adequate number of people from its neighbors and help in allocating its land more evenly and conveniently, nothing else would be left to desire for its affluence but that the King of Spain were to view Biscay less so as foreign to his crown. As it is indeed noticeable that there is as much tax on Biscayan products when they come to Castile, as when they are shipped abroad. It is in the same vein that one cannot bring in more than 2,000 *reales de vellon* (123 Thaler, 18 pennies, the Friedrichsd'or calculated at five Thaler) from Castile to Araba, just as is the case from

---

12. These pieces that are subject to majorat law are called *fincas vinculadas. Finca,* property that can be burdened with mortgage, derives from *fincar,* in today's Spanish *hincar,* and is used to mean as much as to remain. Thus to reside. In medieval Latin: *finchare.* S. Du Fresne *h.v.* and in the old Spanish poem of the Cid: *fincanza,* sojourn. "*Que sopiesen que mio Cid alli avie fincanza.*" Sanchez *Colección de Poesías Castellanas anteriores al siglo XV. T.* I, p. 251, v. 571. From this finally property. The word derives perhaps from *finire.*

Catalonia to France, without a special permit, known as *guía*. Hence, whoever lives in Araba but at the same time owns property in Castile, as is so often the case, will lose 5 p.c. of his income whenever he carries it in cash, or brings it into the country illicitly, or falls back on bonds, but this is not always easy nor good value here.

Araba, and in particular Vitoria-Gasteiz, does not lack insightful and patriotically inclined men who, having stood at the top of its affairs, sufficiently know the needs of the province and would actively work on the aforementioned points with great effort. Also, they would find themselves less deserted by their countrymen's industriousness and diligence once these advantages came into place. It would be thus decisive that an insightful and enlightened minister reached out his hand and supported these plans at court. The realization of which could never be anything but beneficial to the interest of the crown. For the rest of Spain's advantage, if in good faith, can never possibly stand in direct conflict to the advantage of the Basque provinces, regardless of their privileges and liberties.

Araba's legal foundation is based on the charter of voluntary incorporation *(la voluntaria entrega)* by which the province subjugated itself for all future times to King Alfonso XI of Castile in 1332. Until then it had been free and had elected its leader by way of its own sovereign rule; ever since to this very day its relations to Castile rest on a certain, written contract that has been henceforth confirmed by all Spanish kings.

Among writers the name Araba is first mentioned in the eighth century by the Bishop of Salamanca Sebastián.[13] Around this time, just after the invasion of the Moors, the names in this corner of Spain underwent great change albeit without known cause. Until that point, the Cantabrians (under which the smaller peoples such as the Autrigonians, Caristians, etc. are subsumed) and the Vardulians had owned the coast right to the borders of Aquitania.[14]

---

13. He lived in the ninth century but covered the history of Alfonso I of León between the years 738 and 757 in his chronicle. According to Astarloa (*Apol.* 229) the name means wide plain.

14. According to Pomponius Mela: *Tractum Cantabri et Varduli tenent*, and Idacius, when he speaks of the year 456 and the Herulians: *qui ad sedes proprias redeuntes Cantabriarum et Varduliarum loca maritima crudelissime depraedati sunt* ["While on the return journey to their own parts, they most cruelly ravaged the maritime reaches of Cantabria and Vardulia"]. Publisher's note: This translation on page 143 is taken originally from Robert G. Latham, *The Germania of Tacitus* (London: Taylor, Walton and Maberly, 1851), xcv; quoted in E. A. Thompson, *Romans and Barbarians: The Decline of the Western Empire* (Madison: University of Wisconsin Press, 1982), 180–81.

All at once it appears as if Bizkaia, Araba, and Gipuzkoa gained borders very similar to those that they currently have; Vardulia or Bardulia retreat to the southern shores of the Ebro toward today's Old Castile and also slightly over the northern ones as well, beyond the Beronians, and the name of Cantabria disappears at the coast and survives only in the minor district of the old Beronians, in today's La Rioja, from where the Kings of Navarre call themselves Kings of Cantabria, and where still to this date the Cantabrian mountains (*Cerro de Cantabria*) are on the other side of the river opposite Logroño.[15]

In spite of the fact that among all Basque Provinces Araba is the most vulnerable to hostile invasions because of its plains, it was able to stay clear of Moorish occupation. Having expanded farther south compared to today, it protected its borders against this new, terrible enemy with three small fortresses, one of which can still be seen on the road to Madrid at the end of a long, very narrow pass: Pancorbo (actually Poncorvo, Pontecurbum, curved bridge).[16] Everyone who has gone this way will surely remember the steep, bare, bizarrely shaped rocks with grotesque figures that come to eye shortly behind Miranda del Ebro in the lowlands; the Moorish forces foundered twice, in 882 and 883, on this now so insignificant bulwark of the fort;[17] the first time after a three-day-long battle.[18] It seems that in Araba merely one raid twenty years prior, in 861, had been carried out more successfully.[19]

---

15. Cf on this P. Manuel Risco, *Castilla y el más famoso Castellano*, Madrid in Blas Román. 1792, 4, p. 2–4. This work contains a detailed discourse on the name, the location, and the history of Castile, and a copy of the chronicle by the famous Cid, which Risco had found among the manuscripts of the St. Isidro Monastery in León. It describes the history of the valiant Rodrigo Díaz, in what seems to be an utterly authentic way free of any adventurous or fantabulous tales unlike the older chronicles that have so abundantly embellished the life of the hero in the epic poem about Cid, as in Sanchez *Colección de poesías anteriores al siglo 15* and the *Romancero del Cid (recopilado por Juan de Escobar,* Cádiz, 1702). This aspect alone should merit a translation – at least in parts.

16. Publisher's note: Although originally part of the *hermandades* of Araba, Pancorbo was ultimately incorporated into Burgos.

17. The Spaniards erected a new fortress in these very mountains against the French during the last war with France.

18. Landazuri, II, 21. Risco's continuation of *España sagrada*, XXXIII, 224.

19. D. Juan Francisco de Masdeu *Hist. crítica de España y de la cultura Española.* XII, 147. A very extensive work that nonetheless leaves a lot to be desired, especially sound criticism and an unprejudiced philosophical view of history.

It is thus truly wrong, when some intend to delineate the name *Alava* from the Arabic. It is rather purely Basque, and Mr. Astarloa relates it, as the local inhabitants of the province pronounce it Araba, to *ara, aria*, plain, thus denoting an extensive, large valley. The name of the city Alaba or Alba[20] mentioned by the ancient writers is thus similarly of Basque origin. That is to say that a part of the Roman road from Astorga (Asturica) to Bordeaux used to go through this province. Hence a lot of inscriptions and milestones are still being found, and, just to mention one example, the church of St. Román (a village in the *hermandad* of San Millán, not far from Agurain) is mostly made up of inscribed steles, most of them, however, are no longer decipherable. The place where the road enters Araba from the east is marked with an inscription of the Emperor Aulus[21] Constantius Chlorus, where the same road leaves to the west, with a different one of Constantius Constantine, and also on its route in between there are many traces of the same to be found. D. Lorenzo Prestamero has sought to find, with the utmost diligence, as many as possible on several trips carried out for this purpose, and determined the direction of the entire road accordingly. Hailing from Briviesca via Pancorbo it enters the province at Larrazubi [Puentelarrá], approaches the River Zadorra at Artzi [Arce, Navarre], ascends then almost completely in the same direction as today's road from Vitoria-Gasteiz to Miranda, but bears west before it reaches the former toward Agurain, and runs through the Arakil [Araquil] Valley in Navarre toward Iruñea-Pamplona. Alba, which used to be a station (*mansio*) of the same, must, according to these explorations, have been situated close to Agurain.[22]

In the direction of this road, close to Komunioi [Comunión] on the Ebro, a few years ago the remnants of a Roman house were found during

---

20. Pliny, III, 4. (*Ed. Hard.* I, 143, 8) Ptolem. II, 6. P. 46. *Itin. Anton.* (?)

21. On the first name Aulus see Gruter, p. 119. (?)

22. Mannert, Geogr. d. Gr. u. Röm. I, 354, holds it to be Estella [Lizarra in Basque] in Navarre, which in the light of this seems incorrect. For anyone who is interested in old geography, I list the *mansio*s of the ancient road according to the Itinerarium and today's locations in the direction that Mr. Prestamero traced, for comparison: The ancient mansions were: Vindeleia (in the vicinity of today's Sta. Maria de Rivarredonda), Deobriga, Veleia, Suissatium, Tullonium, Alba, Araceli, Alantona, Pompelo. Today's locations are: Larrazubi, Komunioi, Bayas, Artzi, Estavillo [today part of Armiñon], Burgeta [Burgueta], Argantzun [Puebla de Arganzón], Iruña [Yruña], Margarita, Lermanda, Zuhatzu [Zuazo], Armentia, Arkaia [Arcaya], Ariarza, Argandoña, Gazeta, Dulantzi [Alegria], Gazeo [Gaceo], Agurain, Bernedo [S. Román de Campezo], Ilarduia [Ylarduya], and Egino.

the excavation of a field; it had several delicate and tastefully laid out Mosaic floors. On two of which were figures, one representing the four seasons in the form of female figures with their attributes, the other Diana [and] how she, bearing a bow in her left and drawing an arrow from her quiver with her right, is followed by a bitch. D. Lorenzo Prestamero saw to it that both were copied and sent the drawings to the Academy of History in Madrid.

Araba was ruled by counts in the oldest of times, before its unification with Castile. The first to be mentioned in history is Eylon around the year 866 who rebelled against Alfonso III of León but then was besieged and taken prisoner. Furthermore, from 947 until 1200, when all Basque provinces cast their lot in with Castile, it was united with Navarre with only minor interruptions. Nevertheless, during this time it also remained in a state of independent liberty and exercised its sovereign rights by way of their own people's assembly. Perennially, the nobility, the peasants (*los fijos-dalgo y labradores de Alava*) and the clerics of the province, to which also the Bishop of Calahorra is counted, came together on the field of Arriaga (stone-place) not far from Vitoria-Gasteiz, and this assembly had, as witnessed in several records, under the name of the brotherhood of the field of Arriaga, (*la cofradía del campo de Arriaga*), all rights of majesty in their own hands, signed valid pacts, alienated townships and lands, and at last transferred supreme reign to the King of Castile in 1332 in a ceremony of self-disbandment.

It is impossible to determine with certitude the date the brotherhood came into being; some writers refer to a document from the year 1000, the inauthenticity of which is however proven. There is debate about the location of the gathering; some make reference to a field at Arriaga that is called *el campo de la Aqua*, while the place of the assembly in the mentioned false document is called Ocoa; while others opt for another one close to it. Either one is bare now, but presumably they were formerly covered with trees. For it seems to have been a habit of the Basque peoples to gather beneath oaks and trees. An as yet unpublished Basque record, of which I will speak in more detail later, which in itself could hardly be authentic, but trustworthy nonetheless with regard to the customs mentioned in it, comes to it right away: this custom has survived till this day in the oak woods in front of the church[23] and so on and in the

---

23. *En la robledad que está etc.* Basque: *Andramendico jauregui aurecco arestian Eleaiaun aurrian etc.* In front of the Andramendic ruling house, in the oak forest in front of the church etc.

assembly of actual Bizkaia underneath the tree of Gernika [Guernica]. In addition, it is noteworthy that women were not excluded from the brotherhood of Arriaga; but presumably only those belonged to it who were not married, or who owned their own estates as widows. The cities, in turn, were not part of the free constitution of Araba. Being founded by the privilege of the kings, they received governors from them, and thus Vitoria-Gasteiz and Treviño, for instance, remained always separate before and after 1200.[24] The *cofradía* appointed in their yearly meetings the four *alcaldes* who functioned as judges throughout the year amid one who carried the name of a supreme judge, *justicia major*. In extraordinary meetings they elected their princes or military leaders, and did so with complete liberty. For, according to the chronicle of Alfonso XI,[25] Araba was "always an exceptional dominion, the nobility and local peasants would always have it their way; at times they took one of the sons of the king, at times the Lord of Bizkaia, sometimes that of Lara [in Burgos], at times that of Cameros [La Rioja]."

Sometimes the princes carried the title of the *merinos mayores*.[26] In matters that the *cofradía* could not bring to a close in time, they were handed over to a commission that in turn dealt with it (*con consejo y otorgamiento*) with the brotherhood's consent and authorization, as it is referred to in several records.

---

24. Landazuri, I, 208, 209.

25. *Crónica de D. Alfonso el Onceno*. 2 ed. *por D Francisco Cerda y Rico. Parte I.* Madrid, Sancha, 1787. ch. 4, 100, p. 177. This is part of a collection of Spanish chronicles published by the same publisher with great elaboration.

26. Merino (to the same effect *mayorino*) is someone, as explained according to the law *de la Partita* (*Part. 2, tit. 9, l.23*), who bears the right (*ha mayoría*) to speak justice in a city or land. From *merino* comes *merindad*, a name that is carried by several districts in Spain, as e.g., *la merindad de Durango*, etc. The institution of the *merinos mayores* is ascribed to Ferdinand III, the Saint, (reigned from 1217–1252). It is known that also the Spanish rambling sheep are called *merinos*. Perhaps this name was given to them as those that enjoy legal privileges or stand under the influence of an *alcalde mayor*. This is at least more probable than P. Sarmiento's opinion, who believed *merino* to hail from *marino* while thinking of the transports of sheep from England to Spain in former times. By the way, it is true that they attempted to improve the Spanish race with English sheep. The Baccalaureus Fernán Gómez de Cibdareal states explicitly in his letter to Fernán Alvarez, Lord of Valdecorneja, in the year 1437 that Alfonso XI (the actual donator of the royal herds, *Cabaña Real*) had deployed a judge of the Mesta [an influential association of sheep owners] when sheep were brought in freight ships from England to Spain for the first time. The attempt thus seems to have been repeated recurrently during this time. *Centon epistolario del Bachiller Fernan Gómez de Cibdareal y generaciones y semblanzas del noble caballero Fernan Pérez de Guzman*, Madrid 1790, Ibarra. 8, *ep.* 73, p. 174.

It is a well-known fact that King Alfonso VIII conquered Vitoria-Gasteiz in 1200 from King Sancho of Navarre, and it is right at this time that the province of Araba, together with Gipuzkoa and Bizkaia, united with Castile. It thus seems odd why there should have been a second hand over 132 years later? Also, some writers claim that Araba had already from 1200 onward been treated as a subversive, indeed conquered province of Castile. History reveals quite the contrary though. The handover in the year 1332 was utterly free and unforced. This is what Alfonso XI himself admits to in his document that he had issued the Brotherhood of Arriaga and that is still existent in the original at the regional archive. "The nobles, clerics, and others, whomever they may be, Brothers of Araba," as it says, "have handed over to me the land of Araba (*otorgaron*) in order to reign over it, that it may be royal, and we have incorporated it under the crown of our kingdoms for us and our successors in Castile and León;" this is language that could not possibly make any sense in the context of a province supposedly acquired through conquest more than one hundred years beforehand. The right that the Kings of Castile had exercised already prior to that and since the conquest of Vitoria-Gasteiz over Araba had been granted to them by the province on a voluntary basis and the difference between this handover and that of the last transferal was that the former was always only for a period, the latter one forever, the former only in commission, the latter by complete forfeiture of their own right.

For prior to 1332, the *cofradía* still existed as always next to the kings, and just how their powers were separated becomes apparent in the treaties they entered. The king possessed, as mentioned above, the cities Vitoria-Gasteiz, Treviño, and since 1256 also Agurain, founded by Alfonso X the Wise, with full authority and had them governed by his commanders. They were surrounded, however, by the territory of the province. For the end of increasing the territory of the cities, the kings sought to acquire properties in the vicinity by way of barter or purchase. The brotherhood of the province did not enjoy the sight of it and set itself against it. It finally solemnly yielded a number of villages to the king, though, by means of a certificate of title issued on August 18, 1258, in which it is distinctly written: We Brothers give You, our Lord and King etc. and also later, always before 1332 though, a couple of similar documents occur. It becomes most vivid that the real and highest authority and ownership of the land had remained in the hands of the brotherhood of the province also after 1200, and that the kings had only exercised a temporarily commissioned and limited authority. This double relationship ceased entirely with the year 1332; the *cofradía* dispersed, the province was merged under the crown of Castile, and the king became the single lord of it bound solely to the conditions he had set himself.[27]

Alfonso XI was just sojourning in Burgos when he received the Brotherhood of Arriaga's offer to assume the lordship for this land. To that end he traveled to Vitoria-Gasteiz and from there to the assembly on the field at Arriaga, and it is here where the pact between the two parties was solemnly sealed. The most outstanding rights that the province secured through this treaty regard personal liberties. The king shall never, neither in whole nor in part, divest the land to whom it ever may be, but remain incorporated forever under the crown of Castile.

He shall not place any tributes or duties on the residents, but they shall remain free of them as they have been, and only certain rights will be reserved for him pertaining to those peasants (*colonos*) that are not free residents, but belong to churches or nobility and that are known as *collazos*. He shall only appoint natives of the land as *alcaldes* or high judges (*merino*), and the high judge shall not execute a native of Araba, nor arrest him without prior indictment and subsequent sentence by the *alcaldes*. Besides these main points the treaty of the handover contains several more with special regard to the relationship of those *collazos* to the nobility and to the king, grazing rights, prohibition of setting up new ironworks—which would desertify the woodlands—and specific liberties of single locations of the province.[28] These rights and liberties of the province have been confirmed on oath henceforth by all subsequent

---

27. The abovementioned new edition of the chronicle by Alfonso XI contains the following statement at the aforementioned place: since Araba had been conquered and taken from the Navarrese. *Acaesció que antiguamiente desque fue conquista la tierra de Alava et tornada à los Navarros, siempre ovo señorío apartado* ("so it happened that in ancient times since the land of Araba was conquered and taken from the Navarrese, there was always a lordship apart"). It is only the earlier editions of 1551 from Valladolid and the 1595 from Toledo that mentions: *desque fue conquista la tierra de los Navarros, la tierra de Alava era etc.* so that Navarre, not Araba, is referred to as conquered. Should the text of the new edition be correct as well, one cannot interpret the conquest in a strict sense, for the author of the chronicle would contradict what he had just claimed regarding the freedom of Araba at the very same place. Also the authenticity of the interpretation is highly dubious. The new edition follows the manuscript of the Escorial, and the editor gave preference to this one on the sole grounds that it is written beautifully on parchment and he therefore held it to be the copy that the son of Alfonso XI had sent to King Henry II, which according to the words of the chronicle was deemed: "a very honored, very royal, very rich, very glorious and very precious treasure."

28. The text of the entire treaty can be compared in Landazuri, II, 116.

Kings of Spain. And when Queen Isabella came to Vitoria-Gasteiz in 1483, the magistrates of the city and province came toward her outside of the gates of Arriaga and kept the gates shut until she had performed the confirmation and had reinforced it on oath. It is only then that she gained entry through the reopened gates.

Right after the unification of Araba with Castile there is a void in the history of the province's constitution that only ends with the institution of the *hermandades*. One only knows that the administration of justice was in the hands of the higher and, subordinated to him, the *merinos* and the *alcaldes*; but what general assembly stood in the place of that of Arriaga? On this, historiography has no answers. King John II (governed from 1407–1454) first instituted the *hermandades* in Araba, or, given that some had already existed in the land, a general and legal frame. The *brotherhoods*, as one has to translate it literally,[29] owe their origins to King Ferdinand III, the Saint; they were originally intended to keep public order in the land on account of a great number of disturbances that, especially in the fifteenth century, flared up between individual parties in Biscay and thus provided the immediate cause for their establishment in Araba. Their charter includes a mass of regulations on how to persecute criminals, to seek each other's help, and how, in cases in which they neglect their duties, they are bound to pay compensation to the affected party. Their jurisdiction is limited to a certain number of offences, and to determining the rights of mutual rights between them and the common local *alcaldes*. These offences especially bear the characters of those that disturb the public peace, such as murder, assault, arson, violent housebreaking, depredation of seed plots, and so on.[30] The ordinances that John II had decreed for the *hermandad* of Araba were later changed twice again, and the one that is currently in use dates back to Henry IV in the year 1463. The kernel of Araba's current constitution lies in the foundation of the *hermandades*. The whole province is divided into fifty-two of them; they send delegates to the country's general assembly, which in turn comprises all authority. These assemblies originated at the same time as the *hermandades*; according to Henry IV's ordinance, they are to be held twice a year and their decisions (*acuerdos*) have survived uninterruptedly since 1512. Currently one is held from May 4–8, the other from November 18–25, the latter in Vitoria-Gasteiz, the former in

---

29. From *hermano* (*germanus*) brother.

30. Landazuri, I, 239–267.

wherever it has been determined during each November assembly. Not all *hermandades* send delegates to these, though. The seventeen that make up the *cuadrilla* of Vitoria-Gasteiz have abstained from doing so for a long time, yet the city that represents them on their behalf has only two votes nonetheless.[31] Given that these meetings only last for a few days, authority must be executed by individual magistracies in the meantime. Between the beginnings of the *hermandades* until the end of the fifteenth century, two commissions were appointed to this end, one of which came from Vitoria-Gasteiz or one of the other locations (*la ciudad y las villas*), the other one from the rest of the province (*las tierras esparsas de la hermandad*). From round about 1476, however, the authority that rested in their hands transferred to the dignity of office of the still existing chief delegate. Albeit, they managed to survive alongside him if with rather limited esteem. The chief delegate was originally just the judge in charge of executing the legal cases that came before the *hermandad* (*juez executor de los casos de hermandad*). In the beginning his term of office was lifelong, but it was limited to three years as of 1533. He subsumes all executive powers, he has the chair in the assemblies of the province, and proposes the items to be debated; but he cannot avoid that other members do the same and he has no vote of his own.

All the same, he represents the province only in the time between their assemblies, and while these are in session his powers in all political and economic matters of the land cease completely. Whenever the chief delegate deems it necessary, he calls for an extraordinary meeting, equal to a tighter panel consisting of two commissioners and four that are elected for this purpose in advance at the respective general assembly in November; and should they not dare to decide the matter at hand themselves, they call in a general assembly. The delegate is only allowed to schedule such a meeting immediately in cases of crisis. In the extraordinary meetings of this type no other points may be put forward for debate but the ones mentioned in the call for the meeting.[32] The chief delegate is elected by six persons who are appointed especially for this task, three of whom are elected from the province in the November meeting; the other three, however, consists of the attorney general and the two aldermen (*regidores*) of Vitoria-Gasteiz. In addition, never may anyone else but a resident of Vitoria-Gasteiz be taken for this. This double privilege of the

---

31. Ibid., I, 291–300.
32. Ibid. I, 268–278.

city draws on a treaty entered between the city and the province in 1534 that terminated a longstanding conflict about the matter. The city based their privilege above all on the premise that because in 1498 the office of an executive judge in the *hermandad* had been abolished, they stipulated the right with the king to have a chief delegate from their midst, and thus deemed him to be belonging to them. The province however disputed this privilege. Several *hermandades* immediately set themselves against this settlement, and even today they still protest formally against it.[33]

In Araba nobles exceed the commoners by far in numbers. Some *hermandades* are indeed noble. Their privileges are of little significance. They pay duties just the same, of which even the clerics are not exempt. At times, a nobleman is even a commoner's tenant. Moreover, in political terms the former is in no way inferior to the latter. They just as well elect the delegates to the general assembly, and can be elected to it themselves. It is in some *hermandades* that the estates alternate in the elections, and in others of two delegates one must be common and the other noble.

In former times, the dominion of Araba was considered to be very profitable. "Whomever the Arabans," says the author of the chronicle of Alfonso XI, "transfer the reign of their land to, they give them plentiful tributes;[34] in addition to the legal taxes, the *semoyo* and the March oxen as well." *Semoyo* refers to a certain amount of wheat that the landlords who reside on the land receive from their vassals for each yoke of oxen. In today's standards, however, the king does not draw considerable revenues from the province. The so-called voluntary donations amount to a relatively little quantum. Taking the average sum of forty-eight years, it comes to 43,750 *reales de vellon* (2,734 talers Friedrichsd'or)[35] per year. All sums that the province pays to the crown in terms of royal privilege can be best viewed in the following compilation.

---

33. Landazuri, I, 283-287. II, 137–177.

34. Ch. 100, *dábanle servicio muy granado*.

35. The individual sums in the various years were:

1744	240,000	*r.d.v.*	
1747	240,000	-----	
1761	660,000	-----	above all used for the reconstitution of the Cantabrian Regiment, which returned from the Americas in a very bad state.
1765	480,000	-----	for the wedding of the then Prince of Asturias
1780	480,000	-----	
	2,100,000	*reales de vellón*	

reales de vellón

1—	Voluntary donations on average	43,750
2—	*Alcavala*. (Bourgoing, II, 16)	116,738
	It is for the most part fixed at a certain rate across all of Araba. In Vitoria-Gasteiz it is paid on the sale of immobile goods, the local resident gives 5, the foreigner 6 *p.c*	
3—	Rights of the Seigniory and Services (*Derechos de Señorío y Servicios*)	20,124
4—	A large part of the two last mentioned charges is alienated to the communes and the *hermandades*. The sum of these alienated duties amounts to 741,495 *real*. 22 *mrs*. If one calculates with 5 p.c. on this capital there is an income of	37,074
5—	The king has sold or relinquished another part of the Alcavales. The province pays for this	25,987
6—	*Derechos de Señorío* and *Servicios* sold in the same way	19,912
7—	Guilds-fines, can be estimated on average at	4,000
8—	Duties from the clerisy, namely:	

	a) *Subsiduo*	22,415	
	This fee was granted to Philip II by Pius V in support of his war against the infidels		
	b) *Escusado*, or the right to claim the best tithe within the parish. (Bourgoing, II, 22) for 400 houses in Araba. Reckoning for each house with 50 *pesos* (one *peso* at 15 *r*.) this duty amounts to	300,000	322,415

9—	Extraordinary expenditures, such as e.g. costs for governmental change, royal obsequies, births of royal princes, furthermore for the marching-through of troops, rewards for those catching contrabandists etc. All these diverse costs can, more or less, be estimated per year at	25,000
	Total	615,000

(38,437 1/2 Taler Friedrichsd'or)

Besides direct duties, the king also draws indirect ones as well from this land, but one can hardly call them duties as it depends on the province itself whether they procure the articles, on which a duty is levied, from Castile or elsewhere.

It is only the bulls, the revenues of which also go to the king's treasury,[36] which need to be excluded from this as they essentially belong to those tributes that flow toward the crown, even if the amount depends on the land in question.

---

36. Bourgoing, II. 19–21.

In 1787, 84,400 papal dispensations of all sorts were collected in the province of Araba, and, at different prices, these gave the royal treasury an income of—209,676 *reales* (13,104 3/4 Taler Friedrichsd'or). However it is odd that amid this tally there were 15,711 with which the piety of the Arabans had provided for their decedents even after their death.

The main articles of consumption for which money moves from Araba to Castile are the following:

reales

1.— Salt. The Biscayan provinces can procure their salt from
wherever they desire. Araba, however, with the exception of
a few *hermandades*, entered a contract with the king to fulfill
their demand from the salt works of Añana, and by dint of
this contract the price of the *fanega* was fixed at 11 *reales/*
fanega. The province consumes about 8,000 *fanegas*, which thus
amounts to   88,000
Since Añana is further away, the people of Araba also buy from
Salinilla at the higher price of 17 *reales* yearly in some cases.   1,360
The salt works of Añana and Salinilla produce about 51,500
fanegas of salt per year, which earns the king, minus the cost of
production and administration, 1,061,734 *reales*.

2.— Chocolate. According to a precise calculation, Araba yearly
consumes the immense sum of 200,000 pounds of cocoa, which
can only be comprehended accounting for the widely diffused
and frequent consumption of this drink. The king receives for
each pound 1 *real* minus one *Maravedì*, thus this levy amounts
to   194,117

3.— Sugar. The quantity of the demand that is drawn from the
kings' states amounts to about 100,000 pounds, so 16 *reales* for
each center comes to   16,000

4.— Oil. From Andalusia and Castile, the province consumes 25,000
cantaras, each at 35 *reales*, amounts to 875,000 *reales*, of which
the king according to the most recent tariff, receives 4 p.c.
which, together with another minor duty, make   37,941

5.— Wine, soap, etc. according to the same calculation valued at   35,000

6.— The sum that the royal post services generate throughout Araba
province can be estimated at   162.000

               Total   615,000

(33,401 Taler Friedrichsd'or)

According to these figures collected in the land itself, insignificant articles not included, the crown receives:

1.	from direct duties	615,000	*reales.*
2.	duties for dispensation bulls	209,676	———
3.	from indirect duties	534,418	———
	in sum	1,359,094	*reales.*

(84,943 Taler Friedrichsd'or)

Vitoria-Gasteiz, the capital of the Province of Araba, has the appearance of a blossoming provincial city as a result of its trade and industriousness. One sees life and affluence everywhere, and one notices many large newly built buildings among which the market square, finalized only in 1791, features especially. It is rectangular, built completely of stone, and consists of thirty-four houses among which the city hall (*la casa consistorial*) is the largest. The master builder did not deviate in anything from the usual building style of Spanish market squares. Here, too, an open arcade runs all around below, and every window has its iron balcony, a feature that is practical in so far as that in those cities that do not have their own amphitheaters for bullfights, it is in the market squares that they are carried out. On the exterior sides, the market is surrounded by four wide streets, so that each house has a second entrance that is not obstructed by the market turmoil.

The city owes its emergence to King Sancho the Wise of Navarre. It was after numerous border disputes with the King of Castile Alfonso VIII, the Noble, that they could finally come to an agreement that the Zadorra River should become the eastern border of his territory. In view of reinforcing the border, he surrounded the town of Gasteiz with walls, brought new residents there to enlarge it, fortified it according to contemporary style with towers, and gave it the name *Victoria*. This happened in the year 1181. Since then Armentia, which had been the seat of the bishops [and] still today consists of only a few remaining houses, has been in constant decay, while Vitoria-Gasteiz, due to the privileges that Sancho and the succeeding kings had granted, ascended to becoming the capital of the province of Araba. On the north side of the collegiate church, one can still glimpse the tower and a considerable wall piece of the fortress that Sancho drew up here.

According to the claims of Biscayans, the name of the city is of Basque origin; they delineate it from the word *bitorea*, splendid, outstanding. Alone, given the time during which Sancho founded this city, it is more probable that he gave it a Latin name; presumably, he even sought to enhance it by changing its rather insignificant name in the vernacular to a more erudite Latin name.[37] Perhaps one also believed that an older, same-named city used to stand in the same place.[38]

The traveler will gladly use the time that he will have to spend in Vitoria-Gasteiz anyways while his luggage is being examined with the viewing of some paintings in churches and private collections, of which there are many here. Among them my attention was especially drawn to a Titian Magdalena in the house of the Marquis of Alameda. The sculpture is life-size, standing, and fully clothed. Her head is turned to the right, and her hair falls over her shoulders onto her bosom. The beauty of this sculpture resides above all in the supreme dignity that the painter had managed to retain in the figure and the physiognomy, right up to the expression of remorse. Free of the petty intention to lend the beguiling depiction of feminine beauty a thus higher allure with the confession of guilt—whereby one so regularly witnesses that one of the noblest motifs of modern art is degraded to one of the meanest—Titian to the contrary treats his object sublimely. The Magdalena that he presents us with does not divest herself of any adornment that has no bearing on her misdeeds; she does not lift her begging eyes to heavens with weak and anxious tears; her hand grasps her heart, her gaze is turned inward, though timid and fraught, dry and rigidly fixed upon one place. She does not shiver before an unfamiliar chastising judge, but discerns in horror the relentless, condemnatory one in herself. She does not abandon human dignity with rueful contrition, but to the contrary senses its return, and is embarrassed by it, yet strengthened.

Rich in good pieces from various schools is the art collection of the Marquis of Montehermoso, one of the most knowledgeable and patriotically inclined men I encountered among the grandees of Spain.

---

37. In Sanchos's founding charter in Moret and his *Investigaciones históricas de las antigüedades de Navarra*, p. 669, the city is explicitly called Victoria. *Vobis omnibus populatoribus meis de noua Victoria* [to all you people of mine from the new Victoria] and furthermore: *in praefata villa, cui nomen nouum imposui, scilicet Victoria, quae antea vocabatur Gasteiz* [in the aforementioned city, the name of which has been repaced by a new one, namely Victoria, which was previously named Gasteiz].

38. Oihenart p. 22, asserts here that Sancho merely reconstructed the Victoriacum built by the Goth King Leovigild (reigned from 568–586).

Durango

I was longing to leave Vitoria-Gasteiz, which I already knew well from my previous journey, and to engulf myself in the secluded valleys of Bizkaia. After a two-day sojourn we resumed our journey toward Durango.

Until Otxandio [Ochandiano], the border town of Bizkaia, the landscape is rather plain and insignificant. It is from there, though, that it begins to become more wooded and mountainous, and at San Antonio de Urkiola (a farmstead with an *ermita* close to it) the landscape is the utmost romantic. A gloomy face of rock runs across the road from east to west. But split in three magnificent masses (Anboto [Amboto], Untzillatx [Uncilla], and Alluitz), between them narrow valleys plunge down toward the side of the sea. White wisps of fog sped through the long, bare wall of rock, torn to wild spikes by incalculable gouges; in the middle stood an isolated pyramid, clear and free, at the foot of which two fertile plains winding down gorgeously, and a thick cloud still rested on the round vaulted head of the rock. But how multifarious the views come about on the descent, where the road, gracefully planted with trees, leads down between the rocks. One sees flush vegetation from all sides in lovely contrast to the bare and steep cliffs. Soon a dark forest hangs down from the steep heights; soon a small garden is landscaped in a flatter corner of the rocks, the rocks serves as the supporting wall, and to the left the remnants of an old fortress look over the hedges. At the foot of these mountains lays Mañaria, the loveliest village I ever saw in Bizkaia. Around the church, as the center and purpose of their union, are the houses standing closer together here, but more scattered farther down, surrounded by chestnut and walnut trees below large and ivy-twined oaks. And to the side the village green leads to the pass of this mountain range and bids the force of imagination to new vistas in another, equally romantic valley. On account of the surrounding mountains, just as a protective wall against the cold and wind, fig and mulberry trees prosper here, which does not occur a few thousand steps from here, on the heights of

Otxandio,[1] owing its name to the harsh climate, and in the whole rest of Araba.

The road from Mañaria to Durango does not have any additional such surprising locations in store, but many equally graceful and lovely places nonetheless. Inasmuch as this mountainous area varies in terms of nature, as monotonous becomes its ever-repetitive description, and perhaps the lure of recalling images that have been imprinted tightly and vividly into my phantasy has already taken me too far. The description of a journey through a small, isolate living farming folk cannot evoke great interest, and it has been too long already that I have left the reader in these valleys with objects that, without richness and variety, can only appeal by means of the pure uniqueness of their form. Now I will hasten to lead the reader with accelerated paces through the rest of my wanderings; it shall suffice for me to outline the image of this small but remarkable people and pin it to their soul; as it, anyhow, can only be colored in by the one who, these pages in hand, travels this land. It is only for this purpose that I seek the permission to linger with a few points, which present characteristic features in a most exquisite way.

One such point is the scattered houses of the country people in the valley of Durango, where the old simplicity of Biscayan customs is yet purer conserved. As I will show more clearly in the following, the kernel of the Basque people actually consists of the farming people who live scattered around and by themselves, often deep in the mountains. The cities are an alien and later addition; whoever lives there enjoys his most treasured privileges only because his house belongs to this or that village. Bearing the expression of pride on their faces that this conviction instills, and a defiant courage that a rough and laborious way brings to life, the country people come to town on Sundays and feast days. And when one sees them then with their arms crossed, leaning against their long walking sticks, in front of the church, one realizes at first glance that it is they who are the true lords and chieftains of this land. More than elsewhere, to this day one has known to defend oneself against the domination of the cities in Bizkaia; but far more noteworthy yet is that beyond their walls sovereignty is not held by the hands of one single detached class; it rests within the nation itself and to the greatest part among the farming parts of it. No kind of feudal constitution has crept into this happy corner of Europe. It is with these terms that one needs to enter the *caseríos*

---

1. From *otza* (Bizkaian *ocha*) coldness, and *andia*, large.

[farmsteads], if one wants to comprehend its utter beautiful peculiarity, life and the inhabitants' character in its entirety.

But just as presumably during its population's earliest times, people in the inner parts of Biscay still live scattered about and isolated, the various *caseríos* often lie lonely in considerable distance to each other, their occupants only constitute a municipality in the sense that they belong to the same church, and it is only here that one sees a number of houses built together in a village like manner. Moreover, the Biscayan villages are merely called *anteiglesias*, squares in front of the churches, a name that is unusual for the rest of Spain. It is in these isolated houses that the Basque nourishes his spirit of freedom and independence, which characterizes him, not being surrounded by anything foreign he clings with passionate love to the peculiarities of his way of life, of that of his nation and his language; the small field, from which he toilsomely wrings the nourishment for his family, produces the strength, the mountains on which he lives provide for the agility of his limbs, and thus his build and his physiognomy acquire the imprint of the power and the courage that makes him recognizable at the very first glance. Nowhere did this occur to me more than in Durango when I visited the market on the morning after my arrival, where I came across the incoming peasantry gathered there.

Already their garb is utterly distinct, and contrasts advantageously with the more Castilian one of the city dwellers. Already Campomanes[2] had a clearly critical stance—and rightly so—against the two most characteristic pieces of Spanish garb, the mantle and the hairnet. The former impaired on the work and encouraged idleness; it is also remarkable that the inhabitants of the more industrious provinces, the spry Catalans and the almost Moorishly dressed Valencians, use them a lot less. The hairnet (*la cofia*) causes uncleanliness and rashes, from which often eye infections follow. The true Bizkaian has his own unique dress. Instead of shoes, he wears bull-leather soles that have just a small turned edge and are tied by a string; the *abarcas* already received mention during the oldest times.[3] In comparison to shoes, they are more comfortable for climbing in the

---

2. In keeping faithfully to his general scheme, that is to render the Moors responsible for nearly all objectionable habits in Spain, he also delineates the constant use of the mantle from them. But he admits so much that the Spaniards have rendered it yet a lot more uncomfortable and impedimental to physical movement. *Discursos sobre la educacion popular de los artesanos*, p. 122.

3. Cf. Du Cange Glossar. v. *abarca*.

mountains, and Sancho, King of Navarre, made use of them for himself and his army in the tenth century in order to traverse the Pyrenees, from which he received his nickname *Abarca*.[4]

Stockings have only recently become customary among the Bizkaian peasantry, and mostly among the women. The men wrap woolen cloths, usually fixed with narrow black strings, around their legs, that are tied down with the cords of the *abarca*. The color of the pants is mostly black, and that of the vest is red. A band (Spanish *faxa*[5]) is worn around the vest. The place of the mantle or coat is taken by the *longarina*, a wide jacket with long shirttails and sleeves. Those who wear them according to old custom have the sleeves fastened to the jacket with ribbons or buttons in order to unfasten them whenever necessary and throw them high and above and thus become freer at work. The *longarina* is commonly black or dark brown. The head is covered by a black, pointed, helmet like hat with a triangular lapel of black velvet in front. They hold a long cane in their hands, sometimes underneath their jacket also a short one, a bludgeon running thicker toward the end, called *cachiporra*—a kind of dagger for them, given that, as I have mentioned above, the long cane takes the place of a sword. One sees them in this attire on the markets of the cities after church, for the mountain dwellers, in order not to lose time throughout the week, tend to their minor shopping on Sundays. Of all ages they are alone and calm with the cane placed under their shoulders and with crossed legs, before long in a group in lively conversation, for the most part in marvelous postures and gesticulation, as the natural movements of a people with a free spirit and elaborate physique in itself have always been beneficial for arts.

The sight of these strong and cheerful people enticed me to visit them in their houses, and almost every afternoon I undertook a walk to one of the farmsteads located nearby. Durango lies in a fertile valley, and whichever side one turns there are charming winding footpaths through fresh thickly grown oak groves, many of which are fenced in by living hedges. Plentifully and thoroughly sprinkled with small creeks, they bear the nicest grass and the most aromatic scent of flowers; vegetation everywhere pushes forward in merry lushness, and bridges, tree trunks, and fences are covered with the thickest of ivy. One imagines to be losing

---

4. The *abarcas* of southern Spain are *alpargatas* in Valencia and Catalonia, soles that are bound together by cords of spartum.

5. From *fascia*.

oneself in these small groves, they appear so thick at first sight. Suddenly one sees light; one steps outside and a happy sown field lays there again surrounded by small woods through which one again sees country homes shining through.

Should one arrive at such a free space just at twilight, one comes to enjoy the most glorious spectacle; thick masses of clouds linger on the top of the southern mountains; to the north the milder mountain range cuts away from the bright skies with amicable clarity, and crimson-glowing evening skies are flooding in from the lower openings in the northwest at the sea. One day I went to visit a farmstead in the mountains toward Mañaria. All the houses, with only a few exceptions, built in the same way. Generally with two stories, half of wood, half of stone, with flat descending roofs, no chimneys. There is a bower where one enters supported by a wooden or stone pillar, and two stout grapevines stand to either side and their thickly leafed tendrils intertwine in a brotherly way toward the house's center. Sometimes one of them suffices to shade the house from all around. In the bower stood the cart and the agricultural equipment, and foliage was heaped together as future dung below an aged oak. The kitchen serves as the family's meeting point in the few hours that are free from fieldwork. The adjacent small chambers are only used for sleeping and for certain household tasks, such as linen-weaving. Above is the loft and directly next to the kitchen the stables.

The house was occupied by a widow and her children. The grown up son came back from his work with the yoke. We could hear the squeaking sound of the cart long before the oxen ascended the mountain's cumbersome winding path. Upon his arrival his younger brothers assembled around him and helped him to unyoke, shove the cart with its surrounding basket above into the bower, and let the oxen into the stables. Hardly inside, they trustingly stretched their heads into the kitchen and demanded pay for their sour day's work. For the loyal companion in labor is here not excluded from the close family circle. The manger is set up in the kitchen at the wall that separates it from the stables, and there are two openings in the wall that the beasts put their heads through. In this way uncleanliness is avoided and the peasant has his two most important pieces of his husbandry under his immediate supervision at all times. Also, he can make no pretense as to how he keeps them, for any neighbor or stranger visiting have them permanently before their eyes and thus acquire an unmistakable understanding of his husbandry or carelessness. Whenever there is talk of the industriousness, the integrity, or affluence of a peasant, his oxen and their strength are never left unmentioned.

Horses are seldom seen in Biscay as their use is not easy in the mountain areas. Also, it seems as though the horse is designed for the two extremes of human civilization, the nomadic and the highly civilized life, rather than for the transition from one to the other: farming. More suitable for this is the bull with his untiring strength, his heavy-trotting yet powerful tread, and dutiful, obedient sense of labor. It is undeterred in the bitter labor of treading the same piece of plow land days at a time for the purpose of cutting furrow upon furrow into the firm soil, and in the evening it is content with the frugal and meager feed, in this it is more apt to the slowly but surely maturing hopes of the peasant, in a life whose cycle ends in the fall only to commence again each spring.

Descending from the mountain we encountered the daughters of the house, with heavy sacks on their heads carrying flour from the mill. It was already late; the evening star was twinkling bright, and fire of brush was shining across from the opposite mountains, burning it to loosen the soil for future cultivation.

There was more prosperity to be found in one of the other farmsteads. There was a large barrel of cider in the kitchen, the chambers were cleaner, the beds artfully carved, and below each one of them was a blanket of straw for a more comfortable getting in and out of bed. A talkative old man showed us all the bits and pieces and he especially liked to linger over his clothing, almost all of which this industrious farmer made for himself. Above all the *abarcas* were not forgotten as the most distinctive piece. In the corner laid a half way prepared piece of cowhide for that purpose. The skin is merely stretched out, dried, slathered with salt and ashes, and then cut into long stripes. On these, the wooden form of a single *abarca* is traced, and as soon as these are cut out, the work is as good as complete. For now merely the hair is scratched off a little bit on the sides (the rough side remains, as the sole, turned toward the floor) and holes are hammered in through which one threads the strings that attach the woolen cloths serving instead of stockings when putting on the *abarca*. On the larger farms one finds two additional buildings, the wheat and cattle house.

The former, *garaija*,[6] has a wonderful form if built according to the actual custom of the land. On four large stones stand four stony blunted

---

6. From *garaitu*, to climb, a high place.

pyramids. On each one lies a round hewn stone, just like a millstone, and on this rests a rectangular wooden cabin, similar to our free-standing pigeon loft. Around it is a form of passage on which the beehives stand. Stone stairs lead up to it, but it misses the highest step, so that one must take a step that is twice as big. However, since mice and rats are no longer the most dangerous enemies of the granaries, the type has become very rare, and we had trouble to find even one of them on our long walks.

The cattle shed, *abelechea*,[7] is an open shed under which the live-stock is gathered and fed.

To go through the details of this small economy offers its own, rewarding joy. The independence, the prosperity, and the buoyancy of the occupants of these places demonstrate that it is neither need nor suppression that coerces them to this way of life; it is, rather, their own choice and custom that invites them to it. The imagination takes pleasure in this limitation because it exceeds it, in a kind of hope, with any aim arbitrary, any ambition to which the spirit is devoted in its most free and daring flights, and with this it imparts those same limitations with meaning, which does not exist for he who lives naturally in them. It is one more pure and noble form in which man tests himself, and one would be mistaken to ever attribute the enchantment it brings with it the observation of a simple lifestyle, even in rough and uncivilized peoples, only to the annoyance of excessive civilization, and also to merely senti-mental feeling, strengthened by such contrast. Wherever man is, whether civilized or simple, pure in his customs or however he has been, more or less corrupt, since the first moments of his existence, only through his spirituality and the instantaneous impression of moral liberty in which he thus appears as a natural being, that is where he displays a more sub-lime and reassuring dimension. If a free-spirited people is seen to create a language, which expresses the whole range of human sentiment and contains within it the mark of order according to a plan, without discov-ering any of the stages by which it has reached that point, or rather with one feeling that there have been no such stages, that this admirable work came suddenly out of nothing; if the elements of the highest and most delicate feelings are to be found in it, in which its nature gives in, without any embossing, to its primitive impetus; then that is when one gains trust in humanity and nature, and the fundamental forces of each, still deeply unknown, are believed to be related. In the final spiritual refinement, to

---

7. From *aberea*, livestock, and *etxea*, house. Publisher's note: should be *abeletxea*.

which man only arrives in times of a higher culture, the human being
seems like a solitary stranger in nature, cutting himself off with a certain
arch fearlessness from his usual ways. These scattered rural dwellings
seem even more pertinent and interesting, however, if one considers their
influence on the land and the people's character. It is undeniable that
Biscay has advantages over the rest of the Spanish provinces, that the Biscayan provinces are at the very least equal to the other provinces in terms
of bustle, industriousness, and skill. And that in terms of the people's
enlightenment, true patriotism, and real national pride, no other provinces may consider themselves equal to the Biscayan ones. Inasmuch as
this may be dependent on other circumstances as well, it is the described
allotment of the land, and the way of life of the agricultural part of the
nation that contributes the greatest part to it. It does not suffice for man
to have property; he must also live detached and, where possible, isolated
and close to nature if a certain feeling of independence and power should
ever develop inside him. That in so many of Spanish provinces the peasantry does not live in villages, but in cities and market towns, is surely
disadvantageous to their character. It is only where the proprietor has his
property right before his very eyes that he can become one with it; also,
in the cities there is always more uncleanliness, neediness, and idleness
and the latter two are less humiliating as the individual gets lost among
the crowds. Whoever has traveled through France, Spain, and Italy will
have noticed with bewilderment that in most areas of these countries
the peasantry does not constitute a class apart in terms of house, garb,
and custom as compared to Germany. And whoever endeavors to ponder
on the causes and consequences of this phenomenon will find that the
disadvantage this carries can be discerned not only immediately in the
national character, but even in the nation's most educated society, in the
language and literature.

Given that it was Sunday on the occasion of my visit to Durango,
I did not fail to visit the open dance square where, in the smallest locations, in the center of the land, people tend to assemble with far greater
interest than in the bigger cities, where the love for the national customs
has already grown cold. In Biscay dance still has the character of a completely popular merriment. One dances in public in the main square,
without any difference of class, on all Sundays and feast days, at the cost
of the town council and under public control, and the different locations
differ from each other by way of different dances that are exclusive to this
or that, just as they do by way of constitution and dialect. Immediately
after the afternoon service the *tamborilero* [tabor player] paced around

the square playing. He has a tabor [small snare drum] on a strap hanging over his shoulder in front, and in his mouth a small flute [*txistua*] that has no more than three holes. The drum has no jingles and is thus indeed different from the so-called *Tambour des Basques*, which, by the way, has no business in carrying that name, as it has nothing to do with the national music, nor the Basques' national dance. The *tamborilero* plays the drums and the flute at the same time. The flute that hangs down from the mouth in a straight line is governed by the left hand; with the right hand he beats the drum with a drumstick. He is supported and paid by the town council, given that the Sunday dances, just as much as anything else, is part of the national constitution. For quite some time the tabor remained alone in the square and served merely to entertain the children. The adults were still gathered at the pelota game. For this game's lure outweighs everything else for the Biscayan, and the maidens had to wait impatiently for a long time at the dance place before the male dancers appeared. The dance commonly danced on a Sunday is called *karricadantza*.[8] Once an old *alguacil* (bailiff), with a soiled mantle and a long cane, had cleared the square of children and other spectators, twelve to fifteen young people took each other by the hand, and proceeded as part of a kind of procession around the square a few times, the *tamborilero* at its head. Only the leader of the dance performed the actual steps, but they had nothing peculiar about them, the others just followed him walking. After a few rounds a dancer left the row, took a girl, and gave her to the leader of the dance. He received her with compliments and a new procession began. The girl, even if the most noble, may not decline anyone, not even of the lowest kind, if asked to dance. But the more separated they are socially by class, this applies to Biscay as well, they detach themselves from the rest of society and the old customs fall asleep, the more this dance is left to the people's lower classes. At times, the leader of the dance and the girl have their own dance once she has been welcomed. This is called *chipiritaina*[9] and consists of formations that both carry out with each other by themselves. Following a few more

---

8. Dance on the open road. One should not prematurely take the word *dantza* as the mere adoption of the French. This term is signified by this sound in many languages, which is presumably an Onomatopoeia of the stamping of the feet (dan, dan). Also in Gaelic, *damhsair* is a dancer; in Breton: *dansa*; in Irish *yun donnsy*, to dance.

9. *Tipia, Chipia, chiquia*, means small [today *ttipia* or *txikia* —ed.]. Just how much this dance got its name from this word I cannot say as I never had the opportunity to see the actual dance.

rounds a second dancer is picked out and she is given to the man in the last row. As soon as these two places of honor, often cause for bloody altercations between whole towns, have been given away, all the dance's formalities come to an end and exuberant merriness takes their place.

Everyone runs as fast as he can and takes a girl of their liking; again just as before rows are formed, but now everything is in movement, all jump, swing and pull to and fro, and the male and female dancers try to bump into each other *dos à dos* in an ungentle kind of way. These so-called *culadas*—a most peculiar part of this Basque dance—play the major role, and it is just as good that the female dancer is usually not of frail nature or she would soon suffer being jerked, run into, as her two fellow dancers will not spare her. During this part of the dance, *zortzicos* are played that give the adequate beat for it.

Fandangos follow. The rows separate, every male dancer faces his female partner on his own, and starts the fandango. Until this point the dance was pure merriment for the people, a boisterous running, bouncing, dragging and hitting, kept in order only by the rhythm of the music, but there was nothing to embarrass the morals. The fandango, here just as elsewhere, has its own more or less distinctive character. But one has to know it in order to recognize it here.

It is disputed whether the fandango, in the way some derive it from La Mancha, is an originally Spanish or Latin American dance, and presumably both claims are contemporaneously true. Standing by itself (as one should not confound the real fandango with what one sees in the theaters of Madrid and elsewhere, and, even less, judge it according to the ever so exaggerated reports of the travel writers) the fandango is a simple dance, which lends itself so very adequately to the natural outbreak of merriment that it would be ridiculous to take its origins from beyond the ocean. The specific modifications, however, that it acquired later and especially in southern Spain have undeniably come over from the Americas. At least, everyone who has been over there affirms that one rediscovers the same dances on the islands and in the Spanish-American territories, just more complete, more diverse, and far more salacious and lascivious. The utterly unique and characteristic agility of the movement of the hips, as I have been assured by eyewitnesses, is practiced on the islands early on by young girls in front of a mirror that is put in front of them, and the entire character of the lewdness that governs these dances shows its origins. For it has no northern rawness, but the vivid imprint of a climate that, by inflaming the power of passion, unleashes the forces, the entire body seems to dissolve into a number of joints, and it seems to

be a sensation that the entire soul succumbs to. Its very essence is lascivious voluptuousness; its most important part is not the interlacing of the
turns and the steps, but the positions and twists of the body. The forceful movement of the arms, especially in the shoulders, the stamping of
the feet, the perpetual briskness of the back and the hips, let alone other
movements that every witness will always remember, all of it expresses
the presence of heftiest lust; and it is this that makes this dance, if viewed
objectively, neither noble nor gracious, but rather monotonous in its more
decent rendering, and its genuineness is remarkable only for its peculiarity. Meanwhile, its fire always enraptures the audience, and the first hit of
the *castañuela*, as I often saw with bewilderment, brought forth a true
frenzy among the Spaniards. Men and women, young and old, everything accompanies the tact with facial expressions and movements. The
masters of this dance are the gypsies from Andalusia and the kingdom of
Granada. Some of them I saw there were truly ideals, natures that would
only succumb to the most sensual joys. Many among them, such as the
Phaiakians at Alcinous's court, engage in nothing but dance and entertainment. Hostile to any form of work or toil, their body, for the lack of
any nourishing food (for they are only fond of fiery drinks and cakes),
seems to run on its own fire. Meanwhile they are tender, well-natured,
and even gentle; nature people who, without any other consideration, let
themselves adrift to the influences of the unnerving climate.

Utterly divested of this character of delicate lewdness is the fandango in Biscay, a raw, and I would like to say, primordial nature dance,
arguably also indecent and obscene (however not generally and as part
of its nature, only with the one or other dancer) but never salacious.
Moreover, its variants are unfamiliar in Biscay and the *bolero*, *zorongo*,
zapateado, and so on are unknown names, yes even the fandango itself is
probably a foreign addition like the English contradance that terminates
the Sunday merriment. Biscay's genuine national dances bear a superior
and more noble character, that of a popular fair, and are far more distinguished by way of decency and dignity and this was even more so the
case in former times when the nation's more genteel parts less than today
detached themselves from the people and their national customs, when
the authorities gave dance more of their special attention or when the
clerics either disapproved less or their zealousness was less venerated.
A dance that is mentioned as especially grave is one that begins with a
circle in which the male and female dancers hold on to each other via
handkerchiefs. In those days, the dance was more artful and the steps

were calculated precisely according to the melody and the verse structure of the *zortzico*.

It is more the public authority under which the just-described *karricadantza* is danced than the actual dance that is noteworthy. It is exclusively the Basque national dances that are presumably of an older origin that resemble our ballet, they are images of story lines, or likewise social games. Almost every town has its own individual dance, performed as a public procession but usually only on the Feast of Corpus Christi, or on St. John's, or on the day of the town's patron saint.

Thus, the *acheridantza*, the fox dance, is common in Hernani. All dancers crouch down behind each other in row, each one with two short and thick bludgeons in his hands, the person behind holds the foot of the one in front of him. Only one stands upright and has a charred stick in his mouth. He tries to kiss the others with it and they must defend themselves without losing their balance in this difficult position. Upon this game follows an entertainment with a young bull. Some of the young men go into the stables to provoke it to go outside. The others deny him his exit. Once the animal has finally jumped through them to the outside, it is teased and hounded. The joy of chasing a bull is common throughout Spain. An old man on a *caserío* in Durango showing me his oxen as it went after his hand when he teased it rejoiced like a child over how wild it was going to be at the next *novillada* (bull-baiting). And every time before a bull is slaughtered, it first serves to entertain the city. One lets it run around on a square fixed to a long rope, and teases it with coats, hats, and handkerchiefs, or pulls him here and there on the rope which mostly lies loosely on the ground. The *tamborilero*, the constant companion of any popular fair, plays to it and once the bull begins to tire, it is tantalized with dogs. Some *alcaldes*, however, forbid this game for the workshops are quite empty whenever it happens and I myself saw about fifty to one hundred people running after such a bull.

Another dance that is common in Azkoitia (*toalladantza*) consists of a foot race. Pairs of runners hold a long cord in each hand and run next to each other in this way. The pair running from behind tries to overtake the one ahead by throwing their cord beyond them and this makes for many comical scenes when one becomes tangled up in the cord; but sometimes however, when the cord entangles the runner and he becomes dragged away, it causes injuries and accidents. Most of these dances have their own special music reserved for the occasion.

Even more dangerous, but truly national, is the bludgeon dance, *trokiua*. Eight young fellows, each of them with a thick and long cane[10] in their hand, carry out all sorts of dance figures while striking each other with a bludgeon. All strikes occur according to the rhythm and with great precision; and while one strikes, the other parries by holding the stick beneath, now above, and with both hands horizontally to the front. Given that the dancers blow very heftily it can happen that the bludgeons break while parrying and cause injuries, but this is usually not the case as they have great dexterity in hitting and parrying.

More peaceful, just as the business that it simulates, is the weeding dance, *jorraidantza*. The dancers have a small spade in their hand, and firstly pretend to weed the soil according to the rhythm then they hoist their spades in the air and carry out a number of swings with them.

It would be of little use to list additional dances whose character are illuminated sufficiently from those mentioned above. I shall dwell on two for a moment for they seem to be noteworthy as they possibly bear the ancient remnants of the original customs; these are the *espatadantza* and the *dantzariadantza*.

The *espatadantza*, sword dance, requires thirty to forty young people. They are all in shirt sleeves and a scapular around their necks; they alternatingly hold the swords in both their hands, one at the rapier point, the other the coquille. The leader unites the rapier points of four swords in his hands; those that hold the coquilles also grasp other tops and thus the line becomes ever wider toward the end. In this way, accompanied by music they twist and turn through the streets of the town toward the church. Upon arrival, five or six of the most skillful, each bearing two swords, approach the high altar, kneel down and then perform moves and contortions with their bodies and both swords to such an extent that one should think that they would injure themselves and pierce themselves at any moment. While at it they from time to time look up to the altar and kneel down in the process.

I would like to relate this dance that is common in Gipuzkoa—I did not have the occasion of seeing myself—to a second one that belongs to Durango and that one is better called a shield dance. Today it is only danced by children and is one of the celebrations at Feast of Corpus

---

10. Publisher's note: In the Spanish translation of Miguel de Unamuno, Unamuno makes the point that the original German *Strick* ("cord") is likely an errata for *Stock* ("cane"). We have conserved this difference.

Christi. Four boys stand behind each other in four pairs, and one, called the king, stands in the middle with a flag. He commences the dance, starts waving the flag, and covers the dancers with it, then they dance and change their positions among each other several times. Thereafter individual dances alternate with communal ones, with the former performed at first by one of them alone, then by two, and finally by the four in such a way that the dance goes through the row each time and all get their turn individually. Once this has been accomplished each one of them receives a round metallic, shield-like plate with an iron handle; the boys separate into two groups, and hit this plate in a regular beat while they continuously change their positions and a quiet beat is always followed by a loud one. After this has gone on for a while, they all come into order in one row one behind the other; the one at front dances on his own and turns toward the end while turning one cartwheel after another; all the others follow his example. Once everyone has joined together again the final scene occurs. Two step forward and hoist the shortest of them all up in the air while balancing him on their extended hands closely kept together, so that he rests lengthwise on the furthermost part of their fingertips. While he just lays there still letting only his feet shiver to the rhythm, everyone else dances around him.

As disfigured as the dance of these small Curetes may have become, the representation of a war scene shines through, whether it means the burial of a fallen soldier, or whether it means the elevation of the victor. Perhaps it belonged to the sword dance that is today even more elaborated. At least, it is not unusual to see pagan games and ceremonies transcend into Christianity. And just as the national first names in Biscay have given way to the Christian Saints, perhaps also these former war dances have become part of ecclesiastical ceremonies, or at least relate to them.

Unlike elsewhere, in Biscay such popular things (like dance and revelry) are not left to the private sphere, but are, in a sense, part of the constitution, subject to public supervision. They are steadfast traditions handed down, truly national, and, moreover, traditions that have a fixed form depending on the individual's place of birth. The character of the Biscayans, for the most part, recurs on these very things, and it is these aspects of their character that are praised, in preference to other nations. It reinforces the Basque's tie with his land and his compatriots, and nothing can supersede the power of this tie in terms of the beneficial influence it has on the strength and the upright integrity of his character. Even the highest of culture could not fully take its place as it cannot lend itself to all branches of society; love for the homeland and national ambition, however, are readily adopted by both, the beggars and the elites of a people, if in different shape. It is only natural, though, that with increased commerce with foreign countries, these institutions will ever more fall into oblivion. In fact it is deplorable that the authorities have ceased to see to its preservation. Thus, one public custom after the other continues to fall asleep.

In Durango there used to be a festivity that was very instructive for ethical purity on the Day of St. Maria de Ulibarri[11] and St. Anna. One usually gave a small donation on these days at church (mostly a small piece of money, often just an *ochavo*). Men and women did this without any further ceremony. Only the unmarried girls gathered according to streets in their Sunday attire. Every street was led by the oldest and proceeded to the church door accompanied by the *tamborilero*. Here the procession was welcomed solemnly by two priests and led into the church accompanied by the whistles and playing of the tambourine and also afterward back out again. Given that the defining difference in traditional custom between girls and married women is that the former wear their hair openly while the latter wear a cap, all girls showed their bare head, and went to church like this. This is normally quite unusual as even the *aldeana* (peasant woman), when walking to the town's church over the fields, always carries a folded white scarf on her head serving as a veil in church so that in all of Spain a foreign women who sets foot into a church without will be instantly shown out. Should one of the girls in town have been unfortunate enough to become a mother, she lost the right to proceed with open hair; the others would not suffer her to join their part of the procession and because they were watched upon closely and since no one was permitted to absent oneself from the ceremony for whatever reason, the procession became an actual muster of morals. Today even the difference in garb is often neglected. Generally, it is remarkable that moral breaches of unmarried women, inasmuch as they are rare, occur more often in Biscay than in Castile, but, one rarely encounters adultery in this community. Moreover, fallen girls have no difficulties in finding a husband, in some cases even easier than other girls.[12]

---

11. Newtown, *Ulia* for *Uria*, town, and *barri* or *berri*, new.

12. Publisher's note: Unamuno has inserted a curious note here that we translate from the Spanish. "It should be noted that the boy who is the author of the mess is considered more obliged to act well than foolish reformers of values have later counseled" (159, n. 23).

On the same day of St. Anna and on that of Santiago, there also used to be a regular inspection by the authorities through all the streets, where every head of household had to present himself with his rifle at the door. This custom, however, has also fallen into disuse. But all Biscayans are still bound to amass in the event of a hostile attack; alas, one has witnessed in the last war just how little such a gathered force is useful and if there is anything among their liberties and rights in which the Biscayans should be less insisting, it is the introduction of an orderly and regular recruitment of troops.

The market town of Durango, which counts only about four hundred and fifty families, was once an affluent and respected town on account of its sword factories. Witness of this was the civil unrest that occurred repeatedly in former times during the election of *alcaldes*; reaching the highest degree of factional spirit, these often had a bloody outcome. To avert this for future times, one surrounded the elections with a lot of distractions and ceremonies and one lets it pass through so many different hands that the constitution of this small republic Durango belongs to the most entangled that I know. The office of *alcalde* does not make much and only lasts for a year. Hence one can add here, just as with Ariost's knights:

"A war not waged for empire or domain, But that the best should buckle to his side

Good Durindana, and Baiardo ride."[13]

The city's supply of bread, wine, meat, oil, and so on lies in the hands of five *regidores*, and the people have given great care that they carry out their duties in an orderly fashion. For not only were they equipped with two custodians but also with a third whose duty it was to control the first two. Also, the people elected these three magistrates who concerned their closest interests in a more immediate way, and only upon the mediation of twenty-five electors who were appointed by him. The supply is carried out, just as almost throughout Spain, by *abastos*, that is, persons who are given the task to deliver the necessary goods with adequate quality for a fixed price; the privilege is obtained in a public auction by way of the lowest bid. Every head of household, however, can fulfill his demand wherever he wants and even the farmer may engage in the trade; yet obviously he will not find his buyers so easily.

---

13. Publisher's note: Lodovico Ariosto, *Orlando furioso* (London: J. Murray, 1823) Canto 33, LXXVIII. Translated by William Stewart Rose.

Bilbao

The road there from Durango comprises of all the natural delights that are typical of this land; it is variant and mountainous, yet less rough than the road between Markina and Berriatua, which however also supersedes it in terms of picturesque beauty. Without wishing to dwell on single places, I will solely mention that in order to enjoy the beauty of the area to the fullest, one must leave the main road at Zornotza and continue past the ironworks at Astepe [Astapa] via Lemoa [Lemona]. The beauty of this way—on which one rides nearly uninterruptedly along the banks of a stream that is clear yet darkened by overshadowing, delightful bushes—is a more than sufficient recompense for the minor detour. One looks down into a new land from a mountain that is not far from Bilbao. The city lays there confined by wonderfully garlanded mountains and hills and its white and friendly houses shimmer through the green of the trees. Beyond it one can nearly see the entire way to the sea and the beautiful Serantes Peak, upon whose regular pyramid-form the eye so gladly rests and which remains to be in one's view continuously, firstly appears here.

Even though Bilbao is by far the most impressive and prosperous and in many regards also the most delightful city of Biscay, I will have little to say about it nonetheless. For partly other travel writers have spoken of it in detail, partly it is the least noteworthy with regard to my ultimate objective. The continuous commerce with foreigners has pushed out the national customs that should only be sought in the country and mountains; and even the language is impure to a high degree and intermingled with Castilian.

You will rather wish to visit the delightful banks of the Ibaizabal,[1] whose picturesquely covered hills are equal to the most beautiful and diverse English gardens, than read a description of it. Whoever remains here for a few days will wish to visit the heights of Altamira from where

---

1. *Ibaia*, river, *zabala*, wide. It carries its name only after merging with the Nervion.

one all at once overlooks the most endearing scenery, the shimmering sea in the distance, and Serantes together with the other pyramid-shaped mountain tops that surround it; or to immerse oneself in the valley on the other side of the river and to walk along its rolling stream toward the new bakery (*panadería*) at the weir's whooshing fall and do not forget upon your return to look out for the lovely oak groves in front of the church of the wonder-working picture of the Virgin Mary in Begoña. Even from the *Arenal,* the city's square for strolling at the river land-scaped with avenues of shady linden trees, one enjoys splendid country views of the banks on the other side of the river.

Even if one does not come across actual Basque customs in Bilbao, there is possibly no other city where one more readily perceives the ben-eficial influence of the Basques' national spirit. For there are only very few Spanish cities where one will encounter as many useful and valu-able institutions that are geared toward the common weal and there are only very few in which the traveler will find more men inspired with an enlightened and patriotic sense for improvement. Only Cádiz is compa-rable to Bilbao in terms of cleanliness and beauty of its cobblestones. It is worth making a note of the facilities that supply the city with water on a continuous basis. A large container at St. Juan *el antiguo* serves all the city's wells that are not intended for drinking, many of which flow consistently to clean the underground canals and water all the streets keeping down the summer's dust. Drinking water flows into town in iron pipes from the mountains on the other side of the river from a consid-erable distance. They cut through the river not far from the *panadería*. Of all the public institutions, it is the *Casa de Misercordia* and the hos-pital that are most worth mentioning. The former when I went there sustained about ninety men and women of whom everyone who is suf-ficiently strong works toward the advancement of the house. The men produce canvasses and ribbons, also some kind of faience; the women spin. Also, the house gives young boys an apprenticeship for any kind of trade they wish. As the house receives part of its income from a duty that each entering ship must pay, it suffered terribly during the war. When I was there one was just about to introduce Rumford's soups to feed the poor.[2] The building is the former Jesuit college. The hospital distin-

---

2. Publisher's note: According to Unamuno "an economical nutritious soup invented by the Count of Rumford made of bones, blood, and other cheap materials" (165, n. 3). An early pioneer of the soup kitchen, Count Rumford's famous soup more generally consists of barley, peas, and potatoes.

guished itself by its exceptional cleanliness. Other public buildings are the meat market (*carnicería*); the slaughterhouse (*el matadero*), which indeed can be regarded as an exemplary house of this type, both in terms of cleanliness and for the prevention from all kinds of dangers; the granary in the former theater; the city hall and what is known as the Consulate; the newly built theater with space for about nine hundred to one thousand people; and the general flour mill and bakery situated outside of the city. As the city had suffered immensely and repeatedly from rising prices, they decided to bake bread at their own expense, by the way without putting any constraint on the free wheat and bread market. The only thing is that the mill is too expensive and too grandly designed. As the flour and bread trade outside was disappearing, only about five thousand pounds were baked per day during my stay there.

I could not obtain any more recent figures than those of 1797 for the population size of Bilbao. According to these, I found them in the city archives, there were 10,953 persons that occupied 781 houses. Among them, 4,684 men and 6,269 women; namely 2,565 unmarried men and 3,552 unmarried women; 1,925 married men and 1,940 women; 194 widowers and 777 widows. There were 39 monks to be found, 61 nuns, 132 clerical persons (to which many are counted who are merely employed by the churches and can marry). Because the population is quite large in proportion to the amount of foodstuffs that the surrounding area produces, no one, neither a muleteer nor a teamster, may carry goods from Bilbao overland unless he supplies the city with products in return at the same time.

In an *anteiglesia* situated close to Bilbao I saw a *romería* or village festival, something I had not had the opportunity to see so far. The dance floor was in front of the town hall standing opposite the church. In one corner sat the *fiel* (judge, juryman) of the place, on a red velvet canapé that bore the coat of arms embroidered in silver, with a long cane with which he sent back the boys who pushed to the front. There were two pikes stuck in the ground in front of him, and two red and white flags were hanging from the windows of the church. An incredible amount of people had streamed in from Bilbao and it was the most pleasant spectacle to see underneath the shade-giving trees partly hanging about in the most diverse groups of people, partly wandering around, partly dancing. Refreshments, food stalls, games of all sorts; there was no lack of anything, not even a peep box with the story of the lost son. Men and women went about separately for the most part, almost all of the women in the *Basquiña* and *mantilla*, and those from the simple folk wore incredibly thick and black braids that would often reach even beyond their hips, they were nothing less than charming. The dances were the usual; but joviality was all around and exuberant. The *fiel* determines the duration of these merriments according to his own will, usually he does not let them go on after eight, eight thirty in the evening.

The houses in Bilbao are not as large and grandly designed as in the other, even more elegant commercial cities in Spain; but some whose lower stories are completely clad in marble mark an exception. The market square (*la plaza*) looks marvelous. It lies at the river and derives its distinct appearance above all from the church built in a gothic style and the city hall overladen with gilding. From there two bridges lead across the river, one built of stone at the church and a wooden one with a very keen arch that was erected in place of a stone bridge that had been washed away during a flooding. It leads to a monastery surrounded by trees, and right on the other side of the river a large, wonderfully formed mountain rises. Whenever bull fights are held, it happens in this square and a great number of people flock to the mountain just as in an amphitheater. Ordinarily they only hold *novilladas*—at which the bull is not killed; the real bull fights are too expensive. At the last one they held in 1799 the acquisition of thirty-six bulls (they were killed over three days) at 5 ounces (115 Talers) each one 57,600 *reales* (4,168 Talers); and alone the *torero* (bullfighter) Romero, who had been contracted from Madrid especially with his eight to nine men, was given 90,000 *reales* (6,512 Talers). So the complete cost ran up to 13,000 Talers. This Romero, whose truly characteristic portrayal by Goya I seem to remember seeing in Madrid, supposedly derives from his properties alone that he by and by bought from his wages—60 to 70,000 *reales* (4,300–5,000 Talers) annually; now that Pepeíllo has lost his life, it is uncontested that he is the only one left of the illustrious bull fighters.

Pepeíllo's death was announced in Bilbao just as I was there. He died in Madrid in the arena while carrying out his profession and retained his glory also in death. For just when the bull pierced his horn through his body reemerging on the other side at the shoulders, Romero too dealt a deathblow to him and they both collapsed simultaneously. The games continued as usual, but the fallen was buried in the soil with great splendor. Prior to him Candido had died in a similar way, the most famous among the *toreros* and the one who, according to Pepeíllo's own admission, was the first to have given the art of bullfighting its dependability and beauty. He had slipped on a melon skin that a spectator had tossed into the arena and was killed before he could take vengeance on the bull.

Pepeíllo, his actual name was José Delgado,[3] is possibly the only one to have written about tauromachy or bullfighting and to have given this art its formal system. As his short text[4] published in Cádiz will be scarcely known in Germany, only by its title, if at all, and yet nonetheless noteworthy in more than one regard, I allow myself, even if slightly out of context here, to dwell on it for a few moments and to provide my readers with a short understanding of it and the art it treats.

He is presented on the title page carrying a sword in his hands and with the bull only just killed at his feet with the subtitle: the Sevillian swordsman (*el diestro Sevillano*).

In the preface to this little work, which is addressed to the people of his profession, the dilettantes, and everyone else who has a taste for bulls, he spreads out about the usefulness and necessity of his project. "In an age" he writes, "that is so illuminated that even the castanets can find someone to write about them, no one has written about the art of bullfighting, and this in itself has spurred me on to be the first who drags his own tauromatic ideas into the light (*sus pensamientos y ideas tauromáticas*). Perhaps the reason why people have been so silent about this art is the fact that one can only speak of it by experience, not by mere speculation (*por la especulación*). I, thank God, he continues, can tread on firm ground and present myself, as it were, as a master." He calls his work useful, because the love for bullfighting is universal; because it distinguishes the whole nation from others, and because the nation's most illustrious and famous arms have excelled in it; and lastly, because the conflux of a mass of beautiful and pleasant items and the sight of peril and a cast of fortune render bullfights a fetching spectacle.

He explicates these three points one by one. Noble and lesser women alike, he says, speak of our actions and are never missed in our squares, circuses, and amphitheaters. Any bad cow one leads through the city on a rope makes everyone leave his occupation and run after her, to see or tease her. In short one can assert that the liking of bulls is inborn in people (at least, he should have added) in Spain.

Then he goes through history and assures that the art of bullfighting has been blossoming in Spain as long as there have been bulls there.

---

3. Pepe is the known Spanish abbreviation for José and illo is a byname.

4. *La Tauromaquia ò arte de torear. Obra utilísima para los toreros de profesión, para los aficionados, y toda clase de sayetos que gustan de Toros. En Cádiz. Por D. Manuel Ximenes Carreño*. Calle Ancha. año de 1796. 4. 58 p.

Among the heroes who have excelled in it for him stands Spain's national hero, Cid Campeador, at the top followed by Charles V, Philip IV, Sebastian of Portugal, Pizarro, the discoverer of Peru, and others. Still today, he says, it is part of the knights' most noble exercises to be able to fight with bulls on horse and foot.

But today it is possible that this is no longer entirely true. I do remember, however, a not-so-old man of nobility in Spain who as a student in Salamanca had slain a bull during a bullfight. In terms of older times, I do not recollect, neither in the Romances of Cid, nor in the Moorish romance novels (*Moriscos*), nor in the poems of the *Cancinero general*, not even in the pieces that deal with the attainment of knightly perfection, to have found any mentioning of bullfighting. Also, they could have hardly been greatly regarded while the tournaments lasted.

Furthermore, he does not pass over the objections against bullfighting; what he finds especially ridiculous is to condemn them on the grounds that here and there a fighter loses his life while at it. Danger is a part of many other physical exercises and greater, too, at the end of any given year there will be at most one man who will have lost his life or have been wounded in a bullfight.

In the end he passes through the history of his art. Apparently, fighting on foot was still very little known at the beginning of the eighteenth century. José Candido was the first to determine the various kinds of attack and the according demeanor, and his principles have been further developed and expanded by Joaquín Rodriguez, also known as Costillares, Pedro Romero, Juan Conde, and the author himself. Now, according to him, the art has reached its highest pinnacle and nothing more is missing at the moment than to let the rules be better known to the spectators and thus enable them to judge more accurately the fighters' merits.

In the small theory, which is not all uninteresting to sieve through, the author explicates above all the fight on foot and on horseback. In the former, which he carried out all alone, he feels very much at home; he lists the individual cases and then explains each one in methodological terms based on simple principles. For everything depends on the bull running toward the cape the fighter holds before him in a direct line, without diverging, and that it lowers its head before him with the intent of charging into him, and thus suffers the mortal blow in its neck. The danger comes about when the bull runs to and fro in fright or because of fatigue comes to a halt before reaching the cape and thus renders the fighter uncertain, or when it becomes aware of the deception and throws itself at the fighter instead of the cape, or even the most dangerous case yet, while doing this it raises its head and disarms the fighter by detracting its neck. All these cases are individually discussed. Even if his instructions commence with the pompous assertion that every kind of attack entails its own steadfast, never erring rules, Pepeíllo does have to admit that the chief thing is to remain cold-blooded when seeing the bull charging toward you and that even good fighters sometimes do not make an appearance out of fear; moreover, cases do occur when, again according to his own admission, there is nothing left to do but to throw the cape on the bull's eyes and make a run for it as fast as one can. As everything depends on the bull running at the cape in a direct line, he implores his readers to hold their silence and keep very still during bullfights, at least during the moment of the death blow, so as not to distract the bull's attention. Thus it becomes vivid with every line just how unsafe this art is and how great the danger.

It goes without saying that such a popular and longstanding trade that has always been carried out by a particular sort of people has its own language, incomprehensible to the uninformed; and Pepeíllo has thus appended a small dictionary to his text. It is remarkable to see how many adjectives are given to the bull according to his various character traits. He is *claro* (clear), *sencillo* (simple), *franco* (frank), *boyante* (buoyant) if he charges straight toward the deception; *de sentido* (with sense) if he turns toward the fighter and goes after him; *revoltoso* (rebellious) if he catches the cape but turns around with it, which is the most amusing and frequent case of all; *abanto* (punch drunk), *temeroso* (fearful), or deceitful, *bravucón* (rowdy), when he comes out calmly at first but then charges, and so on.

King Charles III allowed bullfights only in Madrid and Cádiz. Had this system remained in place, bullfights—especially now that Romero is the only remaining famous bullfighter—would have ceased to exist by and by. However, it is undeniable that the courage with which a single human opposes a raging bull without any protection or armed only with a sword, the pictorial positions of two of the most sublime creations, the bull and the horse, never fails to offer the densely crowded masses of people in the large amphitheaters under the open skies a fascinating spectacle. In addition, bullfights are the only remaining events in our times that an entire people take an interest in equally and where they can freely and directly express their dismay or approval. Alone, this is about all that can be mentioned in their favor, their detrimental consequences leap to the eye, and one cannot even make the claim that they help to maintain courage and bravery in the nation. It was particularly in its weakest and most unnerving times that Rome held its bloodiest and most dangerous games. I think that one can just as little call nations barbarian that find pleasure in these dangerous battles. Very often the human emotion just focuses on individual things; and should the sentiment of humanity and compassion give way to the fires of passion stirred up during a bullfight, one can still not claim that a whole nation is generally desensitized, also for other things.

Somorrostro

After a short sojourn in Bilbao, I rushed toward the sea again to visit the rest of the coast from Portugalete to Ondarroa and thus complete my wanderings around the whole of this charming little country.

The Desertu (Desierto) must not be forgotten on the way from Bilbao to Somorrostro. This small peninsula, which is created by the Ibaizabal where the Galindo, a small mountain stream, disgorges into it, is one of the most beautiful spots in all of Spain as one can all at once overlook the area of Bilbao, the sea with its pyramid mountains, and the Somorrostro from there. The road there from Bilbao follows along the right-hand side of the river through Olabeaga, Bilbao's actual port. To one's right there are for the most part picturesque and high rocks; on the opposite river-banks a charming, densely cultivated and planted area. An old rectangular tower, standing on this side just where a small river unites with the Ibaizabal at the market town of Lutxana [Luchana], is a reminder of the feudal system of the previous centuries. For this tower once had the right to block the river and exact a toll from the ships passing through. Beyond Lutxana lay the scattered rural inhabitations of Barakaldo [Baracaldo] in a dainty valley, and surrounded by bushes. The Desertu is connected with the firm land here and coming from Bilbao one must be ferried across the river to get there. The nicest view is from this side too, even though one has an unobstructed view of the whole area from one particular mountain that stands right where both rivers come together and on which the monastery was built.

For also this indeed divine place has dedicated itself, as so many in southern Europe, to pious devotion; and sixteen Carmelite friars lead a lonely life here. Their entire lot is surrounded by high walls for no female being is permitted to set foot inside and it is only in a chapel before the monastery where the open mass is held to which the people from the surrounding area stream to in heaps. Whoever has lost his peace of mind or his soul's happiness in the world's turmoil, could surely regain it here under the shady oak trees that cover the whole mountain, on the fertile *vega* (lowlands) that the monks' industriousness has wrested from the waves of the sea, which penetrate thus far up the river, and that now have been secured by dams and walls in such a way that whereas the floods come roaring in on the outside, inside there are vineyards heavily laden with grapes. To be banned to this place for a while, as occasionally happens to young people, must be light punishment indeed.

There are four small hermitages in the woods. But there are no actual hermits here. It is solely the monks wanting to retreat to undisturbed meditation during Lent that lock themselves away here; and they only leave the hermitage to fetch wood from the forest. This desire for seeking to exchange the deepest solitude for an even deeper one seems strange enough; but never will this desire be greater though than among those that are condemned to live their life in a dense and never-ending community with the very same people.

The monastery is surrounded by cypresses, aloes, and a few date trees—charming strangers that I was thrilled to see again after a long time. For these plants are unusual in northern Spain as even oranges only survive in some rare and favorable places. Oranges and citrus groves, aloe bushes, palm trees, and thickset cactuses only begin toward Cordoba, beyond the Sierra Morena where snow is no longer to be seen. There is a Moorish tale that King Ben Aceit of Seville had the mountains covered with almond trees for his wife, a Castilian princess, in order to give her the pleasant illusion rendered by the white perianth as she longed for the snow of her rougher, yet much favored home.[1] It is peculiar that it is at the most northern part of Spain at Santoña, between Bilbao and Santander, that a lot of citrus and orange trees thrive shielded by a small hill whose fruits are sold in Bilbao. That also for the rest Bizkaia should not be characterized as rough comes to the fore in its *txakolina* [*chacolí*], which is a splendid wine if made with care that could rank midway between Champagne and Moselle wine.

While riding up the Somorrosto I rested at a small mill, of which there are many in this country. Visiting this mill was to widen ones understanding of all the various kinds of human existence. On the wide field with four narrow walls and a roof riddled with holes, a whole family's sleeping and living space in one, a wide gap instead of a door, the stables

---

1. *El Conde Lucanor, compuesto por el ecelentissimo principe D. Juan Manuel hijo del Infante D. Manuel y nieto del Sancto Rey D.* (circa 1330), truly a sourcebook, yet full of naive and flimsy tales, and peculiar wisdoms.

for the goats and mules and a double millstone. Right upon entering one stumbled across the fire place, a kneading-trough stood opposite it and a cupboard with all sorts of old pieces of equipment. The stables adjacent, farther left one of the two millstones was turning, next to it a few steps lead up to the freestanding conjugal bed and the places for the children to sleep with the other millstone right next to these, and some sort of scaffolding made up of poles above the stables that lead to the attic. And it is in such housing that humans lead their life, are born, and die in it!

Hearing that the Somorrostro is taken to be a mountain that according to Pliny[2] rises up steeply where the ocean washes against the coasts of Cantabria and apparently consists of iron one would expect a peak such as the Serantes or the mountain standing opposite, the Pico de Muñatones. However, the Somorrostro is not even one single mountain but in actual fact a range of mountains where no peak really stands out between the others. There is a valley between them that actually bears the name and there is a village at the end of it called S. Juan de Somorrostro. The mountain only corresponds to the descriptions of the Roman explorer of nature in so far that it is so ferrous that at several places the ironstone lies directly under the black earth. The more correct assumption is that Pliny did not mean this mountain at all, but rather one on the same coast but farther toward Santander, the Cabarga.[3] Supposedly his descriptions seem to fit this mountain far better, but I never saw it myself. The Serantes and the Muñatones do not contain any ironstone.

Situated as it is and neither cultivated nor covered with bushes, the Somorrostro may not be ranked among the more charming areas. Its gloomy and barren heights, where the eye can merely distinguish the redly shimmering footpaths of miners and muleteers, have the sole purpose of serving as the antithesis to the beautifully cultivated and delightful plains of Barakaldo and Lutxana, even if seen from as far as Desertu. Despite all of it, there are some good pasture grounds on the bare heights of the Somorrostro and there are traces everywhere of mines that were designed throughout various ages, in fact the whole mountain has been rummaged. Most of the mines are located on one particular level called Triano; individual parts have individual names; the royal mines for instance are called *Minas de Janizuela*. It is right in their midst that Mr.

---

2. *L.34. c. 43. Metallorum omnium vena ferri largissima est. Cantabriae maritimae parte, quam Oceanus alluit, mons prearupte altus, incredibile dictu, totus ex ea materia est. Cf. also L.4. c. 34.*

3. Florez, *Espana sagrada, v. 24. Discurso preliminare*, p. 17.

Pensel from the Bayreuth area has his lonely home in a small caldron of rocks up on that level. Yet his isolation is compensated by a marvelous view from the upper story of the lowlands, a part of the sea, and some grotesque-looking rock formations in the vicinity. These royal mines have only been in existence since 1792 and their purpose is to produce the necessary iron for the ammunition foundry at Santander. As it had been supplied with enough stock to last some years, there was no mining going on while I was there.

It is well worth seeing the additional mines here as well for their distinctiveness. According to Bizkaian law, every native Bizkaian can start digging as long as he leaves ten feet between his and his neighbor's mine. If one digs underneath the other and is ahead of the one above, the higher one has to yield to the other. If one leaves ones mine unused for more than a year it becomes ownerless.

As much as these laws appropriately reflect the maxims of the simple constitution of this small land, in which everything seems to be geared toward personal liberty, they are just as damaging to the mining industry. Also, one can assert with confidence that nowhere else has a richer mine been ever built so badly. As anyone could get in the others' way at any time and thus frustrate one's efforts, no one dares to invest heavily. Moreover, the whole point of this form of mining is to produce at the smallest possible cost enough ironstone for the worker to make a modest daily wage.

Nowhere is mining carried out less skillfully than here. Peasants who have absolutely no understanding of it, who have never seen anything beyond their mountain, who are so little to be called artisan miners in that they not even distinguish themselves by the right clothing, choose a piece of land by chance, dig a hole, cut into the ironstone that they find beneath their hands with a pickaxe, and once they have worked it for some time and the pit becomes too deep for their comfort or the waters become too powerful, abandon the place and make a new hole just as unskillful as the previous one. They do not come even close to considering setting up ordinary shafts with traps, much less carefully quarried adits. The only piece of machinery they put to use is a wretched pump. As unbelievable as it seems, they use oxen to remove the ironstone. They tread through a burrow, often very steep coming in and out, with a basket (*rastro*) into the mine, and one has to admire their patience, strength, and dexterity. Where it becomes too steep, several people just hand each other the ironstone in hand-baskets. The gathered ironstone is heaped up in front of the mine on a flat place (*rastrero*) where the rough and finer pieces are separated by men and women with a rake. The rough ones are carried down to the rivers by carts or mules where they are hoisted into boats and brought away by water; the finer ones are delivered overland by mules.

It would be simple to give the mountain's water a natural outlet by digging an adit underneath; subsequently, one could dig deeply undisturbed. Because the workers here shy away from taking any measures that do not yield immediate returns, they commence their digging from above and then move diagonally into the earth. As they do not care to secure their tunnels with struts, the soil often collapses and many workers die. Mr. Pensel has often had the occasion of having to rescue these unfortunates and it was only recently that he succeeded in freeing ten of them at once.

As so often in production, it is the merchant who has the real advantage in this branch of Bizkaian industry, the middle man between the miner and the ironworks. The former would seldom get more than 45 piastres for a boat load (*barcada*) of 225 centners, calculating with 100 pounds per centner. The transport costs about thirty though, the extraction of such a quantity from the mine twelve to fifteen piastres. Therefore, the mineworker is often left with a mere pittance at the end of the day. Often the workers join together and own the mines themselves. When working for a day's wage the man is paid five *reales* (eight gross and eight pennies at the Prussian exchange rate).

It would be pretty accurate to estimate that about nine hundred thousand centners[4] (at one hundred pounds) are loaded aboard per year; it is difficult to give an estimate for the finer ironstone as such is transported overland. This quantity is produced by about 230 workers and the number for its transport is not much less for which they also depend on children as I saw girls aged seven to ten that all by themselves led mules down the mountain to the boats. Mining is carried out only for six months, though, from May to October; by discounting the Sundays and festivities that fall into this period, there are 140 work days. For each centner (according to local standards, namely 150 pounds) of ironstone that leaves the province (for royal use being the exception) the government is paid a duty of (*recargo*) of 25 *maravedis* (1 ¼ gross). Sales to

---

4. For a more accurate calculation one would have to add 4 9/16 p.c. to this sum in order to arrive at our Berlin weight as the Pound in Bilbao is this much heavier than the one in Berlin.

Gipuzkoa and toward the mountains of Santander were down during the war and the prices were lower for shipping was blocked on all sides.

By the way, there are two kinds of ironstone here, one white with a ca. 80 p.c. yield and a black one with a mere 40 p.c. In Biscay they refuse to process the former, though, because they deem it to be of inferior quality.

The ironstone that they produce is commonly referred to with the truly Latin term *vena*.[5]

Also in the Somorrostro is the ancestral seat (*solar*) of the Salazar family that is so famous in Spanish history. It is the most mighty castle or *casa de bando* as it used to be referred to in the Middle Ages when Biscay was torn apart by several factions—there are still remnants of it in the land. Today the castle belongs to the Mazarredo family that the last daughter-heir of the Salazars married into as I already mentioned above. In the fifteenth century Lope de García de Salazar lived here, who had no less than 125 children, 120 natural ones and 5 in wedlock. His personal history had been written by his son, it remained unpublished though. He was so unfortunate as to quarrel with his younger son to the extent of forfeiting his liberty and ultimately his life. Having set up a majorat which favored his firstborn, the younger one tried to seize it for himself; he overpowered his father and locked him into a tower of the castle in which he perished out of despair and grievance.

---

5. Plin. l. 33. c. 40. *Romam perfertur vena signata.*

Portugalete, Plentzia, Bermeo, and Mundaka

I traveled through this part of the coast quicker as I was already familiar with the customs of this land and it therefore had less interesting things to offer. For the same reason, my readers, too, will not need to dwell here for long. The Ibaizabal feeds into the sea at Santurtzi [Santurce], beyond Portugalete, making it a large, picturesque bay. There is a sandbar at Santurtzi that often puts ships at peril and a village called Algorta opposite. The bay is surrounded by the mountains Serantes and Muñatones on the Santurtzi side; the shoreline opposite consists of a row of white and craggy chalk cliffs that end at the Galea Point (*la punta de Galía*).

The river has well preserved quays on both sides.

Portugalete is a small, rather badly built town. It mainly lives on the up and offloading of the incoming and outgoing ships. The pilot that comes to the assistance of a ship in trouble receives a double bonus. It is for this reason that they often hasten too quickly beyond the sandbar and drown.

When I was ferried over the Ibaizabal close to the estuary at Portugalete during the evening to reach Plentzia [Plencia], the sea was very rough. The sea was completely black, but white foam danced on the rims of the dark waves in parts and in between them I saw the white sails of the fishing boats shimmering through.

The road to Plentzia goes through Algorta, first through the sands of the shore, then overland. The only things I noticed on my way were the mountains of Unbe (*las peñas de Umbe*), which are a range of rocks with many gashes and rugged edges in the middle of the land. Besides Monte Candina, which you can see already from the Somorrostro and that I spotted behind me at sea, there are the mountains of Santoña that stand out like large foothills and obstructed any farther view toward the west.[1]

---

1. Publisher's note: Mount Candina and the port of Santoña are in Cantabria, to the west of the Basque Country.

Plentzia is small, yet it has, perhaps more than any other town in the region, a clean and amicable appearance. It appears especially nice from the hills before it. There is a bridge across the river bearing the same name that runs into the sea at the town.

On the way from Plentzia to Bermeo one must traverse two high mountain ranges, that of Lemoiz [Lemóniz] and that of Bakio; between these mountains a little stream flows down into the sea. There is hardly a more cumbersome and dreary route to be found anywhere else in Spain; one barren mountain backs behind the other, without any houses, trees, or fields, merely fit for pasturing. It is only where here or there the lonesome path winds down into a small valley that one can spot the familiar country houses surrounded by trees and fences made of vines.

The sea, which one always continues to see from above, was marvelous on the day I took this path. It was on a May day with fog and alternating showers of rain, intermittently the sun would often bring forth the most magical illuminations. Soon all the mountain tops were dressed in a thick, immobile veil, soon the fog would rush toward the sea and threatened to envelope me with its wet clouds. Suddenly the depths of the sea and the valleys turned dark and the peaks of the foothills reared their heads like shining islands. Then the fog would rise up again and the skies were laden with heavy and darksome clouds of rain that descended their wavelike edges down to the sea.

Halfway, right about at Bakio, there are the foothills of S. Juan with an island before it with the same name. According to what I was told by my guide, there is a hermit who lives on it.

There are the foothills of Matxitxako between Bakio and Bermeo confining the sea's shallow turn at Portugalete on the eastern side just as that of Santoña on the western side. For the mountains of Santoña, Cape Matxitxako, the island of S. Anton in front of Getaria, and the Higer Point, are the four most prominent landmarks that dominate the form of the whole Bay of Biscay and, in turn, divide it into three smaller and more shallow bays.

It was before Bermeo that I was fortunate enough to enjoy the sunshine. The ancient city with its black, sea-washed towers, the marvelous cliffs and small bays, and the pleasantly cultivated fields around the river that flows into the sea here, lay before me clearly and brightly. The sunshine that lit up the scenery was heightened by the shadows of the dark clouds that covered the western part of the skies, it was raining far beyond, and a splendid rainbow unfolded its glittering colors above the sea.

Nowhere can one overlook this as well as from the way from Bermeo to Mundaka, which is delightful and brief as a mere stroll. As it keeps running along between fields and vineyards, up and down, one oversees both, the larger bay of Bermeo and Mundaka, and the smaller one that is, again, formed at Bermeo with its bush clad rocks and small foothills with the most manifold views. From here it alternates between the most magnificent views and a full perspective of the sea and the sea looking through small openings between the rocks.

A small island called Izaro lies before the bay of Bermeo. Here once stood a Franciscan monastery, founded by Queen Isabella in 1500, which was later moved to Bermeo for the sake of convenience.

My garrulous muleteer, occasioned by the monastery, told me a Bermeo fable regarding the island. Allegedly, a monk on the island kept a lover in Bermeo and, as the island was not a great distance from the shore, swam across to her every night. For these nightly crossings she always held a torch out from her window. Once, however, the Devil lit the torch at a different, very distant location down the coast and the tricked monk drowned.

As I was struck by the similarities of this fable with that of the story of Hero and Leander, I inquired whether there exist additional tales of that sort. I came to know that many Greek fables resurfaced in Biscayan stories with only minor differences. The story of Polyphemus, for instance, called Gargantua[2] on account of his voraciousness. Also the works of Hercules and the fable of Deianira which is attached to the *Chomin sendo*[3] (the mighty Dominicus), and the tale of the golden fleece that is transformed into a shepherd's tale, and so on.

There is possibly no other people that has a greater taste for fables than the Basques. And a great number of them are exchanged among the people, and they even have different classifications for them. One of such is that of the Kobolds, *de los duendes*.[4] There is a well-known one that belongs here: *Santon bildurbaguea*, Anthony the Fearless. The Impossi-

---

2. The devourer, from *garganta*, the gullet.

3. *Chomin* [today *Txomin*—ed.], the Basque version of Dominicus, *sendoa*, the forceful.

4. *Duende* from *Dueno, Dominus*, Lord, is actually a house ghost. For *Duendo* means "part of the house," tame. Also in the Basque such a ghost is house-haunter, house-scare (unless the words *naspecha, icecha*, in Larramendi have not been merely invented by him). Perhaps the delineation of the word *Kobold* from *Kobel*, the High-German for house, should be preferred to the other scholarly contributions.

bilities, *de los impossibles* belong to a different class, as for instance the life story of the unborn and the like.

It would have been a great pleasure to have gained more knowledge about the people's tales. However, since they only exist in the mouths of the people, it would have required complete fluency and understanding of Basque and a longer stay to collect them from this source. Men, though, who are not part of the people, are unfamiliar with them or who have contempt for any engagement with them. Also, some of them assured me that their attraction is so closely connected with language that they lose all their charm in Castilian. Indeed, this is always the case with all folk poetry, to which fables belong as well in a sense, as they are the most natural and inherent expression of a national fantasy.

I doubt that one should be looking for half-vanished traces of an ancient common delineation in the similarities between certain Basque stories and Greek fables. It seems to me as though such similarities come about on their own, even in languages that are doubtlessly known to be related. The field on which tales-inventing fantasy bustles about, must in fact be the same everywhere, for it is the fantasy and the human passions and also individual locations on which certain fables (e.g., the story of Heros and Leander) recur and return to perpetually. The only thing the individuality of a national character does is that a people persists to remain in one part of the field while a different people dwells elsewhere in that field and the random multifariousness of the imagination regroups all possible combinations ever differently together over and over again.

Certainly it would be of interest to run through the whole domain of the fables and scrutinize it in this regard, even if only to hint at the hazy fringes of the cycle that the imagination wanders through. Moreover, by this we would again stake out the inherent areas of particular times and nations. For it becomes apparent that, for example, the Greek fables, the Eastern tales, and the knights' adventures in western Europe constitute their own, if large, class within which one can distinguish various finer nuances yet.

Mundaka lies at the estuary of the river that comes down from Gernika. It is an *anteigleisa*. Its delegates are the first to be called up at the assembly of the Bizkaian estates. The reason for this, however, is merely one of ancient tradition. For precedence holds no sway in these assemblies, the call occurs as a formality just as any other.

Gernika

A charming way leads inland along the river to this small town consisting
of a mere hundred families, yet well and cleanly built. First one passes a
mountainous and woody area that then opens up toward Gernika into
well-cultivated plains. The river is deep enough to carry barges laden
with wheat and ironstone to the city. During the time I spent in Gernika
I bore more than enough witness that it could swell up as much to even
threaten its own banks. In one night it flooded the whole area so terribly that the water stood at seven to eight feet high above the bridge so
that all communication with the neighboring towns was cut off. Stuck
in a wretched lodging house for three days my situation was less than
comfortable. Although I fortunately found a Don Quijote, which seldom
goes wanting in a Spanish Inn; alone, as I was given a very dark chamber
I had no other room to do my reading than that of the host; yet every
afternoon I was beckoned to move even from this and into the kitchen in
a polite yet no less pressing manner for his not-so-short afternoon rest.
Meanwhile, I used my time to become more accustomed to the Biscayan
constitution that has its seat and center point in Gernika as all public
hearings always commence with the words: *so el arbol de Guernica*, under
Gernika's tree.

For just as, as I have mentioned above, the boroughs of Araba had
convened on the fields of Arriaga until their voluntary dissolution, they
still to this day congregate underneath the tree of Gernika, even though
they hold their meetings not right there anymore, but in a chapel erected
right next to it. Nonetheless, they hand over their authority and always
begin their festivities underneath that tree. One would wish to see an oak
ample with leaves and dignified with age in a beautiful, unobstructed,
and rural place that would spark the reminiscence more vividly of the
times when the nation's affairs were dealt with in a simpler manner than
a mere family would be administered today. Alone, although one finds
a pretty large, yet not so picturesque holly oak with a cracked up trunk
twisted by the wind and some desiccated branches, an image, if one so

desires, of the constitution that, too, has defied several storms yet has been beaten down by them as well and has transmuted from its original state in more than one part. Younger trees have been planted next to the actual one to take its place as soon as the old one dies. Not one of them stands freely by its own as there is a form of stone barrier and a stage in front of them that one reaches by climbing a few steps. During the assemblies the persons who make up the government of the province sit here on a bench with seven seats separated by armrests made of stone. The *corregidor* takes the central seat, next to him on either side the two chief delegates, syndics, and secretary. The Castilian coat of arms is displayed on the tall, stone backrests in the middle and the Bizkaian ones are both to its sides, two running wolves with a cross covered with leaves behind them. On both sides and up front, these seats are surrounded by a parapet that has an opening opposite the *corregidor*'s seat. There is a longish rectangular square in front of it paved with ashlar blocks and four columns on it. These used to carry a roof under which the deliberations took place prior to the erection of the chapel.

Ferdinand the Catholic confirmed the privileges and rights of the Bizkaians by oath at this location and one can still see these festivities depicted above one of the chapel's entrances. The king is seated where now the *corregidor* has his place. His wife, Isabella, is among the women scattered around.

The chapel, or as it is actually called, La Iglesia Juradera de S. Maria la Antigua, was built close by; it has an elongated hall with three rows of seats plainly made of wood that are elevated behind each other and can seat about three hundred persons; it has two entrances, one on the short side opposite the altar, the other one at the end of the long side to the right of the altar. The hall is paved in red stone, one sees the rafters of the roof above and instead of ornamentations, there are very mediocre paintings of the former independent Lords of Bizkaia. There were only two among them that struck my interest: Iñigo Esquerra and his son next to him. The father has a wrathful stance and bears full armor as though intending to fence; the son is barefoot, in his shirt and grasping a spear with no spearhead. The account goes that the father had challenged the son to a fight and the son appeared in this way as though to show his innocence, but killed his father nonetheless. The delegates sit on the benches of the hall, the government is provided with a long table and chairs before the altar, the doors remain open and the hall is filled with listeners. They sit indiscriminately among the delegates; only the women have their place next to the door. The delegates from Mundaka alone take the higher seats as they are the first to be called, although they hold no specific right for it. The delegates wear no special clothing and one sees the old national rural garb mixing equally with those bearing our contemporary city dress in a colorful blend.

The archive of the province is kept in the sacristy. The oldest files, concerning the country's assembly, do not go beyond the fifteenth century. Since the noble Bizkaians share a disdain for the city life, the fact that the tree of Gernika—the figurative representation of the entire constitution, as it were—is to be found within the town boundaries, causes bewilderment. However, the place where it stands (that of the *anteigle-sia*) belongs to the village of Lumo [Luno], which lies on the mountain opposite; it is only because it served Lumo as some form of quarters or precinct (*barriada*) in ancient times, and called Gernika, the tree bore the same name, even before the construction of today's town.

Bizkaia was originally, and is still for the most part, a true free state of land ownership. Inasmuch as there existed a feudal constitution in France and Germany, they here had a free peasants' constitution; every *pater familias* was a free citizen, for everyone (just as today) took part in the election of the delegates that decided on the general matters of the land. Solely the city dwellers and artisans shared the same fate, like everywhere else, of being excluded by the dominant part of the nation. And just as it was with us the armored knight, it was here the landowner, proud of his isolated and independent mountain house. The cohabitation within closed walls and the engagement with sedentary work produced a sense of dependence that was equally abhorred by both. The Bizkaian landowner's true spirit of liberty becomes evident by the sheer isolation and dispersion of his dwellings. Driven neither by the fear of hostile attacks as in the rest of Spain, where a planning of open villages was rendered impossible by the continuous raids of the Moors and the fact that these required a solid location to which one could instantly rescue the goods and herds, nor by being subject to the will of a lord and crowded together with many, he chose his dwellings preferably where he had free reign.

Originally, the entire constitution rested exclusively on the inhabitants of the plains (*los moradores de la Tierra-Llana*), who constituted a separate party to that of the towns, only the *anteiglesias* sent delegates to the land's general assembly (*junta*); when a town caused offense to someone in their midst, they by law[1] joined to come to his defense, and to

---

1. *Fueros de Vizcaya.* Tit. 30. l. I. p. 167.

exchange ones father's dwellings in the country with one in a town was considered an ignoble, demeaning act. The unification of the *anteiglesias* and *villas* occurred merely in the last century, and it is only since then that the latter enjoy the same rights as the former and dispatch delegates to the assembly. Bizkaia's constitution is not as consistent as that of Gipuzkoa and fraught with far more exceptions. Already the way the province is represented in the *junta* is odd. For every town, whether it dispatches one or several delegates, whether big or small, has only one vote. Moreover, not all parts of the province have the same rights. The towns were incorporated only late into the constitution. Although the *Encartaciones*, districts beyond the Ibaizabal where Basque is no longer spoken, dispatch delegates to the assemblies, they enjoy neither active nor passive electoral rights, they can neither vote for a chief delegate nor can they be elected themselves. Recently, however, six of them were incorporated with the other *merindades* [districts] while the others refuse to do so for they would have to carry their equal share of the province's expenditures, whereas they presently only contribute a certain minor sum. The *merindad* of Durango was incorporated into Bizkaia only in 1631. It acquired two votes at the *junta* in return for a pledge to carry its share of the general dues in proportion to its number of hearths. But given the fact that it consists of eleven *anteiglesias*, it used the occasion to be taxed for a greater amount of hearths and thus demand additional votes; they acquired five in 1740. In 1800 it returned with a new demand claiming one vote for each of its *anteiglesias* with the aim of achieving equal status with the other communities of the province. They appealed to the burdens they had born during the last war, to the active service of their men bearing arms for the country's defense, and to the project of again revising upward the number of taxable hearths. The matter has not been decided though, but handed over to a commission that will address it during the next assembly.[2] The number of all votes in the *junta*, which, as seen, have increased from time to time and still can, was 107 in the year 1800. Should two delegates of the same place differ between each other, the place loses its right to vote for this particular time for the vote cannot be split.[3]

The general assembly is held every two years, in June or July. The masses of people that come together in spite of the minuteness of the

---

2. *Acuerdos de Juntas Generales del Señorío de Vizcaya celebrados en el año 1800,* p. 68, 73, 83.

3. One finds an example of this ibid., p. 85.

land and the extent of the patriotic interest in these debates renders this small Gernika a most lively and populated place during that time. The purpose of the assembly is twofold: the ordering of the communal matters of the land and the election of the chief delegates and that of other people for government. The issues to be debated are listed in the call for convocation (the *convocatoria*). They concern all that which regards the well-being of the whole province, the demands for voluntary duties on the part of the king, internal financial matters, the institutions for the public peace in addition to the land's police, the appointment of certain offices determined by the *junta*, the export of wheat and other commercial goods, the condition and maintenance of the clergy, and finally the claims of single municipalities and individuals directed at the province. The debate regarding all these issues is free throughout. There is, though, the disadvantage of disarray, as anyone without having been given the floor begins to speak from his seat and thus frequently there is more noise and confusion than tempered discussion. For the most part, after futile to and fro, the issues are handed over to a commission which then withdraws to the sacristy and furnishes an opinion that is subsequently put before a majority vote.

The election of the chief delegates is the *junta*'s last act. Its tenure runs from one General Assembly until the next, thus for two years. For this end, all towns of the province are allocated to two parties (*parcialidades*), that of the Oñacinos and that of the Gamboinos. This division stems, just as the names themself, from the time when the entire land disintegrated into factions that would never stop quarreling with each other. Either party chooses one of its own as a delegate, and all other elections are carried out in the same way, so that each has its own elected magistrates. This difference regards only the election, though, and has no bearing whatsoever on additional matters. The election is carried out in the following way. The names of all places that have a vote are put into a ballot box and three are drawn from it by a boy. These three then become the actual electoral towns and as soon as they are determined, the *junta*'s part in the process ends and the meeting is considered closed.

In the afternoon of the same day, however, the delegates of the electoral places assemble in the chapel behind closed doors, swear on the Bible to elect impartially and in all conscience, and then each put forward a subject aloud. For each electoral place has two votes that can either be given to one or two subjects. In the case that objections are raised against one of the proposed that in turn are deemed valid, this candidate stays behind; for the rest all the submitted names are put back into the ballot box and three are drawn from them. The first one will be the actual chief delegate for the next two years; the two others become his possible substitute.

The election of the other magistrates occurs in a similar fashion, and that of the other party is carried out in exactly the same way. The Oñacinos vote first according to tradition.

The chief delegates receive a salary that is so inconsiderable, however, that it does not even recompense them for the costs of the sojourn for those that do not generally live in Bilbao, yet are required to be there by virtue of their office. Upon termination of their office they are called Provincial Fathers (*Padres de Provincia*), by virtue of their office they keep a seat in the General Assembly, are allowed to join the debate—albeit not vote—yet they are even called up first at the convention. Furthermore, they are frequently used for the commissions. There is no estate that is excluded from the office of chief delegate and even merchants have executed the office in recent times.

In the time between assemblies they administer the matters of the province collaboratively and with equal rights and they, amid the syndics and the *corregidor*, constitute the actual government (*gobierno*) of the province. The syndics have at their side a *consultador perpetuo*—with a substantial salary; he is a jurisconsult and expected to always furnish them with his legal opinion. The *corregidor* is appointed by the king. Even though he has no vote in the debates of the government it is he who tips the balance in the case of a split vote.

Through this his influence becomes very significant, and the crown through him maintains sufficient means to push through its intentions. According to the law of the province, no royal edict (*cédula*) is valid that runs counter to the once granted liberties. This is expressed explicitly in Bizkaian law; any such ordinances shall be met with respect, yet not acted upon, and any judge that decides in accordance with it, even if renewed twice or thrice, shall be punished.[4] What has not been determined, however, is who it is that evaluates the ordinance. Once upon

---

4. *Fueros.* Tit. I, l, II, p. 20. *Otrosi dixeron: que avian por fuero et ley et franqueza et libertad, que qualquiera Carta ò Provision Real, que el dicho Señor de Vizcaya diere ò mandare dar, ò probar que sea ò ser pueda, contra las leyes et Fueros de Vizcaya, directe ò indirecte, que sea obedecida et no cumplida.* And at a different place, Tit. 36, l.3, p. 219, *y que aunque venga proveido et mandado de su Alteza por su Cedula et Provision Real, primera, ni seguenda, ni tercera jusion et mas, sea obedecida et non cumplida, como cosa desaforada de la tierra.* [sic]

a time it was the province; but the court sent an *Acalde de Corte* with a commission to Bilbao in the seventeenth century and changed this. Now, all ordinances go to the *corregidor*, who then informs the syndicus. The syndicus, in turn, sends them back together with his opinion that he always bases on that of his co-signing *consultador perpetuo*. On the basis of this opinion, the *corregidor* decides whether the ordinances shall be implemented regardless of the syndicus's objections, whether the implementation shall be adjourned, or whether they shall be rejected entirely.

The General Assembly, however, is dominated by an almost unrestricted freedom and a true sense of independence, and the presence of the *corregidor* does not hinder anyone from speaking his mind freely. At times it happens that he absences himself and often Basque is spoken, which he does not understand. At times he even dictates that the petitions are to be read aloud in both languages when the debates are of general interest. To refrain from curtailing the freedom of expression is a prudent and wholesome politics. By no means does this offend the pride of a nation; on the contrary, it substantiates the opinion of the old and less restricted independence, nourishes the more noble and higher character and patriotism, which springs from this sentiment and forfeits only little in terms of results. For when, as it occurs nearly always, the issue to be decided comes before one single commission it often acquires a different form than in general debate.

Meanwhile, as one has to admit to the honor of the king and his ministry, the Court wields its power—which is of course in its hands—at all times only with prudent moderation. Even still to this moment Bizkaia enjoys the most essential rights; one should only think that it cannot be taxed despotically, which becomes vivid in the fact that even today the voluntary donations demanded by the crown are rejected at times. Moreover, the Spanish government, one cannot repeat this point enough, will never gain as much through the expansion of their privileges over Biscay, as it would lose from a decline of patriotism and national spirit, which would be the inevitable consequence of any curtailment of Biscayan liberties. Small and only meagerly endowed by nature this distinct little land has no other riches but the amount and force of its inhabitants' character. Being courageous, entrepreneurial, and active at the same time and urged by the combination of a large population and the insufficiency of its soil's produce, they ever find new ways to affluence and fortune and they use whatever they acquire in the process for the improvement and beautification of their country. One man's example is the other man's spur to action and thus there is prosperity and comfort among all the families and greatness and splendor in all the public institutions. Should one ever uproot this sense of community at its core through the curtailment of its political liberties, one would take away from the Biscayan his idea that he is working toward the happiness and the reputation of a people that is secluded, left to its own devices, and inwardly focused; all this would crumble and all at once the province would be condemned to an existence of poverty and insignificance. It is above all for these reasons, not because of petty or selfish local intentions, that the enlightened and patriotic Biscayan is proud of his nation's privileges. Thus to assert such stands in good harmony with the large and lively support among all the truly patriotic Biscayans for the crown, which, should its Biscay ever count more than an insignificant strip of a mere few square miles of mostly mountainous and unfertile soil, has no other means at its disposal than to maintain the national spirit of the people through the prudent protection of its privileges.

A complete list of all Bizkaia's privileges is part of the *Fuero de Vizcaya*[5] that concurrently also serves as the nation's code of law. On April 5, 1526, the General Assembly of the boroughs decided underneath the tree of Gernika to review and improve their *fuero* as it in many regards required corrections and additions. For this, they selected fourteen delegates and assigned them with the task of drawing up a new *fuero* to be finished within twenty days. Indeed such did come to light in time and written down according to the suggestions of the delegates, among them the *corregidor*. As one has retained the form of simple narration of the procedure, it is for this reason that each law commences with the words: "and again they say" (*Otrosì dixeron*). It was then put before Queen Isabella for her confirmation, which she did in Aranda on October 14, 1473, by oath. This oath has to be repeated by each king and it is immediately the first law in the *fueros* that remarks on his duty to do so as soon as he reaches the age of fourteen and it threatens to retract their obedience should he not do so within a year. In theory the new king himself must come to Bizkaia and confirm by oath the liberties of the nation at several locations, among them underneath the tree of Gernika. However, ever since Ferdinand the Catholic no king has shown his presence

---

5. *Fueros, franquezas, libertates, buenos usos, y costumbres del muy noble, y muy leal, Señorío de Vizcaya, confirmados por el Rey D. Philipe Quinto, Nuestro Señor, y por los Señores Reyes sus Predecesores, Impresso en Bilbao* by Antonio de Zafra. 271 pages folio.

in person. One of the main points of this oath is the promise to never sell off Bizkaia, either in its entirety or some place within it, to give it away as a present, or any other form of divestiture; and in Isabella's oath she credits the Bizkaians that they always remained loyal to the Spanish crown even when Henry IV had been so bountiful with the royal lands as to sell off several Bizkaian towns. In fact, the simple language with which the kings in former times straightforwardly confirmed the services of the provinces is touching. Ferdinand the Catholic mentions all the estates specifically, and does not even forget the women and children, and admits that they had done more than they were ever bound to by virtue of their privileges.[6]

All disputes between Bizkaians are to be settled based on this code of law—of which it is specifically noted that it has been conceived according to principles of fairness and common sense rather than legal subtleties[7]—and all additional laws of the kingdom are only to be consulted in a subsidiary manner; and this occurs not only in the land itself, but also in the highest courts of Spain where the trials are carried out in the last instance.

The privilege of the Bizkaians that is highlighted the most in this body of laws is their accepted nobility, for many of the other privileges are based on this. All Bizkaians, it is said, are aristocrats, of noble origin and of pure blood.[8] Who descends from Jews and Moors, or recent converts, cannot buy into Bizkaia or become naturalized. Foreign merchants that wish to take residence in Bilbao must therefore show proof of their family and are thus frequently met with difficulties. In the case that a Bizkaian moves to another Spanish province it suffices for him to dem-

---

6. *(El Rey) dixo: que juraba y jurí, que por quanto después que Su Alteza reyna, veyendo sus necessidades, y la guerra injusta que los Reyes de Francia y Portugàl contra su Real persona y sus Reynos han movido, los Cavalleros y Escuderos, y Hijos-Dalgo y Dueñas y Donzellas, y Labradores y cada uno en su estado de los Vezinos y Moradores deste Condado y Encartaciones y Durangueses, con gran amor y lealtad le avian, y han servido, y seguido, e sirven e siguen, e poniendo sus personas, y caudales, y haciendas a todo reisgo y peligro, como buenos y leales, y sinalados Vassallos y con aquella obediencia y fidelidad y lealtad que le son tenudos y obligados; y aun de mas, y allende de lo que sus fueros y Privilegios les obligaban y apremiaban. Fueros, p. 230. [sic].*

7. *su fuero, el qual es mas de alvedrio que de sotileza y rigor de derecho. Fueros, tit. 36. l. 3, p. 218.*

8. *todos los dichos Vizcaynos son hombres hijos-dalgo y de noble linaje et limpia sangre. Fueros, tit. I, l. 13, p. 20.*

onstrate his origins from this province in order to enjoy the common, yet as mentioned above, not very significant noble privileges.

From this general privilege follow some personal privileges for the Bizkaians as for example that no one can be arrested because of debt,[9] that except for a few crimes[10] not one of them may be tortured nor threatened with torture,[11] and that the properties of a criminal that lay in Bizkaia may never and under no circumstances be confiscated for the benefit of the crown or the state, but must always go to the natural heir.[12]

More important, however, are those immunities that have immediate consequences for the whole nation: exemption from taxation, freedom of trade, and a particular jurisdiction for all Bizkaians.

In terms of actual duties the king merely collects some insignificant rent and interest from certain properties that go a long way back.[13] For the rest he merely receives voluntary donations and there are examples even in recent times, as mentioned above, that he has been denied even these.

The freedom of trade is unrestricted and it is owing to this that Bizkaia can benefit from its advantageous position by the sea in such a fortunate way. The same extends to buying and selling in the villages and towns inland.[14] In the event that two-thirds of a borough comes to agree to procure bread, meat, wine, and so on from certain privileged vendors only, they are free to make such arrangements as well.[15]

With regard to their own jurisdiction, no Bizkaian may be brought before a court outside of Bizkaia in the first instance for any crime (aside from a few) or for any debt.[16] Yes, even if he has taken up residence in a different part of Spain, the only judge he must accept as legally binding is the chief justice in his chancellery in Valladolid.[17] The obligation for general mobilization upon a royal summons has retained its old character of

---

9. *Fueros*, Tit. 16, l. 3, p. 95.

10. The exceptions are the crime of heresy, lese majesty, counterfeiting of coins, and sodomy. Ib. tit. 9. l. 9.p. 66.

11. l.c. and tit.1, l. 12. p. 20.

12. Ib. tit. 11, l, 25, p. 88.

13. *Fueros*, tit. 1, l. 4, p. 15

14. Ib. tit. 1. l. 10. p. 20.

15. Ib. tit. 33. l. 4. p. 192.

16. Ib. tit. 7. l. 1-4, p. 47-51.

17. Ib. tit. 1. l. 19, p. 27.

former times; however, such can be regarded as more than an immunity as they are freed from any forced military service in times of peace. The entire squad fit to bear arms must follow the king without pay. But such an obligation extends only to a particular, specifically noted location in the code of law (*fasta el Arbol Malato que es en Luyaondo*—"as far as the Malato tree, which is in Luiaondo").[18] Should they be required to do service further away, they must be paid for it.[19] Similar remnants of older customs can be found in other parts of the legal codes as well. For instance, when a person is killed by another the relatives of the slain have the right to pursue an orderly accusatorial process against the murderer, they can also, however, pardon him and thus save him from any punitive action; even when more distant relatives intend to take additional legal action. For the law states specifically that the right to press charges or to pardon lies firstly with the ascending and descending line, the uncles and their sons, and only in lack thereof with other, more distant relatives.[20]

Regarding the distribution of his estate after his death, the pater-familias has undisputed authority and he may leave his entire assets to one of his sons and even among his daughters and needs only to compensate the others with any piece of land, however meager it may be.[21] This right is indeed applied rather frequently and the beneficial ramifications this has for the land cannot be ignored. The estates are not subdivided, the cultivation of the land does not suffer, and the excluded children are urged to seek their own maintenance according to their own industriousness.

---

18. Publisher's note: That is, Araba.

19. Ib. tit. 1, l. 5, p. 16.

20. *Fueros.* tit. 11, l. 24, p. 87.

21. *apartando con algun tanto de tierra, poco ò mucho à los otros hijos ò hijas.* Ib tit. 20. l. 11, p. 116. tit. 21. l. 6, p. 125.

Return to Baiona via Lekeitio, Azkoitia, Azpeitia, Hernani, Oiartzun, and Irun

With Gernika I regarded my journey through the Spanish Basque Country as finished and hastened to find a short way back that was not overly devastated by the flooding.

Between Errenteria and Gernika,[1] which lay opposite each other on either side of the river, the water was still too high, even on the bridge, to ride across without danger. A tall strong man whom they had sent from Errenteria to meet me had to wade through the water chest high, and a mule could have easily slipped and fallen off the narrow bridge whose railings had been ripped off. I therefore chose a detour through an area where the waters had already dispersed.

From Errenteria to Arteaga[2] the road leads through pretty land, abundantly filled with houses, brush, and vineyards.

Behind Arteaga toward Ereño, one ascends into the mountains that soon enough encircle the small plateau of the first village. The church of Ereño makes for a gauntly sight, at a considerable height, built tall of dark blocks of stone, opposite a bleak and bare rock. Beyond Ereño one loses oneself in one of the biggest and most picturesque mountain forests. The path, one of the most beautiful I can possibly recall, always leads over considerable heights, in the shade of oaks and chestnut trees, of unfathomable height and multifarious shapes. One looks down onto the smaller mountains that are all shaped pyramid-like and onto the basin-like valleys they form from the center of which yet another peaked mountain arises. Moss-clad rocks loom through the brush everywhere, rolling down, some of them of incredible size they lay there one by one and scattered in between are, albeit sparingly, rural dwellings, free pastures, and well-cultivated lands. One sees in the distance the location of

---

1. Publisher's note: This is Errenteria in Bizkaia, not Gipuzkoa.
2. An oak glade in an adjacent forest of oaks, *encinas*, Basque *arteac*.

the two small harbors Elantxobe [Elanchove] and Ea between Mundaka and Lekeitio [Lequeitio], which is the only place on the Biscayan coast I did not visit. In front of the former appears Mount Bandera,[3] the former lays in the opening allowed by this one and the mountain at Ispaster. I found traces of devastation caused by the flooding along the whole way; sown fields that were torn away, completely submerged roads, the reconstruction of which occupied half the towns, pieces of earth that had tumbled complete with trees and brush, drowned snakes, cats, and other animals ousted from their hiding places by the floods. The skies were covered in gray clouds after the rain that had endured for several days. Only in the evenings did a dimmed and melancholic light appear. The air was still and humid, and not a leaf stirred in the thick woods—a solemn silence of nature following great devastation. Just a few minutes before its setting the sun emerged after all enveloped in rubicund clouds. I was just riding up the long ascent behind Ispaster and relished, often looking back, the romantic sight of the plateau of the village amphitheatrically enclosed by mountains in addition to the deep forest valley to the side from which the trees loom up from the joined waters. In front of me lay the mountain's barren stone cave whose natural reddish color advanced to become truly purple by the rays of the parting sun. The sun disappeared as I was approaching the summit; it began to rain warmly and quietly, and as soon as I had crested the mountain I saw the surface of the sea as a vividly drawn line that was separating the gray of the clouds from that of the skies; an unfathomable gloom-evoking sight; masses so great, so still, so one-dimensional, and colorless. It was nearly night when I arrived at Lekeitio upon the descent from the mountain.

The morning that I spent there ranks among the most enjoyable mornings I can remember. Was it the contrast between the previous dark days of rain and the now returning sun with all its delight, or did the subject really correspond to the impression I had of it? In short, to me Lekeitio seemed the most friendly and vivacious little town on the entire Bay of Biscay. The view from the upper watch tower (*atalaya superior*) at the foot of Mount Otoio [Otoyo][4] is wide and majestic. It takes in the bay from Cape Matxitxako to Higer Point and a few marvelous

---

3. From *bandera*, banner, because the burgees of the harbors are set on this mountain. Publisher's note: As Unamuno also notes, this is an inaccuracy. The mountain he is referring to is Ogoño. There is a Monte Banderas in the Lutxana neighborhood of Erandio, nearer Bilbao.

4. Mount Linden from *ota*, linden tree, and *oyana*, heights.

points that normally do not meet the eye are the mountains of Ea and Elantxobe. The island of S. Nicolas lies before the town's harbor, which forms a finely encircled bay capped off by Cape Karraspio. A hermitage that had stood on it had to make way for a fortress in the last war.

One glance on a stroll here in the morning shows the whole existence of this little town, which really should be called a fishing republic as everything in it lives off fishing and all that relates to it is carried out upon joint consultation. At the break of dawn two signal givers (*señeros*) go to the small watchtower close to the harbor (the higher one is half an hour away) and examine the weather and sea. They do not let any fishermen out when it is stormy. When there is hope for the day, the female callers (*muchachas llamadoras*)—girls whose task it is to waken the fishermen—assemble, they consult once more, and then send out the girls, some twenty in number. Now a cry rings out through all the alleyways of the town: *levanta te en el nombre del Dios!* Get up in the name of God! The fishermen and their helpers come together, the boat owners now discuss among each other, and the majority of the votes decide whether to sail out or not.

Then it is time to visit the harbor where the sale of the fish caught on the previous day and the casting off for the new catch puts everything in motion.

The sales take place on the boats themselves and the buying girls wade from one bark to the next in the shallow water with baskets on their heads. Meanwhile, the men hoist the nets into the boats. The purchase of the large ones (*trainas*) is very expensive and the boat owner thus leaves his helpers only half of the catch and keeps the other for himself. As soon as everything is in order, they cast off and race each other rowing courageously with high hopes for the day between the island and the shore and the small barks sway with incredible speed upon the backs of the uprising swell. Once they reach the level of the island, they disperse throughout the entire bay and now everyone from along the coast intermingles on the free surface of the sea that has no concept of ownership. They would seldom exceed four to five nautical miles on the open sea, though, and each town easily recognizes its own. In the moment a storm threatens, they make smoke on the watchtower and upon this sign everyone immediately returns either to their own harbor or to someone else's, the first they can possibly reach. Hence, all inhabitants on the coast of Biscay live off the very element that is the main source for their subsistence in constant and uninterrupted contact with each other.

As a consequence of the flooding that had ruined the usual road, I was forced to make my way to Mutriku across the highest peaks of the mountains. I was amply compensated for the toilsome climb, though, by the marvelous views of the sea on one side and of the lovely valleys toward Berriatua and Markina on the other.

The highway between Mutriku and Elgoibar was so devastated that the day before I made my way, right opposite the monastery of Sasiola, a muleteer and his four mules had fallen into the Deba River, turned into a torrent by the rain, and drowned.

Behind Ondarroa I reentered Gipuzkoa and the forest road from Elgoibar to Azkoitia is milder and more pleasant than most of the other areas in rougher Bizkaia. Only the Izarraitz range along which I rode for a long time is a steep, bleak, and high face of rock, full of marble quarries, but on its steep side mostly without vegetation. Azkoitia and Azpeitia are the most vivid examples of Biscayan affluence. A mere quarter of an hour from each other and connected by a continuous stone footpath for walkers along the Urola River, they seem to be one town. Each has a large parish church filled with splendor and the architecture of the houses, the cleanliness in the streets, the nicely designed squares, everything bears witness to the abundant income of its residents. But both are mere farm towns, if surely in the most fertile part of Gipuzkoa.

Also here they lament the pernicious damage to the commons that are detrimental to the woodland. One sells too swiftly when the borough is faced with financial need, waste and theft are caused by improper husbandry and lack of supervision, there is not enough replanting. Patriotic men have made suggestions against these malpractices, although to date without the desired success.

Between Azkoitia and Azpeitia a former Jesuit college, S. Ignazio de Loyola, known for the splendor of its building throughout Spain, is situated on a plain from where one can enjoy a nice view of the rock face of the Izarraitz and the fertile banks of the Urola. I wish not to dispute the splendor; in fact every traveler will remain full of admiration for the marvelous play of colors of the local marble, with which it has been so lavished and which comes from the neighboring Izarraitz quarries. Yet at the same time he will regret the absence of taste and style of architecture. The proportions have no simplicity and greatness, perhaps the cupola could be found best but also here just as the rest is overladen with embroideries and scrollwork. Moreover, the building is still not finished by far. Ever since the expulsion of the Jesuits who had intended to give this institution great influence and importance as mostly older ones came here toward the end of their lives, no one has set hands on it and everything still stands and lies around as when they left it. Now the king has given it to a Chapter of Premonstratensians who had been chased away from their residence by the French in the last war. The silver statue of the Saint had reached safety in Castile at the time.

The most peculiar of all is the still standing part of the Saint's house, where one can still see his chapel, and where the front side of the new building has been added. It is a tall, yellow painted house with small windows and interrupted ornamentations that carry on underneath the window in long stripes. This is where this wonderful man lived, who in most peculiar ways coupled the bizarre ideas of the aristocratic spirit of his time with religious infatuations. He could have hardly envisaged just how sizeable and powerful the order he had founded would become and thrive.

I took an isolated path from Azpeitia to Asteasu that is normally only used by smugglers and a few other country people. It is a wild path across the mountains with the thickest forest with magnificent mountain streams rushing through. In terms of houses there are only a few hostels to be found—*ventas*. The highest is the one of Iturriotz[5] behind which one can oversee the entire land to the estuary of the Orio, Donostia-San Sebastián, and the sea.

At Villabona I rejoined the normal king's highway from Madrid on which the stretch from Hernani to Oiartzun is undeniably the most beautiful part.

I now came upon a ferry where the former bridge had been torn away by the waters some time before. Because of this ferry a conflict had once ensued between the residents of Donostia-San Sebastián and Irun that did not go without bloody heads. It was on the occasion of the late King of Tuscany's trip to France. Both wanted to ferry over the king; but both did not get what they had intended as the king chose a neutral fishing bark that was at the river bank by chance.

---

5. Cold spring, from *iturria*, a spring, and *otza*, cold.

The French Basque Country

Just as one refers to the French and Spanish Basques with two different names (Basques and Biscayans), one also has different notions of their character. The French Basques are lauded, and rightly so, for their strength and their physical adroitness, a high degree of warm and lively imagination, a continual pursuit of great ideas that are often distinct and caricatural, a tender sensitivity that is always in action and easily evoked, and a sense of freedom that runs counter to all social coercion. At the same time, however, they have been reproached for their character being one of rashness, for having an uncurbed passion for leisure, and for being so inconsistent with their interests. In contrast, the Biscayans have a more steady reputation among their compatriots and neighbors. No one would ever question their physical adroitness and strength, quickness of the mind, and a noble sense of freedom either, but, in addition, they are considered to be a superior, more industrious nation, persistent in keeping with their plans, and always readily available to accept necessary enforcements.

In fact, they constitute an independent people of their own, they occupy a land rendered remote by the sea and mountains, and they have yielding sources of earnings and wealth, and form a state in the strictest of senses. The French Basques, in turn, are just a minor outlandish tribe of a people that is superior to them in every way. Their land is poor, consisting mainly of pastures; and even if they used to enjoy exclusive rights prior to the Revolution, such would be a far cry from a constitution of one's own and an independent state. Moreover, the national spirit in France had never been as divided along provinces, as is the case in Spain today. Also, the French Basques tend to be judged vis-à-vis the French, no matter of the fact that they would inevitably fail to live up to any comparison in any regard, while the Biscayans in turn are judged vis-à-vis the Spaniards, whom they quite evidently outclass in many respects.

Meanwhile, all these factors still fail to completely explain the phenomenon. To be sure, the Spanish Basques are more slow-paced by nature, more heavy-handed, their features express less agility, less finesse, less spirit and imagination; and yet it seems as if they have retained more solid and more clearly discernible traits in which the character pertaining to both comes to the fore more forcefully and in a fashion that is more straightforward. Thus the differences seem to lie deeper, if not in the actual organization. As thin as the partitioning wall of even the largest of mountain ranges may seem when speaking of spirit and character, one does not know just how important it may be to live on one side or the other. And just as the occupants of the French side distinguish themselves by a more vivacious serenity, the valleys and the ridges of the Pyrenees on the French side, too, have a more cheerful and friendlier aspect. Yes, the dialect of the French Basques itself (which evidently extends to Navarre) has more charm than that of Gipuzkoa and Bizkaia and is more pleasing, at least to the foreigner who shows a degree of interest for the nation's language, in that it is easier to understand. When the Basque character is added to the French (as experienced in persons that have been formed by literature and company) it gives the latter an allure beyond description. It pours the glaze of imagination over their minds and sentiments, and seems to make them rise toward evermore independent ideas, it re-evokes the natural sounds in them while bearing the tint of the large natural objects, the mountains and the sea, and the simple conditions of a poor people, pursuing mere farming and livestock; and yet, at a closer look, just as much or maybe more, one might even feel cheated out of attaining a real sense here of the actual content of the character's simplicity.

The differences between these two parts of the Basque nation, torn apart by mere coincidence, vanish into the dark at once, however, as soon as one likens them to their neighbors, the Gascons and the Castilians. With tribes that have no literature of their own, some not even their own language, and that have not trod the stage of history, at least not individually, in any remarkable way, it is not possible to demonstrate actual evidence of their characteristics; one can merely report one's own observations and, subsequently, invoke the approbation of past and future witnesses. I believe that every attentive traveler will find a greater independence of mind, a more visible display of passion, a more solid content of character, and more forceful expressions in the physiognomy amid the Spanish Basques vis-à-vis their French neighbors. And as soon as the traveler steps into Castile after Vitoria-Gasteiz, he will miss the serenity and the ever active glee, of which the Castilian seems incapable. In turn, the Basque lacks his impulsiveness, and, although strong and agile, his phantasy is less deep and staggering than what the Spaniard stores in his dark eyebrows alone, and what one can tell from his sparkling, mostly down-cast gaze. The Biscayan is more sober-minded than his southern neighbor, and if he could draw on a national poetic heritage, it would hardly enrapture the sentiment and imagination as the Spanish one does. Even the female sex has, as mentioned above, something dry, stiff, and severe in its facial features and stature, and one would come to find single elements of beauty in a face, rather than an actually graceful or voluptuous guise. The foreigner can detect surviving traces of a certain roughness in the French Basque, Biscayan, and Castilian. Amid the Biscayans, one would want to call such a roughness good-naturedness and ascribe it to a mere lack of formation; in the more passionate Castilian it easily takes on a higher, yet more frightening character, the cause of which I do not believe to be remnants of Moorish blood, as purported by Spanish authors. Rather, I believe it to be the effect of a region neglected by nature, an adverse climate with extremes in both directions, political and religious pressure, and finally, perhaps, also the wild and uncomfortable life to which the Castilians, more than any of the other occupants of Spain, had succumbed to on account of the Moorish wars, having been defeated so often, yet never dominated completely and for long. I prefer to interpret the roughness of the Basques, bearing a lighter and more gracious character, as that of the wild savage loathing all social coercion. But all Basques, if in varying degrees, and regardless of their dissemination across various dominions, conform to a real sense of freedom, a noble national pride, a longing for each other, they share a great love for order and cleanliness, serene joyfulness, and a physical and intellectual strength and agility, rendering them a keen, able, and ever inventive mountain people. Given that all classifications of this kind depend on their relation to their respective point of reference, one could perhaps characterize them best as a southern mountain people while being the northerners of a southern country.

I wish to add though that it would be presumptuous to infer the variant origins of the southern French, the Basques, and Spaniards from their differences in character. Having been separated for so many centuries and living in so many different areas, these modifications have developed gradually over time. And irrespective of this and without wanting to render my final opinion on this matter at this point, the ancestors of the Basques could have easily lived in Aquitaine or Castile, nonetheless, and their descendants may well have made up a considerable part of these provinces' current population. The identity of a tribe can never be proven with certitude beyond the identity of its language and the only thing that one can undoubtedly and without contest conclude from its appearance and examination is the fact that all Basques constitute a nation and that the similitude of their character traits, on the whole, may be derived from their shared origins.

National characters develop by the fact that the manifold influences of the climate, lifestyle, constitution, customs, and such are fixated individually by reproduction; nationally by the people's solidarity with one another, further intensified when set against a foreign people; and dynastically through language, by keeping to one uninterrupted line even in the face of continuous change. It is this sole principle with its three equally fundamental factors that provides the explanation for the consistency of certain national characters, notwithstanding their very different environments, climates, and locations.

Among the Gascons, especially in Baiona, the large group of French Basques shares the very same fate that every smaller group persistently seeking detachment experiences when subjugated by yet a larger group. They are called thievish, deceitful, and cowardly, and only daring whenever they can assail their enemies unseen. One is warned of traveling to the peaceful and solitary valleys of Uztaritze, Buigney,[1] and so on as though it were a journey into the wilderness. Fortunately, these opinions are not shared by the nation's enlightened parts and any truth to their cunningness and skullduggery may be explained by the fact that the Basques (above all the French Basques) are quick and versatile rather than big and strong, and that they, being a small mountain people, always had to fight against superior enemies. In addition, as they live on the border today, they are cajoled into making a business from smuggling by the unhelpful restrictions imposed by the very states themselves.

Inasmuch as the three parts that make up the French Basque Country, Lapurdi [Labourd], Lower Navarre, and Zuberoa [Soule], were less conjoined than the Spanish Basque provinces, they nonetheless enjoyed quite different privileges as compared to the rest of the French provinces. They had their own assembly of the estates, each and every one paid only minimal taxes to the government; and the additional privileges the

---

1. Publisher's note: As Unamuno also comments, there is no record of a Buigney Valley. Possibly Baigorri (Baigorry) is meant, or Bigorre, which is not actually in the Basque Country.

aristocracy and clergy possessed were quite insignificant. It is also for this reason that the French Basques had greeted the Revolution far more coldly than one would have come to expect given their sense of freedom. In fact, they could only lose from being made equal to the other citizens having previously enjoyed privileges that took precedence over the others. Moreover, their properties diminished on account of the new legislation as the lands no longer fell to the eldest son, but were divided among all children and thus ended up fragmented.

In Lapurdi, the boroughs elected their own syndic who answered directly to the government even if the intendant of the province functioned as the intermediary between him and the court. All of the voters belonged to the third estate; nobility and clergy were barred from the election. Their gatherings were called *Biltçarreac*,[2] the gatherings of the seniors. They were also in charge of assessing taxes, and although all tax was property tax and although the nobility did not even come close to possessing one-eighth of the lands, they were assessed with one-eighth of all the taxes nonetheless. Moreover, they were given no feudal privileges in recompense for their greater tax burden. As this small land, upon the recommendation of Vicomte de Guitane, had given itself up to the crown voluntarily, it merely paid fifty-two francs per year in the former times, and still no more than two hundred at the end of the seventeenth century. Even in recent times, it was taxed only moderately in relation to the other provinces. Stamp tax had been introduced a mere twenty or thirty years before the Revolution. In Lower Navarre, all three estates took part in the communal assemblies. But the commoners had a veto in all country's financial matters even when the nobility and clergy were in agreement with each other. The privileges normally reserved for the nobility, such as the right to bear arms, hunting, and so on were granted to everyone as well.

The written body of laws in Zuberoa, *les coutumes de la Soule* (it was drawn up in Gascon, that of Lower Navarre in French) comes right to the point by listing the main privileges of the province. Every resident, it says, is free and the land is a free land; everyone may marry as he sees fit, enter the priesthood, or emigrate from the land; everyone has the right to bear arms; every borough may convene as often as the management of their matters requires. In Zuberoa, too, all three estates had the

---

2. *Biltua*, to gather. *Çaharra* (Gipuzkoan *zarra*), old (man). Publisher's note: Today *Biltzarrak*.

right to attend the general assemblies; the clergy, however, forfeited their right gradually as they increasingly ceased to make an appearance and the nobility stayed behind alone among the commoners. Whenever they could not agree, it came to the king to decide.

Given that the French Revolution has made all these individual constitutions tumble, it would be of little use to further dwell on a discussion of them.

I first strayed off to Itsasu [Itxassou] via Uztaritze. The French Basque Country can be neither called beautiful nor picturesque, unless one cuts to the mountains. It has for the most part a rather barren and harsh appearance. Although the individual farmlands and gardens are worked with the care and cleanliness that is so typical for these people, the French Basques mostly live on cattle breeding rather than arable farming. Therefore, they leave a lot of their land to mere pasturing; in addition, they are also far more prone to merrymaking than the Spanish Basques. Thus one finds long stretches of nothing but heather (*bruyère*), which after cutting is spread and made to manure. Even the most industrious farmer may not fence in his part of these lands without the borough's permission for this would reduce the livestock's communal meadows. I do not recall having seen any single houses, whether isolated in the field or in the mountains. But the houses of the villages are scattered, and form incredibly long roads that are always interrupted by gardens and fields. The road from Baiona to Itsasu does not leave the banks of the Errobi very often—a mountain stream that unites with the Atturi at Baiona.

One has the view of the Pyrenees in the distance. Larrun and Mondarrain,[3] a pointy yet, as it seems, not very high mountain, are the most striking features.

There are large subterranean caverns in these two mountains, but especially at the foot of Larrun around the villages of Azkaine [Ascain] and Sara. An eyewitness told me the following anecdote about them. He was on the hunt for woodpigeons when his dog went missing. After searching for it for a long time and having called and whistled for it here and there, he suddenly heard it barking far below in the ground. He could not fathom just how the dog could have possibly made his way down there, he whistled again and he heard his dog respond yet its barking came from many directions and far away. He concluded that

---

3. *Monoa, munoa, montoa,* elevation, hill, *arria*, stone, stone mountain. Publisher's note: Also known as Arranomendi.

there must be a large subterranean cave and indeed, he finally discovered a very deep hole that descended vertically into which the dog, fortunately without injury, must have fallen. Once it became clear to him that he would not be able to rescue his dog without further help, he returned home to fetch a basket and let it down into the hole on a rope. He recounted this tale to his grandfather, a man as old as the hills, but he only shook his head doubting the rescue of the dog. And why? was the question—Why? Because entire villages exist in the mountain villages underground? Why sure. I have often been told this by the old people who had heard it from their people who in turn had heard it from theirs. Our forbearers had constructed underground caves when the Romans tried to subjugate them—which they never succeeded in doing—in order to rescue their provisions, their sick, their old people, women, and children. This is what the people say about these caves; underground granaries are nothing uncommon as it were, especially in Italy and Spain, even if popular belief may have exaggerated in terms of their size and age. Albeit, the dog was rescued in the aforementioned way, regardless of the old man's doubts.

The hunt for wild pigeons (*palombes* or *ramiros*) I just mentioned is carried out here without dogs, and in a most peculiar way. In some distance from each other they erect three or four structures that look like scaffolds, each of them consisting of thirty to forty foot high rods put together pyramid-like with a basket on top. One reaches them by climbing up a rod with pegs fixed to it. Such a structure is called *pentière* in the Gascon dialect (as this form of hunting does not appertain to the Basques). One sets them up about fifty feet from a row of trees and in a parallel line to them, with nets between them. For the catch a person climbs into each basket of the *pentières* and the others hide in small huts next to the trees from where they pull down the nets with ropes. Once a flock of pigeons approaches, the people in the baskets throw pieces of wood at them from above; the poor animals, startled and perhaps under the impression that birds of prey are shooting down upon them, flee toward the ground and toward the trees and most of them fall into the nets in such quantities that one can catch as many as a hundred and more on a single day.

With its scattered houses Itsasu fills a small valley surrounded by mountains. The vicarage I stayed in lies directly opposite the more romantic side of the valley, a narrow gorge from which the Errobi, coming from Baigorri [Baigorry], emerges with a great roar. Next to it are two mighty mountain faces, in front of which stands Artzamendi,[4] a mountain full of sharp and steep cliffs. A gentle slope covered in heather and overshadowed with chestnut and walnut trees lead from the house to the church, and in front of its windows were a few rows of beautiful and tall poplars.

Even if I have not much to say about the days I spent in these peaceful lodgings, these memories will never die in my heart. The owner of the house, an honorable old man, had handed over his parish to his successor after fifty years of pastoral care executed with steadfast loyalty to end his days in peace and quiet up here. His parishioners however continued to hold him in high esteem and gave their love just as much as before. Only shortly before I was there, they had leveled the somewhat steep ascent in front of his house by their own accord as to make it more accessible in respect of his aging vigors. He had been their incessant benefactor and councilor throughout the whole time of his office. For it is custom among the Basques to involve the priest in all the more important civil matters of life and thus his tasks becomes so multifarious that he can hardly find the time to manage them all. The customs of the Basques in this area are more patriarchal, and are much closer to the original state of society; and even today remnants of the former rawness and savagery are vivid. It is no more than 150 years that—according to old Harambillet (the old man's name)—the priest of Artzamendi carried a rifle over his shoulder to church, and about 100 years ago, one was shot at right there in his own house.

Never have I ever sensed a more amicable, undisturbed serenity in an old man, such willingness to instructively discuss and examine even that which went way beyond the confinements of his limited life, such cordial sympathy for innocent entertainments, in one word, such a sense of real indulgence and true humanity, than in valiant Harambillet. Of course, among all things it was his nation that took his interest and just about anything that had to do with it. He would enter a surge of emotions when he spoke of it, its former glory and its language, and it was touching to listen to him lamenting its gradual demise, he who himself was already with one foot in the grave.

---

4. I wish to point out for those that are thinking of the Old German *hart* or *harz* [Transl: German for resin] in conjunction with this mountain's name, that I have not detected any trace of the original word's stem. *Artza*, in Lapurdian *hartza*, however, means bear and this word seems, just as the Irish art, to belong to the same word stem as the Greek αρχτος.

He visibly enjoyed reminiscing about old songs he had learned in his youth, could sit there for hours with others trying to remember half-forgotten airs and stanzas, and always and with fine judgment knew how to distinguish the true intonation of the people from later imitations that had been tainted with other languages. Alas, his memory had become so faint that he would only manage to recall the initial words and at best their melodies.

One of his favorite pastimes was etymology. According to him the small area of Lapurdi did not get its name from *lapurdia*, a horde of bandits, but from the four rivers that provide it with water: the Atturi, Errobi, Urdazuri, and Biduze [Bidouze]. The name is composed of *laur*, four, and *ura*, water, stream, and the "b" in between has been placed there merely for reasons of melodiousness.

He has his own opinion about the etymology of the name of his place of residence. It is striking that Itsasu lies inland and *itsasoa* (also *ichasoa*) means sea in Basque. Harambillet surmised that the Errobi, when it first flooded, formed a lake in this narrowly enclosed valley that appeared to be the sea to the first arriving dwellers. I, on the other hand, thought that its name has to do with the location of the place being enclosed by mountains and thus thought it derived it from *ichi*, to lock in. Whatever we thought, a more knowledgeable linguistic approach has led to the simple meaning "cluster of houses." For *ichea* is frequently said instead of *echea*, house, and *tsua* is a common ending of adjectives that can mean a lot of things. Similar compositions of words are *Ichagoya*, housetop, roof, *Icharguia*, house light, window, and other villages in Biscay, too, of which I know that they do not have such an enclosed position, are called Itxaso [Ichaso], Itxasondo [Ichasondo], and so on. The similitude of the name with that of the sea is therefore either coincidental, or stems from an even deeper underlying etymology, but this is not the place to go into it any further.

Unlike many, the old man's passion for his derivations did not blind him however. He proved this to me just before I took my leave. I had already bid my farewell on the previous evening as it was my intention to ride off early in the morning. He came to me nonetheless as he wished to warn me for my future endeavors. We have, he said, etymologized a lot during these days and you have applauded many of my derivations. But do not trust them too much. I could not fall asleep last night and thus tried to derive from the Basque the names of all the Kings of France, from Clovis down to the Bourbons, and I must say that I managed quite well. It seems that one often just finds whatever one puts into it in the first place.

How fortunate it would be for me and my readers if I could give the impression not to have forgotten this honorable old man's warning!

The minor, yet rapid Errobi River accompanied me from Itsasu right into Lower Navarre toward a copper smelter that used to be quite impressive, but, as it had been destroyed by the Spaniards during the last war, it has only recently been made to run again; it is simply called the *Fonderia*. The multifariousness of this splendid road is beyond description. On both sides of the Errobi, other, smaller mountain streams fall into it, each one forming its own valley, and there are sweet plains surrounded by mountains where they meet. The mountains wonderfully covered, lush meadows in the valleys and on the plains, and everywhere there is mountain water and springs that seem to emerge bubbling from underneath the wanderer's feet; soon splashing down foamingly from the heights above, soon smoothly floating through the meadows and fields. The mountains are laden with rural dwellings, and here too, the houses of the villages are scattered around widely; and here and there a half-ruined tower sticks out among them on top of a steep rock.

Nearly everywhere I went, I found the peasants occupied with the cultivation of Turkish corn. This labor (*artojorratu*)⁵ makes for the main part of Basque agriculture, just as corn, aside from chestnuts, makes for nearly the only form of nourishment amongst the Lower Navarrese. This is often mentioned in proverbs, songs, and tales.

Corn is sown rather spaciously. In the space between, which is usually hoed, they plant beans, turnips, and other vegetables; they work

---

5. *Artoa* is now called corn, and corn bread in contrast to wheat bread *oguia* [today *ogia*—ed.]. Originally it meant all kinds of grain. The similarity with *artos* becomes immediately obvious; it is likely, however, that both stem from the term for plowing, tilling, Basque *areatu*, Greek *aroun*. Just as in Irish *araim*, to plow, and *aran*, bread, and in Gaelic *aradh* and *aran*, with the same meanings. In Gothic, *arian*, to plow, *ar*, grain. Confer what I have noted about the derivation of *areatu*, *arare* on p. 81. [A:C: here p. 172–73]. Should this be correct, the term that determines these words, i.e. that of orderly and artisan labor, carries the very vivid yet abstract image, that of linear rows of furrows. *Arare* originally meant to work, yet not merely with force and power but with diligence and order (thus the terms deriving from *ars*, in Greek *arete*), *artoa* meant grain that was gained solely through craftsmanship and industriousness (indeed, our rye and wheat is edible only if not taken from the wilderness), moreover, *artoa* and *artos* meant bread that was made exclusively of artificially produced grain. The very fact that the field is worked with the sweat of one's brow and arable farming is the first step of civilization is deeply embedded in language. The Basque words *pamichia*, a kind of small and thin bread, and *pampuleta*, a round bread, show that the stem of *panis* is not foreign to Basque either. *Oguia* appears not to be related to any other word stems common in other languages.

every piece of the field with such diligence and neatness that it resembles that of a flower garden. There are various ways of eating the corn. In some areas they make a mash of it and they either eat it fresh or bake it and cut it into pieces. In others they make bread out of it. As this always remains solid, moist, and cakelike, they eat it seldom as we do our bread. Instead, they cut it into thin slices, roast them on the fire, and sometimes cover them with ham. This is then called *chingarra*. Sometimes, they take a piece of corn bread, heat it on the fire, add cheese to it, and knead it into a ball in their hands. Such a ball is called *marakukia* and commonly part of their breakfast. These taste not bad at all, but a lot depends on the hands that make them. As long as the chestnut season lasts, four consecutive months that is, this fruit is the only food that the Lower Navarrese eat in the morning and in the evening. For lunch they will have a soup of beans, without any fat, but with a lot of red pepper. Meat, with the exception of ham, and wheat bread can only be seen in the houses of the wealthy.

I do not think I have ever seen chestnut trees as they are here. They come close to oak trees in size and their stiff roots, manifold intertwined, lay on the rocky ground like labyrinthine veins intertwined with each other, and calk themselves into the cracks of the rock.

In Lower Navarre and the little land of Lapurdi I noticed an odd way of boiling milk. Instead of putting it on the fire, they throw glowing pebbles into it. It swells up at once and acquires a burned taste, but the people seem to love it.

The serene morning I traveled on the romantic road to the *Fonderia* was followed by a dark and gloomy evening. Clouds had risen from all sides and almost the entire sky was covered when I rode across the mountains to Orreaga [Roncevaux/Roncesvalles]. I reached the pass to the mountain range just before sunset, between the Mizpira [Mispira], or Mount Medlar, and the Meharoztegi [Meharosteguy]. The sinking sun still illuminated the farthest horizon and right around it ran a narrow white belt that gave me just enough light to see the distant mountains. The Errobi Valley and the forests of the lower mountains were magically illuminated, just like decorations in a theater. But as soon as the sun had moved behind the farthest mountains, I was enveloped by a thick fog. No longer could I discern a thing, if only the closest items around, high trees, pieces of rock that would suddenly stand before me dark and gauntly. The muffled sound of the bells of the grazing beasts and the calling and whistling of the shepherds came across. I had to ride on for several more hours before I reached the abbey.

I admired my guide's skill, a young Basque, to find the little used footpath, which often went over grass without any visible trace, in this impenetrable fog. In his red jacket and wearing a flat Bearnais hat,[6] a cane in his hand, he walked in front of my mule with his body tilted forward and his head upright, and he followed even the faintest sound and paid attention to every ever so insignificant mark of the road.

So we continued to climb considerably higher, in part over free pastures, in part through thick beech forest. We reached the Spanish border at the highest point. The chapel of Ibañeta stands here right on the ridge of the mountain just like a saddle—a place I got to see the following morning yet again. The mountains send their springs to both sides toward the ocean and the Mediterranean from here. Only the walls have remained of the chapel, for it was destroyed during the last war.

I went to Orreaga to see the relics of Orlando and the battlefield that so many sing about. Both, however, are not worth the toilsome way. The battlefield is a plateau between the abbey and the Spanish village Auritz [Burguete], about half an hour away. The remnants of this mythic knight are kept unceremoniously in a high and firm vault of the church and consist of a large, broken stirrup, two clubs, two pieces of his broken horn, and the golden wreath that was carried in front of the army in battle. The French took the sword with them during the last war. The clubs are straight, have the same width at the top and bottom, and are about one arm in length; a chain of four to five rings hangs from it and a heavy iron ball with several edges is attached to it. Down below, the club has an iron ring functioning as a handle. Every year a solemn requiem mass is celebrated in memory of the soldiers killed in that battle. The market is held at this place on the same day and everywhere there is merrymaking. Dancing is not allowed, though, as the austere residents of the abbey will not have it.

A dark, yet marvelous beech wood led me down the mountain to Donibane Garazi [Saint-Jean-Pied-de-Port]. The often snail-like way changed its scenery from one moment to the other, but stays equally romantic and wonderful; trees striving toward the clouds with trunks clad in moss, wild masses of rock piled on top of each other as a result of numerous thrusts and covered abundantly with bush on each level;

---

6. Publisher's note: In his Spanish translation, Unamuno makes the point that in his 1799–1800 diary of a trip to Spain Unamuno had also referenced this hat, which in Unamuno's opinion clearly refers to the Basque *boina* or beret.

a roaring torrent deep down in the valley, countless springs that hasten toward it from high above roaring and foaming; long trains of donkeys and mules with their drivers in a great rush and scuffle.

There are two roads to Donibane Garazi, one across Oritzun [Orisson, a district of Uharte Garazi/Uhart-Cize], the other across Luzaide [Valcarlos]. I chose the latter. The main king's highway from France to Spain used to go via Donibane Garazi and Iruñea-Pamplona.

Donibane Garazi, with its black tower and its rectangular citadel can already be seen in the distance. It lies right in the middle of a wide plain, yet encircled by mountains everywhere, the high ones toward Spain, the lower ones toward Baiona and Donapaleu [St. Palais]. The Errobi originates in this plain at the point where three minor mountain streams meet. The look of the people is just as pleasant as the location of this little town. It suffices to see the Lower Navarrese parade in their clean and elegant garb, in their white stockings, linen trousers, and vests of the same color, a red sash and jacket, their cane and their flat caps of cloth, to understand that they are a cheerful, always serene, good-natured people, yet prone to merrymaking rather than work. Their gaze, their posture, and above all their gait shows bold and powerful nimbleness. The ease with which they are able to acquire cash money by selling of livestock—they live off the breeding of livestock alone—without any noticeable decline in earnings, fuels their rashness and their inclination to amuse themselves. For the most part they sell their livestock, mostly mutton, to the Bearnais, who, being more industrious in comparison, fatten them up and sell them on.

The inhabitants of Zuberoa, the last of the Basque lands on my way are quite different to their brothers. They refer to themselves as the Italians among the Basques, believe they have better taste and more refined than their compatriots, and they have a distinct proclivity for poetry and music across all social stations. It is a shame, though, that their creative imagination, almost by necessity, expresses itself as empty dalliance and mere poetic babble, based on the fact that they lack any interesting national features. What is even a greater shame is the fact that the Zuberoan dialect is far more intermixed with foreign words than that of the other Basques. Although their pronunciation is soft and has a musical ring to it, it lags behind in terms of power and expression, especially on account of their consistent conversion of the *u* into *ü*. Indeed, as much as the inhabitants of Zuberoa are dedicated to their nation, they would even shy away from marrying someone from Bearn, they should be regarded as a transition from Basques to Gascons, or, should one want to focus more on character than geography, to Provençals.

Zuberoa is the only place where Basque theater is still performed on a continuous basis. They are called *pastorales* here, but they are not necessarily bucolic poems; in actual fact they deal far more with so called state-actions, with kings and emperors. Orlando's deeds often play a big role in them. The actors are young people of both sexes who for the most part are unable to read; they are instructed by people called *Instituteurs des acteurs de pastorales*, who are normally peasant, though. The teacher is, according to true ancient custom, in most cases also the author of the piece. They perform in the open, in Maule, the main town, usually in the main square, an avenue of tall Linden trees providing shade. The performance is part song, part recital; entry is free to everyone and foreigners, to whom the Zuberoans are generally most obliging, are given the first seats. Impromptu rhyming about any conceivable topic is also not uncommon.

The cultivation of land in Zuberoa is carried out with distinct care and order. The cornfields are gracefully set out and resemble the form of a garden plot. This is the reason why the views across the amply vegetated plains from the Citadel to Maule are most marvelous. There is a beautiful waterfall on the bridge of the city. A stream comes crushing down through two mills into the Ühaitza River [Gave de Saison], which cuts through the plains of Maule before uniting with the Atturi.

I laid my eyes on the mountain ridge of the Pyrenees and the snow-covered peaks of Jaca for the last time on the road between Donibane Garazi and Maule. I bid my farewell to the Basque mountain valleys when I left Zuberoa; and while I contemplated anew the various categories of characters of this small people, yet furnished with so many nuances within, I believed to have discerned the remnants of a great nation; a nation that possibly used to own the lands on either side of the Pyrenees and perhaps even farther, on this and that side of the Alps, from where they were driven into the mountains, the only remaining place to provide them with sufficient shelter. The brave and powerful, yet raw Bizkaian and the delicate Zuberoan, in which the spirit of the Provençal troubadour seems to have reawakened, speak one tongue and are merely separated by just a few days' journey; districts that are close to each other refer to the same thing with different names, which nonetheless belong to the same language; virtually neighboring towns can only understand each other with difficulty and yet recognize each other as brothers belonging to one and the same nation. Names of mountains, rivers, and towns that are obviously of Basque origin have survived on the distant shores of Spain, France, and Italy from one dynasty to another. Does it take more to prove that Basque tribes used to occupy vast stretches of land, but time after time, were driven back from all sides, and in the end have become neighbors with peoples from whom they used to be separated by vast spaces?

This certain, if dark voice in history must not go unnoticed. But whoever wishes to go further and explore the where, the when, and the how, encounters a silence and he merely hears the empty echo of his own question calling back at him.

Announcement of a Treatise on the Basque Language and Nation, Amid an Outline of the Perspective and Content of the Same

When deciding to describe a single isolated tribe, that is the Basques, in all detail and minuteness, inasmuch as the available auxiliaries allow, I was led by the demands that in my opinion have to be put to a certain, most necessary treatment of world history (as such a treatment will undeniably leave room for, indeed require, covering various angles).

The human race is divided into nations, tribes, and races; inasmuch as the individual is autonomous and free wherever he is conscious of his own will and his ethical independence, the whole race belongs to nature akin to plants and animals. Race, from which the human descends, the soil in which he originates, the air that he breathes, the area that surrounds him, the skies to which he looks up, all affect his original natural qualities and their development. One tribe is more fortunate than the other; and the most sublime and beautiful that old and modern history presents in terms of national development is not only the fruit of effort, diligence, education, but also the natural product of a fortuitous tension, a sensation and intertwining of the mind's and sentiment's forces. Whatever point in time one intends to look at over the ever uninterrupted, hastened course of coexisting nations, they always tend to wander, detach, unite, mix, and die out, physically through real demise or intellectually on account of degeneracy; they make for new room or reappear in changed form. Yet every advantageous feature, from whatever side it may have been attained, continues to have an effect. It is also a conquest in the area of what presents itself in the actions of mankind; and it is thus that new forms of human society emerge in continuation, which, more or less perfected, keep supporting and benefitting each other.

No less, it is the duty of world history to take this perspective—one that views the human race in terms of its original *division*, mainly caused by physical nature (mountains, seas, rivers)—compared to one that explores each of the grand events and moral transformations that are geared toward the *unification* of the smaller masses and aspire to link the moral existence of all mankind to an ever-more elevated telos. It is not the place here to discuss just how these fertile, in a sense, dual approaches must engage with each other. We are speaking here of merely one aspect of world history, that of tracing the multifarious kinship of nations and races, their mutual effect on each other, their process of refinement and degeneracy, and thus the activity of nature itself. In ceaseless industry nature brings forth ever new creations, it is to directly focus on the human being and the greatness of the idea taking shape within it, to consider the human race as an enormous plant that in changing directions, sprawling parasitically, stretches out around the Earth's surface, and joyfully shoots up wherever soil and sky smile at it, yet for the rest crawls along lowly; and inasmuch as its roots trust the soil, it is freshened and warmed by the dew and sun of a different, higher world. To thus tie the human race directly to nature and, in return, nature to ideas—as both are subjugated to the realm of organic life. And may this stir up the thought in everyone's bosom and fruitfully upheld until the deed: from whose fathers do they sprout and what children and grandchildren will the presently living leave behind.

For the end of a world history, however, we must work ahead in various ways, especially though with precise, detailed, and true descriptions of single tribes—something we hitherto still lack almost completely. Given that the differences between nations come to express themselves most distinctly and purely in their respective languages, the study of the languages must be treated as converging on that of the customs and history. As much as valued contributions have come forth in this regard in recent times, the unified study of language and history has yet to come a long way before it achieves a satisfactory degree of perfection, yes it has not even arrived to a point where the treatment of one particular aspect in this field could be substantially facilitated by some leading, general hypothesis. We still lack a clear basis for determining the degree of the kinship of languages, there is still too little agreement about the signs that prove the shared genealogy of the various peoples; far too often do we still satisfy ourselves with the fragmental comparison of single customs and a few words randomly ripped from a language; there are still too few facts in this boundless field that could serve as reliable points of reference and comparison; our conceptions are still too flimsy of how a nation's language is at once standard and a means for its formation for us to thus recognize the merging of the studies of language, history, and ethnography for the end of attaining knowledge and honoring the human race. Such a study would have to be the sum of a great—in races, tribes, and nations divided—enterprise, bound by the laws of nature and unalterable principles, and yet determined as it were by its own liberty—like a new field that if at all has only be seen from afar, fleetingly crossed, and only now becomes acceptable to be worked on.

I refer to the aforementioned shortcomings not as a reproach for others, but as a preliminary excuse for the work that I have carried out myself. For where everything is most closely connected to each other, it is impossible even to describe one particular tribe in a precise manner, let alone assign it its right place without comparing it to others. But how much is such a comparison further complicated by the fact that, as far as I know, there still exists no other complete examination carried out with a similar scope, there are not even any language studies that could be utilized in preparation for such a comparison. On the contrary, one is always referred back to the raw material, to language books and dictionaries that were devised for utterly different ends, attempts at general philology that cannot go into detail, to etymological works whose authors have often worked without any clear foundations deploying their more or less limited supply of knowledge with great arbitrariness, or indeed referred to a few historical studies—even if these have often valuable and even exquisite remarks, hypotheses, and systems strewn throughout them.

By attempting to submit a single, yet complete description, a real *Monograph on the Basque Tribe*, I will aspire to transcend these obstacles and spare mentioning the far greater obstacles I find within myself as this would prematurely anticipate the reader's judgment. I will endeavor to portray the Basques in detail according to their customs, their language, and their history to which of course belongs also an examination of the indigenous people of the Spanish peninsula, thus enabling me to decide on the question of whether they constitute a separate tribe or whether they are merely part of a greater one. Moreover, to classify them as the one or the other within the family tree of all tribes, in so far as such a thing is ever possible.

However, above all I will direct my attention to providing the materials so completely and arrange them in a most general way and with as little prejudice as possible so that should my own classification cast any doubt, others could carry it out differently, in any case, however, with the help of the delivered facts. Thus I flatter myself to think that this text will always have the merit of being an auxiliary, which, given the shortcomings of that already printed, will be difficult to come by any other way, and render futile any attempt to carry out yet again a work that has already been done as is so often the case in philological studies in which several people work on them one after another.

That it was of the Basques that I chose to make my subject was a matter of coincidence. My trip to Spain had given me an interest in the nation and the land; both became, in a most literal sense, dear to me when I carried out my own journey to Biscay and the Basque districts and spent several weeks in the most remote mountainous areas. Subsequently I was ever so drawn to the particularities of the language, the people, and the land that I continued my studies with lifeless aids. Indeed, in line with the aforementioned purpose, the Basques are a most interesting subject to examine, even if they have melted down to a rather small heap and even if they did not spread out in former times (as did the Germanic peoples, Slavs, and others) and broke apart into different branches. It is also for this reason that I would not dare to call them a family of tribes as compared to a mere tribe. In geographic and historical terms, they constitute an almost closed, separate entity. As certain as it is that they were powerful and widely dispersed within the Pyrenees, we have, in my opinion, no reliable records of how they possibly also played an important role beyond them. Everything that made them great and interesting, when looking back, is the perdition of their nationality, and even that of their language can be predicted with near certitude. Regardless of the current scarcity of this people, the language has possibly retained the same range of vocabulary and variety of forms that it used to have. For a start place and family names, which have remained wonderfully untouched and pure and are for the most part easily comprehensible, have conserved many roots that are more or less foreign to today's usage of the language. Given that each farmstead carries its own name, taken from its position or its surrounding trees or plants, the entire land becomes a living record of language. Therefore, all questions that one could put to the richest and most complete languages with regard to their structure and nature can also be answered with regard to Basque. It is also here the case that there are just about enough—and then again too few—exhaustive, preliminary studies to warrant the possibility and necessity of a new study. The Basque language is of such wonderful and distinctive construction that most of its earlier scholars have denied any similarity with other languages; it seems to bear the character of a language that became divorced from its sister language in the earliest times, was then later spoken by many and numerous tribes, only to end up driven into those few lonely mountain valleys bit by bit and yet to such a degree that the large number of the language's multifarious forms and signs stands in no relation to the limited number of families that use them. Thus the language is most noteworthy in two ways: for the study of languages in general and for its bearing on the ancient history of Europe. The difficult question concerning which people inhabited Spain and Portugal first, which ways they had taken to arrive there, which forms of amalgamation or division they may have undergone, will by necessity shed some light on the original population of France and a part of Italy; the opaque and still not sufficiently solved problem of the Celtic family of tribes, its main seats, migration, and remnants; Basque and its relation to Gaelic and the so-called Cymraeg [Welsh], and several other uncertain matters of this kind are closely related to this present study and can, in parts, only be solved through a more detailed explanation of the Basque language. Finally, Basque serves to delineate many words in Western European languages. In addition, it is such an essential auxiliary for the study of the sources of the Spanish language that without any knowledge of it, any etymological study would be outright impossible.

Now in order to arrive at the overall purpose guiding the mentioned approach in my text, I will divide it into three parts.

I

In the first part I will convey the remarks that I recorded during my sojourn in the Spanish and French Basque Country and I will make an effort to provide the reader with a vivid understanding of this little land and its inhabitants. This is indeed necessary in order to truly understand much of what concerns the language—as the customs of the nation and the locality of the country are interwoven into it; but it is also interesting in its own right to transfer oneself right into the middle of a bustling nation full of courage and talent, one that inhabits the north of a southern country and the mountains of a coast, thus likewise mountain and sea folk. Moreover, this nation's character unites a multitude of traits that one encounters one at a time, a nation that when I came to see it still had a free constitution and a federal state divided into many small localities yet again divided according to individual local customs. In this way, they often reminded me of the small free states in ancient Greece. In order not to impair the form and vividness of the account, I will keep to the format of a very short travel account that gives consideration to the smallness of the country and the short length of my wanderings.

2

The second part will offer an analysis or a deconstruction of the Basque language, accompanied by an appendix of Basque language examples from the oldest times, from when we still have monuments until this day.

To this end I will seek to present, as much as possible, a short but systematic and exhaustive method and to leave as far as is feasible no aspect untouched that could serve as a point of comparison. In addition, I will try to give a complete understanding not only of the Basque's grammatical, but also its lexical structure; at first only the relation of all the parts of the language to each other, followed by the overall language in how it functions as a means of presenting its object of reference, to examine that what is to be depicted (even though this can never be separated from the reference itself). While doing this I will consider as many languages as possible in view of making this adopted method more widely applicable and, by this, attempt to suggest how all languages, bit by bit, could be similarly dissected for comparative use and subsumed in a large, general *language encyclopedia*.

I have been carrying with me for years this idea for a project—obviously one that can be executed only in collaboration with many others but that nonetheless requires one person for its instigation. Albeit, with the subsequent improvement of others—and I will therefore treat the text on the Basque language with that in view and as a contribution toward it.

Regarding the general focus on the whole language study, may I add just a few words about the kind of language dissection that I have in mind.

One can take it as a reliable principle that everything in language is based on analogy and that its structure is an organic one, right to the minutest details. It is solely in cases where a nation's language formation suffers disturbances, when a people borrows language elements from another, or is forced to use a foreign language, either completely or in parts, that there is an exception to this rule. This seems to be the case for all languages known to us today—given that we have been separated by chasms from the original languages and original tribes, from whence there are no more records to help us across—and even in the deepest woods of America will you hardly find a tribe that still has a pure and unadulterated language that has come into existence prior to any adoption of another language. A language begins its assimilating activities at once whenever it integrates a foreign element or intermixes with another and instantly aspires to transform bit by bit into the other's idiosyncratic analogical forms, yet as much as possible, those contents that lose out during the intermingling. In consequence, even though shorter and longer analogical sequences evolve, it is hardly a nonorganic mass that remains.

Furthermore, we are not always fortunate enough to trace the existing analogy into its finest branches. Time obliterates its tracks; intermediate parts of these sequences vanish as the language's elements resemble living individuals in terms of their alternating birth and death. Yes, even the human himself, who has helped forming the language and still does, is not always aware of the analogy that he follows instinctively and the consciousness of a nation—dissected into its many parts—cannot be vividly united in one focal point. One cannot come to the true essence of a language even by means of an ever so detailed dissection. It resembles a breath of air that envelops all and yet is too fine for the eye to see its individual elemental form. Just as a mountain mist only takes form from a distance; as soon as one steps into it, it drifts around formlessly. One draws closer to the essence, however, the more one observes various languages in detail and thus penetrates deeper into mankind's general business of language formation and the more one endeavors to detect the specific individual expression of a certain national character in every single language—and it is for this end that the dissections are indispensable. Obviously, one reaches beyond the boundaries of mere language study should one follow this way correctly. For language always functions as a mediator, in the first instance between the infinite and the finite nature, then between two individuals; concurrently and by the same act, it enables their unification, and comes into being because of it. Its essence never lays solely with one alone, but has always got to be guessed or surmised from the other at the same time. However, language is, nonetheless, still not explainable taking from both, but is (just as whenever true mediation takes place) something of its own right, incomprehensible, something existing, and the idea of its separateness is only in us and our conception of amalgamation—and it is only within this idea that it is perceived as captive. The observation of language, which in order not to become chimaera-like must be initiated with a most dry, even mechanical, dissection of the physical and constructible, leads into the most remote depths of humanity. One has to free oneself from the idea, however, that one can simply detach it from what it signifies, as for example the name of a human being from its persona, and that it, just like an agreed code, is the product of reflection and accordance, or in any way the task of humans (as the term is perceived empirically or even that of the individual. As a true, unfathomable miracle it breaks loose from the mouth of a nation, just as it does from the babbling of every child, and is thus no less amazing even if it is repeated among us every day and yet overlooked with indifference. It is (in order not to mention at this point the supernatural ties of human beings) the most radiant trace and the surest proof that the human being does not have a per se independent individuality, that *I* and *You* are not just mutually demanding terms, but on the contrary identical ones should one succeed in returning to the point of separation; and that there are, in a sense, circles of individuality, from the weak, needy, and invalid individual to the ancient tribe of mankind, or else all understanding would be rendered impossible for all eternity. This is not the place to expand on these themes, but I do believe it necessary to let them be known, precisely because it is my opinion that they represent the right approach regarding the organic life of the human race in tribes and nations and, for the most part, world history itself. Moreover, I wish to repudiate the idea and do not want to make the impression that I intend to scrutinize the wonderful nature of language with mere dry and ever insufficient dissection. It is the primary duty of any writer to express estimation for his or her subject.

Subsequently, and in reference to the above, no analogy can permeate language completely and the analogy at hand (both, among the sounds and by the terms that are signified by it) cannot always be detected. So every language consists of a large amount of analogically formed sequences on the one side, and on the other of basic elements about which nothing more can be said.

A successful dissection must record this twofold language component completely and with precision, it must follow every trace with systematic orderliness and examine the language in all directions; and yet not to get carried away by the thrill of the chase taking good care not to confound real findings with invented ones. At the same time, such a dissection also serves to facilitate the learning process of a language. For this purpose, however, one will have to take a slightly different approach compared to that required for advancing the general scientific study of language. With regard to the former it suffices to line up the most certain and truly decisive analogies; with regard to the latter, it must, even at the risk that future research will not profit from it, draw attention to every point that may yield even a trace of an analogy, even from afar, as it is its duty to follow that lead down to even the most miniscule filament.

The study's ultimate result will be twofold: a system of more or less general, yet certain rules, principles and analogies, the actual organism of language, and an, as it were, inorganic mass of no further dissectible elements.

Obviously, in such a dissection an examination of the system's characteristic style [*Redefügung*] or its grammar is by far easier than that of the system behind word formation [*Wortbildung*] or the lexical, and of course I will have to content myself with not succeeding in laying out the analogical word formation [*Wortbildung*] of the Basque language in its entirety. Conversely, it is impossible to reject the clear, certain, even as it were persistent analogies. Moreover, it would be good to direct the attention of other language scholars toward these points as they require additional investigation. In addition, I cannot leave this aspect untouched if not for the simple reason that the Basque language scholar I used the most has created his own system in this matter, which, correct or false, must be mentioned and reviewed in any case.

At the end of this section I will carry out a general comparison between the Basque language and other languages in order to, wherever possible, categorize their class according to their general character, and their family to which it belongs according to their affinity. While attempting to carry out a classification of the known languages, I keep this reasonable comparison deliberately separate from the treatment of the special characteristics of the language itself, as it is important not to allow the former to have any influence on the latter. Moreover, it must be left to the reader to correct or expand upon it, which, in turn, depends on the reader's knowledge of additional languages.

3

Finally, following an account of the land and its inhabitants, and following the dissection, the third section, resulting from the first two, will contain historical and philosophical investigations into the Basque nation and language. By pulling together all influencing factors, the point here is to determine the place that both take among the nations and languages in terms of their lineage as well as their worth and importance to the history of mankind, in addition to the knowledge and the expansion of the definition of language generally. This last section will necessarily contain the outcomes of my own ideas and convictions; I flatter myself, however, that the first two should be designed in such a way that every qualified scholar can go on to alter or change the third section as he sees fit.

In this vein I wish, inasmuch as this is possible, to round off the examination of my subject and come to its end by approaching this small corner of Europe in a way that light will stream toward it from all points and that it will illuminate some of them in return. Given that even the most detailed text on the matter does not necessarily warrant a large number of pages, I hope to consign mine to the reading public within a year, one and a half at the most.

—W. v. Humboldt.

Index